YORK HANDBOOKS

GENERAL EDITOR:
Professor A.N. Jeffares
(University of Stirling)

A CHRONOLOGY OF ENGLISH LITERATURE

Martin Gray

MA (OXFORD) M PHIL (LONDON)
Lecturer in English Studies, University of Stirling

LONGMAN
YORK PRESS

ACKNOWLEDGEMENT
I should like to offer my thanks for the friendly and invaluable help rendered by Nigel
Wilcockson, the editor of this chronology, and to apologise for taking up so much of his
time. He has worked indefatigably to ensure that it is more reliable and coherent than I
could have made it on my own, and he has had the unenviable task of coaxing me through
the final stages of its preparation. Many excellent details of fact and organisation are due to
his painstaking perseverance. The remaining inconsistencies and inaccuracies are entirely
my own. David Wilcockson has provided essential knowledge about computers at certain
difficult points in the manipulation of the text, for which I am very grateful.

YORK PRESS
Immeuble Esseily, Place Riad Solh, Beirut.

LONGMAN GROUP UK LIMITED
Longman House,
Burnt Mill,
Harlow,
Essex

First published in 1989

ISBN 0 582 96606 X

Produced by Longman Group (FE) Ltd
Printed in Hong Kong
Typeset by Pastiche, London

Contents

Preface

THE INTENTION of this book is to provide some indication of the richness and variety of literature in Britain from the earliest records of its existence to the present age. It attempts also to place works of literature in relation to the flow of historical events. History and literature are brought together in a typographic form that is designed to be attractive and immediately understandable. Here, arranged in chronological order, are enough names and titles to suggest something of the wealth of English literature and literature in English. However, these titles represent only a tiny proportion of the numbers of books that have added to the sum of culture during the last thirteen centuries. A short visit to any good library will make this instantly clear.

Students of literature sometimes lack a sense of the continuum of literature in modern history. The long-lasting inheritance of the New Criticism, and in Britain of F.R. Leavis, is that literature is studied via Great Works, often seen as isolated texts, and not second-hand through literary histories. Though this method has inestimable advantages, it sometimes seems tacitly to suggest that nothing much happened for large stretches of time, between, say, Chaucer and Shakespeare, or Pope and Wordsworth. Survey courses of literary periods may give some impression of the background to the great works, but patchily. Meanwhile many courses and exam curricula are devoted more and more to twentieth-century literature. If literature is to do anything it should develop the imagination, and this should include the historical imagination: the past is a foreign country which we must visit in order to gain a perspective on our own land, and which should teach us sympathy, tolerance and understanding. The present can hardly be understood without relation to the past. This chronology cannot hope to excite interest in past literature simply by listing names and dates, but it does provide a visual display of the development, continuity and variety of literary culture.

ABBREVIATIONS

b.	born	**incl.**	includes
bk	book	**MS**	manuscript
c.	*circa*	**no.**	number
compl.	complete(d)	*p.*	painting
cont.	continued	**pseud.**	pseudonym
d.	died	**pt**	part
ed.	editor/edited	**publ.**	published
edn	edition	*sc.*	sculpture
f.	film	**transl.**	translation
fl.	*floruit,* flourished	**vol.**	volume

Part 1

Old English Literature

FOR ABOUT four centuries, from the invasion of Britain by Germanic tribes in the mid-fifth century till the Norman conquest (1066), the language now called Old English or Anglo-Saxon was spoken in four main dialects throughout England, and as far north as the Forth in southern Scotland. Latin was the language of learned writings. The body of Anglo-Saxon literature that has survived is small and may not be representative. There are about 30,000 lines of vigorous alliterative verse, mostly preserved in four famous codices. Exact dates and circumstances of composition are unknown, and in most cases matters for scholarly conjecture and disagreement. The poems bear traces of a heroic oral tradition, yet were presumably written down by monks. English prose dates from the great religious writings and translations of King Alfred's reign.

All works are in Anglo-Saxon, unless otherwise indicated.

Date	Historical events	Literature
*c.*397		Augustine of Hippo: *Confessions* (Latin prose)
410	Major withdrawal of Roman legions from Britain; Rome sacked by Visigoths	
*c.*413–27		Augustine of Hippo: *The City of God* (Latin prose)
449	Traditional date of first raids on Britain by Angles, Saxons and Jutes	
451	Attila the Hun defeated near Châlons-sur-Marne	
455	Rome sacked by Vandals	
476	Emperor Romulus Augustus deposed by Germanic leader Odoacer; end of Roman Empire in the West	
*c.*518	British defeat Saxons at Mons Badonicus; legends of King Arthur may refer to the British leader who resisted the invaders during this time	

Date	Historical events	Literature
c.524		Boethius: *The Consolation of Philosophy* (Latin prose and poetry)
527	Justinian becomes Emperor in Constantinople (–565)	
c.529	St Benedict founds abbey at Monte Cassino, Italy; Justinian: *Codex Vetus* (codification of civil laws)	
c.530	Establishment of Saxon kingdoms of Middlesex and Essex	
532	Justinian begins building church of St Sophia in Constantinople (compl. 537)	
c.550		Gildas: *De Excidio et Conquestu Britanniae* ('Concerning the Destruction and Conquest of Britain', Latin prose, laments the Saxon defeat of the British)
c.563	Monastery at Iona founded by Irish monks under St Columba	
594		Gregory of Tours: *History of the Franks* (Latin prose)
597	Roman Christianity brought to Kent by St Augustine	
c.600		Aneirin: *The Gododdin* (Welsh bardic poetry)
c.610	Probable date of manufacture of jewellery found at Sutton Hoo ship burial	
616	Accession of Edwin as King of Northumbria (–632); period of Northumbrian supremacy	
622	The Hegira: the flight of Mohammed from Mecca to Medina (year one of the Moslem calendar)	
635	Celtic Christians found monastery at Lindisfarne	
c.640		Composition of early Heroic poems: *The Fight at Finnsburh*; the *Waldere* fragments; *Widsith*

Date	Historical events	Literature
657–80		During the Abbacy of Hild at Whitby Caedmon composes his *Creation-Hymn*; a programme of biblical paraphrases in verse traditionally attributed to Caedmon: *Christ and Satan*; *Daniel*; *Genesis A*
664	The Synod of Whitby establishes dominance of Roman Christianity in the English Church	
*c.*675–700	Franks Casket carved	
698–721	Lindisfarne Gospels illuminated	
*c.*700	Ruthwell Cross carved (inscribed in runes with extracts from *The Dream of the Rood*); earliest extant records in Anglo-Saxon	
*c.*700–60		Composition of: *Beowulf* (epic poem, dated by scholars variously between 680 and 1000); *The Dream of the Rood*; *Exodus*; *Guthlac A*; Exeter Book *Riddles* (poetry)
731		Bede completes his *Ecclesiastical History* (Latin prose)
732	Charles Martel defeats Moslem invasion of Europe at Tours	
*c.*750	Stirrup arrives in Europe from Asia, leading to a new type of warfare with lance and armour; English missionary St Boniface takes Christianity into Germany	
757	Accession of Offa as King of Mercia (–796); his military successes lead him to call himself King of England	
*c.*760–820	Book of Kells illuminated	
782	Alcuin leaves monastery at York to become educational adviser to Charlemagne at Aachen	
*c.*782	Offa's Dyke constructed to defend Mercia from Welsh attack	

Date	Historical events	Literature
c.785		Composition of the Exeter Book 'Elegies', including: *The Ruin*; *The Seafarer*; *The Wanderer* (poetry)
787	First Viking raids on England	
793	Vikings sack monastery at Lindisfarne	
800	Charlemagne crowned Emperor by Pope Leo III (–814)	
c.800		Cynewulf: *Christ II*; *Elene*; *The Fates of the Apostles*; *Juliana* (poetry)
c.810		Nennius: *History of Britain* (Latin prose)
c.832		Einhard: *Life of Charlemagne* (Latin prose)
843	Pictish and Scottish kingdoms joined under Kenneth McAlpin; empire of Charlemagne split at the Treaty of Verdun	
850	Danish army winters in England for the first time	
851	Canterbury Cathedral sacked by Danes	
871	Accession of Alfred, King of Wessex (–899), the only kingdom unconquered by the Danes	During Alfred's reign a programme of translating great prose works from Latin into Anglo-Saxon is initiated: Augustine: *Soliloquies*; Bede: *Ecclesiastical History*; Boethius: *The Consolation of Philosophy*; Gregory: *Pastoral Care*; Orosius: *World History* *Anglo-Saxon Chronicle* begun (prose, –1154)
878	Danes defeated by Alfred at Edington: Treaty of Wedmore sets up Danelaw	
c.878	The Alfred Jewel (pointer for liturgical reading)	
c.900	Magyar raids on Western Europe begin	Asser: *Life of King Alfred* (Latin prose)

Date	Historical events	Literature
910	Foundation of Cluny Abbey, Burgundy, leading to revival of monasticism	
*c.*910	Earliest extant Anglo-Saxon embroidery: vestments for the tomb of St Cuthbert	
910–54	English gradually reconquer areas of the country held by Vikings	
*c.*915		Anon.: *Judith* (poetry)
937	King Athelstan defeats Scots at Brunanburh	Anon.: *The Battle of Brunanburh* (poetry) in the *Anglo-Saxon Chronicle*
*c.*950–1000		Compilation of major Anglo-Saxon MSS of poetry: MS Cotton Vitellius (*Beowulf*; *Judith*; prose works); Exeter Book (*Christ*; *Deor*; *Juliana*; *The Phoenix*; *The Seafarer*; *The Wanderer*; *Widsith*); Junius Book ('Caedmon' scriptural poems); Vercelli Book (*Andreas*; *The Dream of the Rood*; *Elene*; *The Fates of the Apostles*; prose homilies)
959	Accession of Edgar as King of England (–975), during whose reign freedom from invasion leads to revival of monasticism and culture	
962	Otto, King of the Saxons, crowned Emperor by Pope John XII (–973)	
978	Accession of Ethelred II, 'the Unready', as King of England (–1016)	
980	Viking raids begin again	
991	Vikings defeat English at Maldon	
994	Vikings besiege London	
*c.*995		Aelfric: *The Catholic Homilies*; *Lives of the Saints* (prose) Anon.: *The Battle of Maldon* (poetry)

Date	Historical events	Literature
999	Gerbert of Aurillac, mathematician and philosopher, becomes Pope Sylvester II (–1003); he is said to have introduced Arabic numerals and the use of zero into European methods of calculation	
c.1000	Harley Psalter illuminated	
1007–12	Ethelred II makes a number of huge payments of silver to Danes in return for peace	
1014	Brian Boru, King of Southern Ireland, defeats Vikings at Clontarf	Wulfstan: *Sermo Lupi ad Anglos* ('Address to the English', prose)
1016	Deaths of Ethelred II and Edmund Ironside; accession of Viking Canute as King of England (–1035); first Norman adventurers arrive in Sicily	
1026	Canute makes pilgrimage to Rome	
1035	Death of Canute; Harold I and Hardicanute divide English crown	
1040	Duncan, King of the Scots, murdered by Macbeth	
1042	Accession of Edward the Confessor as King of England (–1066)	
c.1050		*The Mabinogion* (collection of prose tales in Welsh)
c.1052	Rebuilding of Westminster Abbey begun by Edward the Confessor	
1054	Schism between Roman and Eastern Churches becomes permanent	
1066	William, Duke of Normandy, defeats Harold Godwinson at Hastings; conquest of England by Normans under William, who is crowned king (–1087)	

Part 2

Middle English Literature

THE VARIOUS versions of English spoken in different parts of Britain from about 1100 until 1400 are called Middle English. After the Norman conquest Anglo-Saxon was modified by contact with the French of the ruling élite. Anglo-Norman, a dialect of French, predominated till about 1350 in literature not written in Latin. From then onwards Middle English became the accepted medium used by poets. Chaucer and Gower were writing at the court of Richard II and using the London dialect; Henryson and Dunbar used Middle Scots (the latter probably attached to the court of King James IV); the anonymous poet of *Sir Gawain and the Green Knight* wrote in his local English somewhere in the north-west of England.

All works are in Middle English unless otherwise indicated.

Date	Historical events	Literature
1066	Death of Geoffrey de Preuilly, reputed inventor of tournaments	
c.1066		A version of *The Song of Roland* (French poetry) performed by Norman minstrel Taillefer
1066–72	Bayeux tapestry embroidered, depicting events leading up to and including the Norman conquest of England	
1068–9	Great rising of the Saxons of the North against William I is ruthlessly suppressed	
1070	William I makes Lanfranc Archbishop of Canterbury (–1089), and institutes reforms to keep the Church under royal control	
1071	William I subdues last outpost of Saxon independence, Hereward's camp of refuge in the Fen district	

Date	Historical events	Literature
1077	Emperor Henry IV submits temporarily to Pope Gregory VII at Canossa in dispute between Papacy and secular power over control of Church affairs	
1086	*The Domesday Book* compiled at the orders of William I, giving details of the extent, value, population, state of cultivation and ownership of land; population of British Isles *c.*2 million	
1087	Accession of William II, 'Rufus' (–1100)	
1095	Pope Urban II proclaims the First Crusade at the Council of Clermont	
1098		Anselm: *Cur Deus Homo* (Latin prose, theological work)
1099	Crusaders under Godfrey of Bouillon capture Jerusalem	
1100	Accession of Henry I (–1135)	
*c.*1100	Work begun on the great Anglo-Norman Romanesque cathedrals: at Durham, Ely, Hereford, Lincoln, Norwich and Rochester	Earliest record of a miracle play, at Dunstable: *Saint Katherine* (Latin or French, lost)
1115	Abelard starts lecturing in Paris; St Bernard becomes first Abbot of Clairvaux (–1153)	
*c.*1120	Foundation of Military Orders of the Templars and Hospitallers; Abelard, mutilated by order of Héloïse's uncle Fulbert, becomes a monk; Héloïse becomes a nun	*Letters* of Héloïse and Abelard (Latin prose)
1122	Concordat of Worms resolves dispute between Empire and Papacy (*see* 1077)	
1131	Cistercian abbey at Rievaulx founded	

Date	Historical events	Literature
1135	Accession of King Stephen (–1154)	
c.1135		Geoffrey of Monmouth: *History of the Kings of Britain* (Latin prose, incl. stories of King Arthur)
1139–53	Civil war between Stephen and Matilda	
c.1140		Anon.: *Le Mystère d'Adam* (Anglo-Norman mystery play, MS fragmentary)
c.1141	Gratian: *Concordia Discordantium Canonum* (codification of canon law)	
c.1150	Paper-making begins in Europe	
c.1150–80	Winchester Bible illuminated (the work of at least six hands)	
1154	Accession of Henry II (–1189)	Last entries in Peterborough copy of the *Anglo-Saxon Chronicle* (prose, *see* 871)
1155		Wace: *Roman de Brut* (Anglo-Norman poetry)
c.1160		Thomas of Britain: *Tristan* (Anglo-Norman poetry)
c.1160–1200		Arnaut Daniel, Provençal troubador, writing verse
1164	Henry II draws up the Constitutions of Clarendon in order to limit the power of the Church and benefit of clergy	
1166	The Assize of Clarendon formalises trial by Grand Jury	
c.1167	Foundation of Oxford University	
1170	Murder of Archbishop Thomas Becket at Canterbury, following disputes with Henry II over rights of clergy	

Date	Historical events	Literature
*c.*1172		Wace: *Roman de Rou* (Anglo-Norman poetry)
*c.*1175	Rebuilding of Canterbury Cathedral in Early English Gothic style starts (compl. 1186)	Anon.: *Horn* (Anglo-Norman poetry)
1178	Sculptor Antelami signs and dates a relief of the Deposition in Parma Cathedral	
*c.*1180		Chrétien de Troyes active at court of Champagne Marie de France (active at English court): *Lais* (Anglo-Norman poetry)
1187	Saladin captures Jerusalem	
1188	Saladin tithe levied to pay for the Third Crusade: first tax on personal property in England	
*c.*1188		Gerald of Wales: *Account of a Journey through Wales* (Latin prose)
1189	Accession of Richard I (−1199)	
1190	Persecution of Jews in England	
*c.*1190		Orm: *Ormulum* (verse sermons)
1192	Richard I makes truce with Saladin in the Holy Land	
1194	Rebuilding of Chartres Cathedral in Gothic style begins (compl. 1260)	
*c.*1195		Fitz-Nigel: *Dialogue of the Exchequer* (Latin prose, guide to financial administration)
1198	Innocent III becomes Pope; his pontificate (−1216) regarded as the culmination of the spiritual and temporal power of the Roman Church	
1199	Accession of King John (−1216)	
1200	Population of British Isles *c.*2.5 million	'Classical' tradition of Scottish Gaelic bardic poetry established by this date

Date	Historical events	Literature
*c.*1200		Gottfried von Strassburg: *Tristan* (German poetry)
1204	Philip Augustus of France conquers Normandy from King John; Fourth Crusade captures Constantinople	
1205	King John rejects Pope Innocent III's choice of Stephen Langton as Archbishop of Canterbury; eventually he submits to Langton's election and does homage to the Pope (1213)	
1209	Traditional date for the founding of Cambridge University by students from Oxford; Pope Innocent III declares Crusade against Albigensian heretics in southern France	
*c.*1210		Anon.: *Aucassin et Nicolette* (French prose and verse romance); *Carmina Burana* (German song collection); 'Katherine Group' of prose tracts; *Nibelungenlied* (German epic poetry); *The Owl and the Nightingale* (poetry) Layamon: *Brut* (poetry)
1215	Barons make King John accept Magna Carta, following disputes over taxation and royal prerogatives	
1216	Accession of Henry III (–1272)	
*c.*1220		Anon.: *Ancrene Riwle*, later reworked as *Ancrene Wisse* (prose devotional manual)
1221	Dominican friars arrive in England	
1224	Franciscan friars arrive in England	
*c.*1225		Anon.: *King Horn* (verse romance)

Date	Historical events	Literature
1235–59		Matthew Paris compiles his *Chronica Majora* (Latin prose history)
*c.*1235		Guillaüme de Lorris: *Roman de la Rose* (French allegorical verse, unfinished, *see* 1275)
*c.*1240		Emperor Frederick II: *De Arte Venandi Cum Avibus* (Latin prose, study of falconry, first printed in English 1596)
1241	Mongol invasion of Poland and Hungary defeated	
1245	Rebuilding begins of Westminster Abbey (compl. 1269)	
*c.*1245		Anon.: *Laxdaela Saga* (Icelandic prose)
1246	Building begins of La Sainte-Chapelle, Paris (compl. 1248)	
1249	Roger Bacon, Franciscan friar, philosopher and scientist, records existence of explosives	
1250	Louis IX of France (St Louis) captured by Saracens	
1258	Rebellion of barons against Henry III; Simon de Montfort assumes control of baronial party; Provisions of Oxford place baronial constraints on royal power (first official use of English since the Conquest)	
*c.*1260		Trinity Cambridge MS 323 compiled: Dominican miscellany of Latin, Anglo-Norman and English poems, including lyrics Aquinas: *Summa Theologica* (Latin prose, major attempt at a theological system, which seeks to reconcile Christian theology with Aristotelian philosophy)
*c.*1263	Foundation of Balliol College, Oxford	

Date	Historical events	Literature
c.1264		Anon.: *The Song of Lewes* (Latin poetry, justification of baronial opposition to the Crown)
1265	Simon de Montfort summons Parliament, including, for the first time, representatives from the towns; Simon de Montfort killed at Evesham	
1266		Bacon: *Opus Maius* (Latin prose, summary of scientific knowledge, including invention of magnifying glass)
1272	Accession of Edward I (–1307), during whose reign many legal and administrative reforms take place, including organisation of the law courts and institution of Justices of the Peace	
1275	Marco Polo at the court of Kublai Khan	
c.1275		Bodley MS Digby 86 compiled: Dominican miscellany of Latin, Anglo-Norman and English poems, including: *Dame Sirith*; *Fox and Wolf*; *The Thrush and the Nightingale* Jean de Meun continues *Roman de la Rose* (French allegorical verse, *see* 1235)
c.1280		Anon.: *Njal's Saga* (Icelandic prose)
1282	Edward I quells revolt by Llewellyn in Wales	
1283	Caernarvon Castle begun (compl. 1323), one of several built by Edward I in Wales	
1284	Foundation of Peterhouse, Cambridge	
1290	Edward I expels Jews from England (*see* 1655)	

Date	Historical events	Literature
c.1290	Invention of spectacles	B.M.MS Harley 913 compiled: Franciscan miscellany, including *Land of Cockayne* and satirical poems Early romances written about this time: *Arthur and Merlin*; *Bevis of Hampton*; *Guy of Warwick*; *The Lay of Havelok*; *Richard Coeur de Lion*
1291	Edward involved in struggle with Scotland, due to rivalry between claimants to the Scottish crown	
c.1292		Dante: *Vita Nuova* (Italian poetry)
1295	The 'Model Parliament' attended by knights and representatives of the towns	
1300	Population of British Isles c.5 million	
c.1300		Anon.: *Cursor Mundi* (encyclopedic verse history)
1303		Mannyng begins *Handling Sin* (confessional manual in verse, filled with exempla, compl. 1338)
c.1304–21		Dante writing *The Divine Comedy* (Italian poetry)
c.1305	Giotto at work on frescoes of the Arena Chapel, Padua	
1307	Accession of Edward II (–1327)	
1308–11	Duccio paints *Maestà* for Siena Cathedral	
1309	Pope Clement V moves seat of Papacy to Avignon in France	
1314	Edward II invades Scotland; defeated at Bannockburn	
1319	Cannon may have been used by Edward II at the siege of Berwick	
c.1320		Anon.: *King Alisaunder*; *Sir Landevale*; *Sir Orfeo* (verse romances)

Date	Historical events	Literature
1327	Edward II deposed and murdered; accession of Edward III (–1377)	
c.1330		The Auchinleck MS compiled: romances and religious poems; B.M. MS Harley 2253 compiled: miscellany of English, French and Latin verse, especially lyrics, probably written c.1300
c.1335	Expansion of wool trade in England	
1337	Hundred Years War begins between England and France (–1453)	
1337–9	Ambrogio Lorenzetti paints frescoes of Good and Bad Government in Siena town hall (early examples of paintings including landscape)	
1340		Michael of Northgate: *Ayenbite of Inwyt* (prose moral teaching)
c.1340		Rolle writing mystical lyrics and prose in Latin and English
1341		Petrarch crowned as laureate poet on the Capitol in Rome
1346	French routed at Crécy by Edward III and his son Edward, 'the Black Prince'	
1348–9	Black Death kills one third of the population of England	
1349–53	Guillaume de Machaut (writer of narrative love poems and lyrics): *The Notre Dame Mass* (musical setting)	
c.1350		Anon.: *The Prick of Conscience* (poetry); the 'Shrewsbury Fragments' (mystery play)
c.1350–2		Boccaccio: *Decameron* (Italian prose)
1351	First Statute of Labourers regulates wages	

Date	Historical events	Literature
1352–3		Anon.: *Winner and Waster* (poetry)
1361	Black Death reappears in England	
1362	English used instead of French in law courts (but not for written records)	
1363	Parliament opened by the Chancellor for the first time in English	
*c.*1369		Chaucer: *The Book of the Duchess* (poetry)
*c.*1370	Steel crossbow used as weapon of war	Langland: *Piers Plowman* (A Text, poetry, *see* 1377, 1390)
1375		Barbour: *Bruce* (poetry)
*c.*1375		Juliana (or Julian) of Norwich: *A Shewing of God's Love* (prose, *see* 1395)
1377	Accession of Richard II (–1399), during whose reign takes place the great flowering of Middle English poetry; first Poll Tax	First record of a Court Disguising (theatrical pageant): *The Visit to Richard II*
1377–9		Langland: *Piers Plowman* (B Text, poetry, *see* 1370, 1390)
1378	Start of the Great Schism: Urban VI elected Pope in Rome, Clement VII at Fondi (from 1379 at Avignon)	Wyclif: *The Schism of the Popes* (Latin prose, anti-Papal tract)
*c.*1380	Wyclif's followers translate the Bible into the vernacular, part of a concerted attack on the constitution and practice of the Church	Anon.: *The Cloud of Unknowing* (prose); transl. of 'Mandeville's' *Travels* (prose) Chaucer: *The House of Fame* (poetry)
1381	Peasants' Revolt led by Wat Tyler	
*c.*1382		Chaucer: *The Parliament of Fowls* (poetry) Wyclif: *Trialogos* (Latin prose)
*c.*1385		Chaucer: *The Legend of Good Women* (poetry); *Troilus and Criseyde* (poetry) Hilton: *The Ladder of Perfection* (prose)

Date	Historical events	Literature
1387		First record of York plays in city's memorandum book Chaucer begins *The Canterbury Tales* (poetry) John of Trevisa translates Higden's *Polychronicon* (Latin prose, encyclopedic history) Usk: *The Testament of Love* (prose)
*c.*1390		B.M. MS Cotton Nero A compiled, including: *Cleanness*; *Patience*; *Pearl*; *Sir Gawain and the Green Knight* (poetry) Gower completes first version of *Confessio Amantis* (poetry) Langland: *Piers Plowman* (C Text, poetry, *see* 1370, 1377) The most important collection of lyrics by Rolle (*d.*1349) dates from about this time
1394	Rebuilding begins of Westminster Hall (compl. 1401)	
*c.*1395		Juliana of Norwich: *Shewings* (prose, long text, *see* 1375)
*c.*1397	Wilton Diptych (*p.*)	John of Trevisa: *De Proprietatibus Rerum* (prose transl. of Anglicus's Latin encyclopedia of natural science)
1399	Deposition of Richard II (murdered 1400); accession of Henry IV (–1413)	
1400	Population of British Isles *c.*3.5 million	
*c.*1400		Anon.: *The Destruction of Troy* (poetry); *Morte Arthure* (poetry); *The Pride of Life* (morality play)
1401	Persecution of the Lollards (followers of Wyclif's beliefs) (–1413)	
1402		Hoccleve: *Letter to Cupid* (poetry)

Date	Historical events	Literature
1403	Rebellion of the Percies (Earl of Northumberland and his son Hotspur) allied with Owen Glendower; Henry IV defeats them at Shrewsbury	
c.1405		Hoccleve: 'La Male Regle de T. Hoccleve' (poetry)
c.1410	Paul and Jean de Limbourg: *Les Très Riches Heures du Duc de Berri* (illuminated calendar and prayer book)	Lydgate: *The Assembly of the Gods*; *The Temple of Glass* (poetry)
c.1412		Hoccleve: *The Regiment of Princes* (poetry)
1413	Accession of Henry V (–1422)	
1415	Henry V revives claim to the French crown and invades France; the battle of Agincourt won by English bowmen; John Huss, Bohemian religious reformer influenced by Wyclif's writings, burnt at the stake	
1420		Lydgate completes *Troy Book* (poetry)
c.1420		Wyntoun: *The Original Chronicle of Scotland* (verse history)
c.1420– c.1509		The 'Paston Letters' written by members of the family of Sir John Paston (*see* 1787)
c.1421		Lydgate: *The Siege of Thebes* (poetry)
1422	Accession of Henry VI (–1461)	
c.1425	Masaccio paints frescoes of Brancacci Chapel, Florence	James I of Scotland: *The Kingis Quair* (poetry)
c.1425–50		Anon.: *The Castle of Perseverance* (morality play) Shirley active in transcribing books and compiling MSS of Chaucer and Lydgate
1426–30		Lydgate (active as court poet): *The Pilgrimage of the Life of Man* (poetry)

Date	Historical events	Literature
1429	Joan of Arc raises the siege of Orleans and pushes the English into retreat	
c.1430		Wakefield Play Cycle developed; 'Wakefield Master' at work on a homogenous group of plays including *The Second Shepherds' Play* Chestre: *Sir Launfal* (poetry)
1431	Joan of Arc burnt by the English at Rouen	
1431–8		Lydgate: *The Fall of Princes* (poetry)
1432		Lydgate: *Henry VI's Triumphal Entry into London* (poetry)
1432–8		Kempe: *The Book of Margery Kempe* (prose)
c.1433	Donatello: *David* (*sc.*)	
1434	Van Eyck: *The Marriage of Arnolfini* (*p.*)	
1437–40		Lydgate: *The Horse, the Goose and the Sheep* (poetry)
c.1440	Fra Angelico paints frescoes of San Marco convent, Florence	
1441	Henry VI founds Eton and King's College, Cambridge	
1443–7		Bokenham: *Legends of Holy Women* (poetry)
1446	King's College Chapel, Cambridge begun (compl. 1515); Van der Weyden: *Last Judgement* (*p.*)	
c.1450		Pecock: *The Repressor of Over Much Blaming of the Clergy* (prose)
1453	Hundred Years War with France (*see* 1337) ends after the death of Talbot at Castillon; England retains only Calais; Turks take Constantinople; death of John Dunstable, mathematician, astrologer, composer and early exponent of counterpoint	

Date	Historical events	Literature
1455	Wars of the Roses begin (–1485), caused by Henry VI's weakness and the rivalry between the houses of Lancaster and York	
*c.*1455	Uccello: *The Rout of San Romano* (*p.*)	Gutenberg prints the '42-Line' Bible at Mainz, first book printed with moveable type
1461	Accession of Edward IV (–1483), after Lancastrians defeated at Towton	
*c.*1465		Henryson: *Testament of Cresseid* (poetry)
1469	Lorenzo de Medici, 'the Magnificent', becomes joint ruler of Florence with his brother Giuliano; flowering of Florentine culture during the period of his rule (–1492)	
*c.*1470		Anon.: *Mankind*; *Wisdom* (morality plays) Malory completes *Le Morte Darthur* (prose)
1471	Edward IV defeats and kills Warwick, 'the Kingmaker', at Barnet; Henry VI secretly murdered	
1473–4		At Bruges, Caxton prints the first book in English, his translation of Le Fèvre: *The Recuyell of the Histories of Troy*
*c.*1474	Mantegna finishes painting the Camera degli Sposi at Mantua	
*c.*1475	Botticelli: *Allegory of Spring* (*p.*)	Anon.: *The Assembly of Ladies*; *The Flower and the Leaf*; *Lancelot of the Lake* (poetry)
1476		Caxton sets up press in Westminster
*c.*1476		Caxton's first printing of Chaucer (*d.*1400): *The Canterbury Tales*
*c.*1478		Hary: *Wallace* (Scots poetry)

Date	Historical events	Literature
1480	Pope Sixtus IV authorises Ferdinand and Isabella of Spain to appoint Inquisitors against heresy	
1483	Death of Edward IV; Edward V, a minor, reigns for two months; accession of Richard III (–1485)	Gower (*d.*1408): *Confessio Amantis* printed by Caxton
1484		Chaucer (*d.*1400): *Troilus and Criseyde* printed by Caxton
1485	Battle of Bosworth results in death of Richard III and accession of Henry VII, the first Tudor king (–1509)	Malory (*d.*1471): *Le Morte Darthur* printed by Caxton
1489		Skelton: *On the Dolorous Death of the Duke of Northumberland* (poetry)
1492	Columbus lands in the West Indies	
1495	Poyning's Law makes Irish Parliament subservient to English Parliament	
*c.*1495		Anon.: *A Little Geste of Robin Hood* (poetry); *The Summoning of Everyman* (*Every Man, A Treatise How the High Father of Heaven Sendeth Death to Summon Every Creature*) (morality play)
1497		Medwall: *Fulgens and Lucrece* (secular drama)
*c.*1497	Leonardo da Vinci: *The Last Supper* (*p.*)	
1498	Savonarola, religious and political reformer, burnt at the stake after attempting to create a stringently Christian commonwealth in the republic of Florence	

Part 3

Literature
1500–1980

FROM 1500 onwards all poetry and prose is listed by date of publication rather than composition, unless otherwise indicated, though until dating printed works became standard practice, the exact chronology of texts is still often a matter for conjecture. Plays appear on the most likely date of first performance; some publication dates of collections of the works of major playwrights are also mentioned.

Details of works that appear in several volumes are given when publication is spread over more than one year. Where appropriate, some information is also provided about serialisation, a common feature of novel production in the nineteenth century. However, prose and poetry are always listed by date of full book publication, except where it is clearly indicated to the contrary. Literary works by non-English-speaking writers appear in brackets.

1500

Pope Alexander VI proclaims crusade against the Turks; Cabral lands in Brazil and claims it for Portugal; population of England and Wales: 3.75 million; Scotland: 500,000; Ireland: 800,000; London: 75,000; Dürer: *Self-Portrait* (*p.*); (*c.*) violin family and virginals developed; Wynkyn de Worde establishes press in Fleet Street.

PROSE
(Erasmus: *Adagia*, Latin maxims)
DRAMA
During the first quarter of the century there was considerable dramatic activity at the English and Scottish courts in the form of pageants, disguisings, tilts and interludes. Few MSS survive of these occasions, but they are mentioned in historical accounts, such as Hall's *Chronicle* (*see* 1548)

POETRY
Lydgate (*d.c.*1451): *The Story of Thebes* (*The Siege of Thebes*)

1501

Arthur, Prince of Wales marries Catherine of Aragon; Giovanni Bellini: *Doge Loredano* (*p.*); Michelangelo begins his *David* (*sc.*, compl. 1504); publication of fine edn of Virgil by the Aldine Press.

DRAMA
MS exists describing pageant, including disguising and tilt, at Prince Arthur's wedding

1502

Publication of works of Demosthenes, Euripides, Herodotus, Sophocles and Thucydides by the Aldine Press.

1503

Marriage of Margaret, daughter of Henry VII, to James IV of Scotland (leading in 1603 to Stuart succession); Grünewald: *The Mocking of Christ* (*p.*); (*c.*) Leonardo da Vinci: *Mona Lisa* (*p.*).

PROSE

Atkinson: *The Imitation of Christ of Thomas à Kempis* (first English transl.)

(Erasmus: *Enchiridion Militis Christiani* ('The Manual of the Christian Knight'), Latin, English transl. 1533)

1504

Parliament passes statute to control retainers and liveries in order to curb private violence, and seeks to regulate guilds and companies.

POETRY

(Sannazzaro: *Arcadia*, incl. prose)

Skelton writes *Philip Sparrow* (publ. 1545)

1505

Almeida, Portuguese explorer, reaches Ceylon.

POETRY

Barclay: *The Castle of Labour*

Hawes: *The Temple of Glass*

1506

Henry VII seeks to secure cloth trade of Flanders for British merchants in the Malus Intercursus treaty (not ratified); rebuilding of St Peter's, Rome, begun (compl. *c.*1625).

PROSE

Rolle (*d.*1349): *Contemplations of the Dread and Love of God* (incl. verse)

1507

Anglo-Venetian treaty renewed on terms excluding Venetians from trading between England and Flanders.

1508

Giorgione: *The Tempest* (*p.*); Michelangelo starts work on ceiling of the Sistine Chapel, Rome (compl. 1512).

PROSE

Rolle (*d.*1349): *Remedy against the Troubles of Temptation* (incl. verse)

POETRY

(*Amadis of Gaul*, popular romance of *c.*1350, probably Portuguese in origin, printed (with additions) for the first time, in Spanish)

POETRY (*cont.*)

(*c.*) Dunbar: *The Dance of the Seven Deadly Sins*; *The Flyting of Dunbar and Kennedy*; *Lament for the Makers*; *The Thistle and the Rose*; *The Treatise of the Two Married Women and the Widow*

1509

Death of Henry VII; accession of Henry VIII (–1547), who marries Catherine of Aragon, his brother's widow; Portuguese start to establish trading empire in India; (c.) Peter Henlein constructs first watch (the Nuremberg Egg); Cranach the elder: *Venus* (p.).

POETRY
Barclay: *The Ship of Fools* (transl. of Brandt)
Hawes: *The Pastime of Pleasure*

1510

Execution of Dudley and Empson, Henry VII's unpopular tax-collectors, on false charges of treason; (c.) Bosch: *The Garden of Earthly Delights* (p.).

PROSE
(Erasmus: *Encomium Moriae* ('In Praise of Folly'), Latin)
More: *Life of John Picus, Earl of Mirandula* (transl. of Latin biography by Pico's nephew)
DRAMA
(c.) *Everyman: A Moral Play* (publ.)

POETRY
Hawes: *The Example of Virtue*
Lydgate (d.c.1451): *Treatise of a Gallant*

1511

Henry VIII joins the Holy League to protect the Pope's dominions against France; Erasmus made Professor of Greek at Cambridge (–1514); Peter Martyr: *De Orbe Novo* ('The New World', history of Spanish exploration in the West Indies, English transl. 1555).

1512

Physicians and surgeons practising in London required to be licensed by the Bishop of London; Torregiano starts work on the tomb of Henry VII in Westminster Abbey (compl. 1518).

PROSE
(Erasmus: *De Ratione Studii* ('Principles of Study'), Latin)

POETRY
Douglas begins translating Virgil's *Aeneid* (publ. 1553)

1513

Henry VIII defeats French at the battle of the Spurs; France's ally, Scotland, defeated at Flodden; James IV of Scotland killed; (c.) Raphael begins his *The Sistine Madonna* (p., compl. 1519); *True Encounter*, early English woodcut news-sheet, issued after Flodden.

PROSE
(Machiavelli at work on *The Prince*, publ. 1532)
POETRY
Anon.: *Flowers of Ovid* (transl. of *The Art of Love*)

POETRY (cont.)
Lydgate (d.c.1451): *Troy Book*
Skelton: *A Ballad of the Scottish King*

1514

Peace made with Scotland and France; Trinity House made headquarters for Corporation of London Pilots.

1515

Wolsey made a Cardinal, Archbishop of York and Lord Chancellor (–1529); he starts building Hampton Court; foundation of Manchester Grammar School.

PROSE
(c.) (Anon.: *Till Eulenspiegel*, folk tales, oldest surviving edn, in High German; Low German original probably dates from c.1480)

DRAMA
Skelton: *Magnificence*

POETRY
(c.) Barclay: *Eclogues* (i–iii, iv–v 1521)
Lydgate (d.c.1451): *The Testament of John Lydgate*

1516

Portuguese merchants reach China; Titian begins his *Assumption* (p. in Frari Church, Venice, compl. 1518); Erasmus publishes edn of New Testament in Greek.

PROSE
More: *Utopia* (Latin, English transl. 1551)

POETRY
(Ariosto: *Orlando Furioso*, in final form 1532)

1517

Luther nails his Ninety-Five Theses to the door of Wittenberg Castle Church, in protest at Church malpractice, especially systems of penances; riots in London against foreign merchants.

DRAMA
Rastell: *The Nature of the Four Elements* (interlude)

1518

Linacre founds the Royal College of Physicians; Pynson, King's Printer, awarded first recorded copyright.

DRAMA
Anon.: *The Entertainment of the French Ambassadors*

1519

Magellan starts round the world voyage (dies 1521).

DRAMA
Heywood, John (?): *The Pardoner and the Friar, the Curate and Neighbour Pratte*

1520

Field of the Cloth of Gold: fruitless diplomatic meeting between Henry VIII and Francis I of France; Henry makes alliance with Emperor Charles V; (c.) Nisbet translates New Testament into Scots.

PROSE
Barclay: *Chronicle of the War Which the Romans Had against Jugurtha* (transl. of Sallust); *Life of St Thomas*

DRAMA
Heywood, John: *The Four P's*; *Johan the Husband, Tib His Wife, and Sir Johan the Priest*

1521

Luther condemned as a heretic at the Diet of Worms; he starts translating the Bible into German (publ. 1534).

PROSE
Barclay: *The Introductory to Write and Pronounce French*
Henry VIII: *Defence of the Seven Sacraments* (against Luther)

POETRY
Barclay: *Eclogues* (iv–v, *see* 1515)
Skelton: *Speak Parrot*; *The Tunning of Elinor Rumming*

1522

Henry VIII joins Emperor Charles V in war against France (–1526); oldest extant harpsichord made; Titian: *Bacchus and Ariadne* (*p.*).

DRAMA
Rastell and others: *The Welcome for Charles V* (royal pageant)

POETRY
(*c.*) Skelton writes *Why Come Ye Not to Court?* (publ. 1545)

1523

(*c.*) Titian: *Entombment of Christ* (*p.*).

PROSE
Barclay: *The Mirror of Good Manners* (transl. of Mancinus)
Fitzherbert: *Book of Husbandry*; *Book of Surveying*

POETRY
Skelton: *A Goodly Garland or Chaplet of Laurel*

1524

Peasants revolt in parts of the Holy Roman Empire, claiming justification in Luther's teaching; Wynkyn de Worde prints translation of *Gesta Romanorum* ('Deeds of the Romans', popular medieval stories).

PROSE
Cox: *The Art or Craft of Rhetoric*

DRAMA
(*c.*) (Machiavelli: *La Mandragola*)

1525

France defeated by Emperor Charles V and Francis I captured; peasant rebellions in Germany severely repressed; Wolsey gives Hampton Court to Henry VIII; Anon.: *Here Beginneth a New Matter, the Which Is Called an Herbal*; Tyndale completes his translation of the New Testament (printed at Worms and smuggled into England in 1526).

DRAMA
Medwall (*d.c.*1505): *Interlude of Nature* (publ.)
Rastell: *Three Interludes* (publ.)

1526

Lutheranism spreads to Sweden; Cranach the elder: *Adam and Eve* (*p.*).

PROSE
Boece: *History of the Scots* (Latin, English transl. *c.*1535)
POETRY
Chaucer (*d.*1400): *The Book of Fame, and Other Poems*

POETRY (*cont.*)
(*The House of Fame*); *The Canterbury Tales*; *Troilus and Criseyde* (the first proper edns of Chaucer's work, 'diligently corrected and newly printed' by Pynson)

1527

Henry VIII seeks annulment of his marriage to Catherine of Aragon, in order to allow marriage to Anne Boleyn, in hopes of a male heir.

PROSE
Colet (*d.*1519): *Aeditio* (developed, with revisions by Erasmus, into the *Eton Latin Grammar*, publ. 1549)

DRAMA
Rastell: *Calisto and Melebea*; *Gentleness and Nobility*

1528

Reformation doctrines accepted in five Swiss Cantons; Anabaptist leader burnt at the stake in Vienna.

PROSE
(Castiglione: *The Book of the Courtier*, English transl. 1561)
Tyndale: *The Obedience of a Christian Man*; *The Parable of Wicked Mammon* (both publ. abroad)
Wyatt: *Quiet of Mind* (transl. of Plutarch)

POETRY
Roy: *Read Me and Be Not Wroth* (publ. in Strasbourg)
(*c.*) Skelton (*d.*1529): *Diverse Ballads and Ditties Salacious*

1529

Treaty of Cambrai ends war between France and Spain; Wolsey dismissed from Chancellorship because of his failure to secure Henry VIII's divorce from Catherine of Aragon; Sir Thomas More made Lord Chancellor (–1532); meeting of the 'Reformation Parliament'.

PROSE
More: *Dialogue of Diverse Matters*; *The Supplication of Souls* (against Fish's *The Supplication of Beggars*)

1530

Wolsey arrested for treason, but dies on way to the Tower of London; syphilis given its modern name.

PROSE
Tyndale: *The Pentateuch* (transl., publ. abroad); *The Practice of Prelates* (publ. abroad)

DRAMA
(*c.*) Skelton (*d.*1529): *Magnificence: A Goodly Interlude* (publ.)

1531

Zwingli, leader of the Reformation in Switzerland, killed in battle; in England, law passed causing unlicensed beggars to be whipped; act regulates construction of sewers in London; Pizarro begins conquest of the Incas.

PROSE
Elyot: *The Book Named the Governor*
(*c.*) Tyndale: *Answer to Sir Thomas More's Dialogue*; *Book of Jonah* (transl., publ. abroad)

POETRY
(*c.*) Skelton (*d.*1529): *Colin Clout*

1532

Henry VIII forbids certain payments to the Pope; Calvin preaching Reformation doctrine in Paris; wholesale price of wine regulated in England.

PROSE
(Machiavelli (d.1527): *The Prince*)
More: *Confutation of Tyndale's Answer* (pt i, pt ii 1533)
(Rabelais: *Pantagruel*, bk i of *Gargantua and Pantagruel*, bk ii 1534, bk iii 1546, bk iv 1548–52, bk v (authorship in question) 1564)

POETRY
(Ariosto: *Orlando Furioso*, final form, *see* 1516)
Chaucer (d.1400): *Complete Works* (ed. Thynne, incl. many spurious attributions)

1533

Parliament forbids appeals to Rome concerning wills, marriage and divorce; Henry VIII marries Anne Boleyn secretly, divorces Catherine of Aragon, and is excommunicated by Pope Clement VII; Cranmer made Archbishop of Canterbury (–1553); Holbein the younger: *The Ambassadors* (*p.*).

PROSE
Elyot: *Of the Knowledge Which Maketh a Wise Man*; *Pasquil the Plain*
(Erasmus: *Enchiridion Militis Christiani* ('The Manual of the Christian Knight'), transl.)
More: *The Apology of Sir Thomas More, Knight*

DRAMA
Heywood, John: *Play of the Weather* and other interludes (publ.)
Skelton (d.1529): *Old Christmas: An Interlude* (publ.)
POETRY
(c.) Wyatt writing his first satires

1534

Henry VIII made Supreme Head of the Church of England; authority of the Pope in England abolished; Parliament regulates number of sheep per farmer to 2,000 in order to limit enclosures; Loyola founds Jesuits.

PROSE
Elyot: *The Castle of Health*
(Rabelais: *Gargantua*, bk ii of *Gargantua and Pantagruel*, *see* 1532)

DRAMA
Heywood, John: *A Play of Love* (publ.)

1535

Thomas Cromwell appointed Vicar General; Church brought under Crown control; Bishop Fisher and Sir Thomas More executed for refusing to swear to Henry VIII's Act of Succession, which invalidated his marriage to Catherine of Aragon; (c.) Parmigianino: *The Madonna with the Long Neck* (*p.*).

PROSE
Coverdale: *Bible* (first complete English transl., publ. abroad)
Fisher: *Spiritual Consolation to His Sister*

POETRY
Wyatt writing his lyrics before and after this date

1536

Execution of Anne Boleyn; Tyndale burnt at the stake in Belgium; Cromwell organises suppression of the smaller monasteries; the Pilgrimage of Grace, an insurrection in the North and West in favour of the old religion, and aggravated by social conditions; Wales given representation in English Parliament; act provides relief for 'impotent poor' but compels 'sturdy beggars' to work; Cartier's second expedition to Canada explores St Lawrence river as far as island of Montreal.

PROSE
Anon: *A Remedy for Sedition*

1537

Jane Seymour, Henry VIII's third wife, dies giving birth to Prince Edward.

PROSE
Coverdale: *Bible* (modified version of 1535 edn; first Bible printed in England)
Cranmer: *Institution of a Christian Man*
'Thomas Matthew' (pseud. of John Rogers): *The Bible Which Is All the Holy Scriptures* (transl., mostly by Coverdale and Cranmer)

DRAMA
Udall (?): *Thersites* (interlude)

1538

Pope Paul III excommunicates Henry VIII; Becket's shrine at Canterbury destroyed; Mercator completes his first world map (in double heart-shaped projection); Titian completes his *Francesco Maria della Rovere, Duke of Urbino* (*p.*).

PROSE
Elyot: *Dictionary* (Latin–English)
DRAMA
Bale: *King John, Pts I and II*; *The Temptation of Our Lord and Saviour Jesus Christ by Satan*; *Three Laws, of Nature, Moses and Christ, Corrupted by the Sodomites, Pharisees and Papists*

POETRY
Lindsay: *The Complaint and Testament of a Popinjay*

1539

Act of Six Articles asserts Catholic doctrine in England; breaches of the Act punishable by burning at the stake; suppression of the large monasteries (total number of religious houses destroyed *c.*3,000); Holbein the younger: *Anne of Cleves* (*p.*).

PROSE
The Bible in English (first version of the combination of Tyndale's and Coverdale's transls, called 'The Great Bible', *see* 1540)
Elyot: *The Banquet of Sapience*

1540

Cromwell disgraced and executed for advising Henry VIII to marry Anne of Cleves; Raynald: *The Birth of Mankind* (illustrations, probably by Geminus, amongst the earliest examples of line engraving in Britain).

PROSE

The Bible in English ('The Great Bible' with added prologue by Cranmer, copies to be placed in every church, private ownership allowed, *see* 1539)

Elyot: *The Image of Governance* (transl. of Eucolpius and Lampridius)

Wyatt, implicated in the fall of his patron Cromwell, writes *Defence* against charges of treason and immorality

DRAMA

Lindsay: *A Satire of the Three Estates*

1541

Calvin returns to Geneva and continues development of Reformation doctrine and practice; first English nautical tables produced by Barlow.

1542

Henry VIII, in an attempt to make Scotland an English satellite, provokes Scottish counter-attack, which is defeated at Solway Moss; Recorde: *The Ground of Arts* (manual of arithmetic).

PROSE

Lily (*d.*1522): *Introduction to the Eight Parts of Speech* (final form of Lily's *Grammar*)

PROSE (*cont.*)

Udall: *Apophthegms of Erasmus* (transl.)

1543

Treaty with Scotland: Prince Edward to marry infant Mary, Queen of Scots; Scots defy treaty; Copernicus: *De Revolutionibus Orbium Celestium* ('On the Revolutions of the Celestial Spheres', supersedes old Ptolemaic astronomy and is banned by the Catholic Church –1758); Vesalius: *De Humani Corporis Fabrica* ('The Structure of the Human Body', pioneering anatomical study); Cellini completes gold salt-cellar for Francis I of France.

PROSE

More (*d.*1535): *History of Richard the Third* in Hardying (*d.*1465): *Chronicle of England*

1544

English invade Scotland; Henry VIII invades France and captures Boulogne; Parliament passes act releasing Henry from his debts; Palatino: *Libro qual s'insegna a scrivere* ('The Book in which Handwriting is Taught'); publication of the Litany in English.

PROSE

Bale: *Brief Chronicle Concerning Sir John Oldcastle* (publ. abroad)

1545

War with Scotland continues; Council of Trent opens (–1563) to reaffirm Catholic doctrine against Protestantism; oldest botanical garden in Europe started, at Padua.

PROSE
Ascham: *Toxophilus*
Elyot: *The Defence of Good Women*; *Preservative against Death*
Rhodes: *Book of Nurture for Men, Servants and Children*

DRAMA
For the following decades records exist of many court masques of which texts have been lost

POETRY
Skelton (*d.*1529): *The Book of Philip Sparrow*; *Certain Books, Compiled by Master Skelton* (incl. 'Speak Parrot' and 'A Treatise of the Scots'); *Why Come Ye Not to Court*

1546

Treaty of Ardres ends war with France (*see* 1544); Cardinal Beaton murdered in Scotland; Scotland starts revolt against Rome; Agricola: *De Natura Fossilium* (attempt to classify minerals).

PROSE
Bale: *Acts of English Votaries* (publ. abroad)
(Rabelais: *Tiers Livre*, bk iii of *Gargantua and Pantagruel*, *see* 1532)

POETRY
Heywood, John: *Dialogues Containing the Number of Proverbs*

1547

Execution of Henry, Earl of Surrey (poet) on the charge of treason; death of Henry VIII; accession of Edward VI (–1553), with Protestant Duke of Somerset as Protector (–1550); Scots defeated at Pinkie; John Knox exiled to France; Vagrant Act: able-bodied vagrants to be branded with letter V and enslaved for two years; publication of the *Book of Homilies*: Cranmer encourages its use by clergy.

PROSE
Boorde: *Breviary of Health, First Book of the Introduction of Knowledge*
Wilkinson: *Ethics of Aristotle* (first English transl.)

DRAMA
Bale: *Interlude Concerning the Temptation of Our Lord*; *Interlude Manifesting the Chief Promises of God* (both publ. abroad)

1548

Heresy Laws in England abolished; Tintoretto: *St Mark Rescuing a Slave* (*p.*); Bale: *Illustrium Majoris Britanniae Scriptorum Summarium* (biographical dictionary of famous British writers).

PROSE
Hall (*d.*1547): *Union of the Families of Lancaster and York* (Hall's *Chronicle*, most complete edn 1550)
Latimer: *A Notable Sermon Preached at St Paul's Church*
(Rabelais: *Quart Livre*, bk iv (compl. 1552) of *Gargantua and Pantagruel*, *see* 1532)

PROSE (*cont.*)
Udall: *Erasmus's Paraphrase of the New Testament* (transl.)

DRAMA
Bale: *Interlude Concerning Three Laws of Nature* (publ. abroad)

POETRY
(*c.*) Lindsay: *The Tragical Death of David Beaton*

1549

First Act of Uniformity, forbidding Catholic Mass and enforcing use of the First Prayer Book; clergy allowed to marry; Kett's rebellion in Norfolk, against the enclosure of common land; rebellions against religious reform in south-west of England; Francis Xavier takes Christianity to Japan.

PROSE
The Book of Common Prayer (mostly Cranmer's work)
Cheke: *The Hurt of Sedition*
Latimer: *Seven Sermons Preached Before the King in 1549*
Leland: *Journey and Search for England's Antiquities*
POETRY
Baldwin: *Canticles of Solomon in English Metres* (transl.)

POETRY (*cont.*)
(Du Bellay: *Defence and Illustration of the French Language*)
(*c.*) Sternhold (*d.*1549): *Certain Psalms* (transl.)
Wyatt (*d.*1542): *Certain Psalms Drawn into English Metre* (transl.)

1550

Duke of Northumberland becomes Protector (–1553), following arrest of Duke of Somerset; peace made with France and Scotland; Von Gesner: *Historia Animalium* ('History of Animals', compl. in 5 vols by 1587); Vasari: *Lives of the Most Excellent Painters, Sculptors and Architects.*

PROSE
Cranmer: *Defence of the Catholic Doctrine of the Sacrament*
Hall (*d.*1547): *Chronicle* (most complete edn, *see* 1548)
Harington, John: *The Book of Friendship* (transl. of Cicero)
Nicolls: *The History of Thucydides* (transl.)
Wyclif (*d.*1384): *Prologue Written in an Old English Bible*

POETRY
Bansley: *Tract Showing the Pride and Abuse of Women*
Crowley: *One and Thirty Epigrams*
Hunnis: *Certain Psalms in English Metre* (transl.)
Langland (*d.c.*1400): *The Vision of Piers the Plowman*
(Ronsard: *Odes*)

1551

Second session of the Council of Trent (*see* 1545) continues doctrinal codification of the Counter-Reformation; foundation of San Marcos University in Lima, Peru; Recorde: *The Pathway to Knowledge* (manual of geometry).

PROSE
Robynson: *More's Utopia* (transl.)
Turner: *A New Herbal*
Wilson, Thomas: *The Rule of Reason*

POETRY
(*c.*) Lindsay writes *Squire Meldrum*

1552

Duke of Northumberland has Duke of Somerset tried and executed; Second Act of Uniformity enforces use of Second, more Protestant, Prayer Book; act passed organising churches to collect funds for the poor; Tallis: *Dorian Mode Service* (simple musical setting for the Litany); Dr Simon Forman starts writing his diary and autobiography (–1602, publ. 1849).

DRAMA
Udall: *Ralph Roister Doister*

POETRY
Churchyard: *A Mirror for Man*

1553

Edward VI dies at the age of 15; accession of Queen Mary (–1558), after Duke of Northumberland fails to change the line of succession under the pretext of upholding Protestantism; his daughter-in-law, Lady Jane Grey, rules for nine days; execution of Northumberland; restoration of Roman Catholicism begins; Belon: *De Aquatilibus* (natural history of unusual marine animals).

PROSE
More (*d.*1535): *Dialogue of Comfort*
Wilson, Thomas: *The Art of Rhetoric*
DRAMA
Anon.: *Gammer Gurton's Needle* (early comedy)

POETRY
Douglas (*d.*1522): *Aeneid* (transl. of Virgil); *The Palace of Honour*

1554

Queen Mary marries Philip II of Spain, but Parliament does not allow him to be crowned king; Protestant rebellion led by Sir Thomas Wyatt, the younger; Act of Supremacy repealed; Cardinal Pole visits England as Papal Legate and absolves Parliament of heresy.

PROSE
Foxe: *Comentarii Rerum in Ecclesia Gestarum* (first edn of *The Book of Martyrs*, Latin, printed abroad, English transl. 1563)

POETRY
(*c.*) Lindsay: *A Dialogue between Experience and a Courtier*

1555

Revival of Persecuting Statutes; Bishop Gardiner heads commission for the trial of heretics and upholding doctrine of transubstantiation and the Pope's supremacy; many clergymen, including Latimer, burnt at the stake; John Knox returns to Scotland and unites Scots Protestants; formation of the Muscovy Trading Company to increase trade with Russia; Belon: *Histoire naturelle des oiseaux* ('The Natural History of Birds').

PROSE
Cheke: *On the Pronunciation of the Greek Language*
DRAMA
Anon.: *Interlude of Jack Juggler* (adaptation of Plautus's *Amphitruo*)

POETRY
Baldwin: *Memorial of Such Princes as Have Been Unfortunate in the Realm of England* (first attempt at publication of *The Mirror for Magistrates*, suppressed, *see* 1559)
Heywood, John: *Two Hundred Epigrams*

1556

Cranmer, Archbishop of Canterbury, after recanting his Protestant beliefs, withdraws his recantation and is burnt at the stake; he is succeeded by Archbishop Pole (–1558); Agricola (*d.*1555): *De Re Metallica* ('Concerning Metals', pioneering mineralogical study); Recorde: *The Castle of Knowledge* (manual of astronomy).

PROSE
The Genevan Psalter (mostly work of Whittingham)
Colville: *The Book of Boethius, Called The Comfort of Philosophy* (transl.)

POETRY
Heywood, John: *The Spider and the Fly*

1557

Queen Mary's alliance with Spain through her husband leads her to declare war on France; French defeated at the battle of St Quentin; Portuguese merchants settle in Macao, China.

PROSE
More (*d.*1535): *Works Written in English* (ed. William Rastell)
North: *The Dial of Princes* (transl. of Marcus Aurelius)
POETRY
Surrey (*d.*1547): *Certain Books of Virgil's Aeneid* (transl.)

POETRY (*cont.*)
Tottel and Grimald: *Songs and Sonnets* (Tottel's *Miscellany*, containing poems by Surrey, Wyatt, John Heywood and others: influential collection of lyric poetry)
Tusser: *A Hundred Good Points of Husbandry*

1558

French take Calais, after 210 years of English possession; death of Queen Mary; accession of Elizabeth I (–1603); William Cecil appointed Secretary of State (–1598); Mary, Queen of Scots married to Dauphin Francis, who dies two years later; first Russian trade delegation to London.

PROSE
Knox: *The First Blast of the Trumpet against the Monstrous Regiment of Women*
(Marguerite de Navarre (*d.*1549): *Heptameron*)

DRAMA
Anon.: *Interlude of Health*

1559

Restoration of Protestantism; Second Acts of Supremacy and Uniformity: all persons should attend Church of England services or be fined one shilling; those who refuse are called 'Recusants'; Pope Paul IV issues *Index Expurgatorius*, listing books unsuitable for Catholics.

PROSE
Elizabethan Book of Common Prayer
Aylmer: *Harbour against the Late Blown Blast Concerning Government of Women*
DRAMA
Heywood, Jasper: *Troas* (transl. of Seneca)

POETRY
Baldwin (ed.): *The Mirror for Magistrates* (*see* 1555)

1560

Reformed Church sanctioned by Scottish Parliament; formal gardens at Penshurst, Kent, established; Nicot imports tobacco into France; Vasari begins the Uffizi Palace, Florence (compl. 1574).

PROSE
The Geneva Bible (mainly work of Whittingham)
The Thirty-Nine Articles
Knox: *The Book of Discipline*; *Treatise on Predestination*
DRAMA
Various anonymous interludes publ.: *Impatient Poverty*; *The Nice Wanton*; *Thersytes*

DRAMA (*cont.*)
Heywood, Jasper: *Thyestes* (transl. of Seneca)
POETRY
Googe: *The Zodiac of Life* (transl. of Palingenius, compl. in 12 bks by 1565)
Heywood, John: *A Fourth Hundred of Epigrams*

1561

Mary, Queen of Scots returns to Scotland, following death of her husband Francis; she clashes with John Knox over religion; sterling standard silver coinage established in England; Fallopius: *Observationes Anatomicae* (pioneering study of anatomy).

PROSE
Hoby: *The Courtier* (transl. of Castiglione)
Norton: *Institution of the Christian Religion* (transl. of Calvin)
(Scaliger: *Poetics*)
DRAMA
Heywood, Jasper: *Hercules Furens* (transl. of Seneca)
Preston: *Cambises*

POETRY
Chaucer (*d.*1400): *The Works of Geoffrey Chaucer, with Diverse Additions, with The Siege of Thebes, Compiled by J. Lydgate* (ed. Stowe)

1562

Religious wars between Catholics and Protestants begin in France (–1598); Elizabeth I makes Treaty of Richmond with Huguenots, and sends forces to Normandy; English gain Le Havre; outbreak of O'Neill rebellion in Ireland (–1567); English trade in West African slaves begins with Sir John Hawkins's first voyage (–1563); Veronese: *The Marriage at Cana* (*p.*); Legh: *Accedens of Armoury* (study of heraldry).

PROSE
(Cellini finishes *Autobiography*, publ. 1728)
Grafton: *Abridgement of the Chronicles of England*
Jewel: *An Apology for the Church of England*
Latimer (*d.*1555): *Twenty-Seven Sermons*
DRAMA
Norton and Sackville: *Gorboduc* (*Ferrex and Porrex*)

POETRY
The Whole Book of Metrical Psalms (first complete edn, by various hands, known as the *Old Version*)
Broke: *History of Romeus and Juliet*
Heywood, John: *Works*

1563

French retake Le Havre (*see* 1562); Parliament attempts legislation to improve unemployment (Statute of Apprentices) and prevent enclosures; work started on construction of the Escorial, near Madrid (compl. 1584); Shute: *The First and Chief Grounds of Architecture*; portrait of Lord Darnley, by Eworth, shows him wearing a watch.

PROSE
Foxe: *The Acts and Monuments of the Church* (usually called *The Book of Martyrs*, first English version, enlarged to include Latimer and others, *see* 1554)
Rainolde: *Foundation of Rhetoric*
DRAMA
Neville: *Oedipus* (transl. of Seneca)

POETRY
Googe: *Eclogues, Epitaphs and Sonnets*

1564

Treaty of Troyes ends war with France (*see* 1562); Puritan opposition to Anglicanism starts; Merchant Adventurers of England granted new charter; Sir John Hawkins's second voyage to South America and the West Indies (–1565).

PROSE
The Scottish Psalter
Bullein: *Dialogue against the*
Pestilence
(Rabelais (?) (*d.c.*1553): *Le Cinqui-*
ème et dernier livre, bk v of *Gargan-*
tua and Pantagruel, see 1532)

DRAMA
Anon. ('R.B.'): *Appius and Virginia*

1565

Mary, Queen of Scots marries her cousin, Lord Darnley; Sir John Hawkins brings sweet potatoes and possibly tobacco to England; Tintoretto starts work on the decoration of the Scuola di San Rocco, Venice (compl. 1588).

PROSE
Golding: *Caesar's Exploits in Gallia*
(transl.)
Stow: *A Summary of English Chron-*
icles (*see* 1618)
DRAMA
Anon.: *Interlude of King Darius*
(publ.)

DRAMA (*cont.*)
Edwards, Richard: *Damon and*
Pithias
POETRY
Golding: *Ovid's Metamorphoses*
(transl., compl. in 15 bks by 1567)

1566

Elizabeth I forbids Parliament to discuss her marriage prospects; Royal Exchange founded; Brueghel the elder: *The Wedding Dance* (*p.*).

PROSE
Adlington: *The Golden Ass of*
Apuleius (transl.)
Grantham: *A Pleasant Disport*
Entitled Philocopo (transl. of
Boccaccio)
Painter: *The Palace of Pleasure*
(transl. of Boccaccio, Bandello and
others, vol. i, vol. ii 1567)

DRAMA
Gascoigne: *Jocasta* (transl. of Dolce);
Supposes (transl. of Ariosto)
Studley: *Agamemnon*; *Hercules*;
Medea (all transl. of Seneca)
POETRY
Drant: *A Medicinable Moral, That Is,*
Two Books of Horace His Satires
(transl.)

1567

Revolt of the Netherlands against Spanish rule begins (–1648); Mary, Queen of Scots is forced by rebellion to abdicate; Drake joins Sir John Hawkins on expedition to the West Indies (–1569); first printing of Anglo-Saxon literature (prose of Aelfric).

PROSE
Fenton: *Certain Tragical Discourses*
(transl. of Bandello)
Paynell: *The Treasure of Amadis of*
France (transl.)
Sandford: *Manual of Epictetus* (transl.)
DRAMA
Pickering: *A New Interlude of Vice*
(*Horestes*)

DRAMA (*cont.*)
Studley: *Hippolytus* (transl. of
Seneca)
POETRY
Drant: *Art of Poetry, Epistles and*
Satires (transl. of Horace)
Turberville: *Eclogues of Mantuan*
(transl.); *Epitaphs, Epigrams,*
Songs and Sonnets; *The Heroical*
Epistles of Ovid (transl.)

1568

After defeat of her forces, Mary, Queen of Scots takes refuge in England and is taken prisoner by Elizabeth I; first Desmond rebellion in Ireland (–1572); school for English Jesuits founded at Douai in the Netherlands.

PROSE
The Bishops' Bible (chiefly work of Matthew Parker)
Grafton: *A Chronicle at Large of the Affairs of England from the Creation of the World unto the First Year of Queen Elizabeth*
Tilney: *Discourse of Duties in Marriage*
DRAMA
Fulwell: *Like Will to Like*
POETRY
Howell: *Arbour of Amity*; *New Sonnets and Pretty Pamphlets*
Lindsay (*d*.1555): *Works*

POETRY (*cont.*)
Skelton (*d*.1529): *Pithy, Pleasant and Profitable Works, Now Collected*
Turberville: *The Plain Path to Perfect Virtue*

1569

Rebellion in the North in favour of Mary and the old religion suppressed with cruelty by Earl of Sussex; Mercator: *Cosmographia* (with cylindrical projection of the earth).

PROSE
Hawkins, Sir John: *True Declaration of His Voyage in 1567 and 1568*
Newton: *Worthy Book of Old Age* (transl. of Cicero)
Underdowne: *Aethiopean History of Heliodorus* (transl.)

POETRY
Spenser: *The Visions of Bellay*; *The Visions of Petrarch*
Underdowne: *Ovid His Invective against Ibis*

1570

Pope Pius V excommunicates Elizabeth I and declares her a usurper; Ortelius: *Theatrum Orbis Terrarum* ('The Theatre of the World', first modern atlas); Hilliard paints his first dated miniature of Elizabeth I; Palladio: *Treatise on Architecture*.

PROSE
Ascham (*d*.1568): *The Schoolmaster*
Foxe: *Sermon of Christ Crucified*
North: *The Moral Philosophy of Doni* (transl.)
Wilson, Thomas: *Three Orations of Demosthenes* (transl.)

POETRY
Barbour (*d*.1395): *Bruce*
Henryson (*d.c*.1508): *The Moral Fables of Aesop*

1571

Convocation sanctions Thirty-Nine Articles of Faith, to be printed in the Prayer Book; Spanish fleet defeats the Turks at Lepanto; Baildon and Beauchesne: *A Book Containing Divers Sorts of Hands* (writing manual).

PROSE
Latimer (*d*.1555): *Fruitful Sermons* (pt i, pts ii–iii 1575)

1572

First Parish Poor Rate; St Bartholomew's Day Massacre of Protestants in France; Archbishop Parker founds the Society of Antiquaries.

PROSE
Parker: *De Antiquitate Britanniae Ecclesiae* ('Concerning the Ancient British Church', Latin)
Wilson, Thomas: *Discourse upon Usury*
DRAMA
Gascoigne: *The Mask for Lord Montacute*
Woodes: *The Conflict of Conscience*

POETRY
(Camoens: *Os Lusiados*)
Churchyard: *The Three First Books of Ovid's Tristia* (transl.)
Fenton: *Monophylo, or A Philosophical Discourse of Love*

1573

Revolt of the Netherlands continues with Spanish massacre of inhabitants of Haarlem.

PROSE
Gascoigne: 'The Adventures of Master F.J.' (in *A Hundred Sundry Flowers*)
DRAMA
(Tasso: *Aminta*)
POETRY
Gascoigne: *A Hundred Sundry Flowers* (miscellany, incl. prose,

POETRY (*cont.*)
interludes, lyrics and sonnet-sequences)
Tusser: *Five Hundred Points of Good Husbandry* (didactic verse)

1574

Roman Catholic mission from Douai to reconvert England; Angola colonised by Portuguese; Dasypodius builds astronomical clock in Strasbourg Cathedral; Burbage receives licence to open a theatre (*see* 1576).

PROSE
Parker: *Lives of the Seventy Archbishops of Canterbury*
Rich: *Dialogue between Mercury and an English Soldier*

PROSE (*cont.*)
Scot: *Perfect Platform of a Hop Garden*

1575

Elizabeth I turns down William I of Orange's request for English intervention against Spain in the Netherlands; Byrd and Tallis: *Cantiones Sacrae* (church music, other collections 1589 and 1591).

PROSE
Fenton: *Golden Epistles* (transl. of Guevara)
Turberville: *The Book of Falconry*; *The Noble Art of Venery*
DRAMA
Gascoigne: *The Glass of Government*; (with others): *The Princely Pleasures at Kenilworth*
Golding: *Abraham's Sacrifice* (transl. of Beza)

POETRY
Breton: *A Small Handful of Fragrant Flowers*
Churchyard: *The First Part of Churchyard's Chippes*
Gascoigne: *Posies of George Gascoigne* (incl. 'Notes of Instruction Concerning Making of Verse')
Rolland: *Treatise Called the Court of Venus*

1576

M.P. Peter Wentworth defends parliamentary freedom of speech and is briefly imprisoned; act provides houses of correction for vagabonds; Pacification of Ghent: the Netherlands agree to unite against Spain; Tycho Brahe establishes observatory at Uraniborg; first theatre in England opens at Shoreditch (*see* 1574).

PROSE

Gascoigne: *A Delicate Diet for Dainty Mouthed Drunkyards*; *The Spoil of Antwerp*
Gilbert: *Discourse of a New Passage to Cataia*
Pettie: *A Petite Pallace of Pettie His Pleasure*

POETRY

Edwards, Richard (ed., *d*.1566): *The Paradise of Dainty Conceits*

POETRY (*cont.*)

Gascoigne: *The Steel Glass: A Satire Together with The Complaint of Phylomene*
Whetstone: *The Rock of Regard* (prose and verse)

1577

Archbishop Grindal suspended for failing to check nonconformist clergy; first execution of Jesuit missionary to England; Drake sets out on round the world voyage (–1580).

PROSE

Eden (*d*.1576): *History of Travel in the East and West Indies*
Hellowes: *Lives of Ten Emperors of Rome* (transl. of Guevara)
Holinshed: *Chronicles of England, Scotland and Ireland*
Peacham, Henry the elder: *Garden of Eloquence*

DRAMA

Lupton: *All for Money*

POETRY

Breton: *A Flourish upon Fancy*; *The Works of a Young Wit*
Googe: *Four Books of Husbandry* (transl. of Heresbach)
Kendall: *Flowers of Epigrams*

1578

Levant Trading Company founded in London for trade with Turkey.

PROSE

Best: *Discourse of the Voyages of Martin Frobisher*
Churchyard: *Woeful Wars in Flanders* (incl. verse)
Lyly: *Euphues, the Anatomy of Wit* (pt i, his highly decorated prose called Euphuism, pt ii 1580)
Rich: *Alarm to England*

DRAMA

Sidney: *The Lady of May* (*The Entertainment at Wanstead*)
Whetstone: *Promos and Cassandra, Pts I and II*

POETRY

Churchyard: *Discourse of the Queen's Entertainment in Suffolk and Norfolk*

POETRY (*cont.*)

(Du Bartas: *La semaine, ou la Création du monde* ('The Week, or The Creation of the World'))
Proctor: *A Gorgeous Gallery of Gallant Inventions*
Whetstone: *A Remembrance of the Life of George Gascoigne*

1579

Second Desmond rebellion in Ireland (–1583); Elizabeth I grants charter to the Eastland Trading Company for trade in the Baltic; Drake sails up the Pacific coast of America as far as Canada.

PROSE
Fenton: *History of the Wars of Italy* (transl. of Guicciardini)
Frampton: *Travels of Marco Polo* (transl.)
Gosson: *The School of Abuse, Containing a Pleasant Invective against Poets, Pipers, Players, Jesters and Such Like Caterpillars of a Commonwealth*; *The Ephemerides of Phialo and a Short Apology for the School of Abuse*
Lodge: *A Reply to Stephen Gosson's School of Abuse in Defence of Poetry, Music and Stage Plays*

PROSE (*cont.*)
North: *Plutarch's Lives of the Noble Grecians and Romans* (transl.)
POETRY
Churchyard: *A General Rehearsal of Wars*; *The Misery of Flanders*
Munday: *The Mirror of Mutability*
Spenser: *The Shepherd's Calendar*

1580

Further campaign of missionary infiltration into England by Jesuits; Drake returns from voyage round the world; (*c.*) El Greco: *The Dream of Philip* (*p.*).

PROSE
Lyly: *Euphues and His England* (pt ii, *see* 1578)
(Montaigne: *Essais*, bks i–ii, bk iii 1588, in final form 1595)
Munday: *The Pain of Pleasure*; *Zelauto, the Fountain of Fame*
Spenser and Harvey: *Three Letters and Two Other Letters Passed between Two University Men*
Stow: *The Chronicles of England*

DRAMA
Sidney: *A Dialogue between Two Shepherds*
POETRY
Churchyard: *Churchyard's Chance*
Gifford, Humfrey: *A Posy of Gilloflowers*

1581

Conversion to Roman Catholicism considered as treason; Galileo discovers isochronous movement of pendulum by observing a lamp in Pisa Cathedral; Beaujoyeulx stages an allegorical *ballet comique* for the French queen, Catherine de Medici.

PROSE
Mulcaster: *Positions*
Pettie: *Civil Conversations of Stefano Guazzo* (transl., compl. in 4 bks by 1586)
Rich: *Adventures of Don Simnides* (vol. i, vol. ii 1584); *Rich His Farewell to the Military Profession*
DRAMA
Heywood, Jasper, and others: *Seneca His Ten Tragedies* (transl., publ.)
Newton: *Thebais* (transl. of Seneca)
Peele: *The Arraignment of Paris*

DRAMA (*cont.*)
Watson: *Antigone* (transl. of Sophocles)
POETRY
Hall, Arthur: *Ten Books of Homer's Iliad* (transl.)
Howell: *Howell His Devises*
(Tasso: *Jerusalem Delivered*)

1582

James VI of Scotland kidnapped by Protestant nobles to remove him from Catholic influence; Jesuit mission to China; plague in London; Pope Gregory XIII promulgates new calendar, with more accurate solar dating system than Julian calendar (Gregorian calendar adopted in Britain in 1752); *The Rheims and Douai Bible* (New Testament, in English for use by Catholics, *see* 1610).

PROSE
Gosson: *Plays Confuted in Five Actions*
Hakluyt: *Diverse Voyages Touching the Discovery of America*
Mulcaster: *Elementarie*
Munday: *A Discovery of Edward Campion*
Whetstone: *An Heptameron of Civil Discourses* (transl. of Cinthio)

POETRY
Raleigh writing poems and circulating them at Court
Stanyhurst: *Aeneid* (transl. of Virgil bks i–iv)
Watson: *Hecatompathia, or A Passionate Century of Love*

1583

Spanish Ambassador and Throckmorton involved in plot to murder Elizabeth I; Whitgift appointed Archbishop of Canterbury (–1604); Newfoundland claimed for Elizabeth I by Gilbert; Cambridge University Press appoints its first printer; Queen's Company of Players formed.

PROSE
Greene: *Mamillia* (pt i, pt ii 1593)
Stubbes: *Anatomy of Abuses*

1584

Revelation of Philip II of Spain's 'Catholic Enterprise' to depose Elizabeth I; Raleigh's sailors land in Virginia.

PROSE
Greene: *Arbasto*; *Gwydonius*; *The Mirror of Modesty*; *Morando* (augmented edn 1587)
Lodge: *An Alarum against Usurers*
Munday: *A Watchword to England*
Scot: *Discovery of Witchcraft*
Warner: *Pan His Syrinx*
Whetstone: *A Mirror for Magistrates of Cities*; *A Touchstone for the Time*

DRAMA
Harrison: *Philomathes's Dream*
Lyly: *Campaspe*; *Sappho and Phao*
POETRY
James VI of Scotland: *Essays of a Prentice in the Art of Poesy*

1585

Following the murder of William I of Orange (1584), Earl of Leicester is sent to the Netherlands to help the Dutch in their war with Spain; Drake attacks the Spanish Indies; Parry expelled from Parliament after opposing anti-Jesuit bill; attempt to colonise Virginia fails; Stevinus: *La Thiende* ('The Tenth', establishes use of decimal fractions in mathematics).

PROSE
Bullokar: *Aesop's Fables* (transl.)
DRAMA
Lyly: *Galathea*

DRAMA (*cont.*)
Peele: *The Pageant before Woolstone Dixie*

1586

Mary, Queen of Scots implicated in Babington Plot to kill Elizabeth I; Mary put on trial; Sir Philip Sidney killed in battle at Zutphen in the Netherlands; to check Puritan pamphleteers, all publications forbidden unless previously approved by ecclesiastical authorities.

PROSE
Camden: *Britannia* (Latin, greatly enlarged edn 1607)
Webbe, William: *Discourse of English Poetry*
Whetstone: *The English Mirror*

DRAMA
Harrison: *Philomathes's Second Dream*
Peele: *The Hunting of Cupid*
POETRY
Warner: *Albion's England* (compl. in 16 bks by 1606)

1587

Mary, Queen of Scots executed; Earl of Leicester returns to England after failure of Dutch expedition (*see* 1585); Drake destroys Spanish fleet at Cadiz; Hakluyt: *Voyages Made into Florida*.

PROSE
Day, Angell: *Daphnis and Chloe* (transl. of Longus)
Gifford, George: *Discourse of Subtle Practices of Devils*
Greene: *Euphues His Censure to Philautus*; *Penelope's Web*
Knox (*d.*1572): *The History of the Reformation of Religion within the Realm of Scotland*
Rankins: *Mirror of Monsters*
Young: *Amorous Fiametta* (transl. of Boccaccio)
DRAMA
Greene: *Alphonsus, King of Aragon*
Kyd: *The Spanish Tragedy* (*Hieronimo is Mad Again*)

DRAMA (*cont.*)
Marlowe: *Tamburlaine the Great, Pt I*
Peele: *The Love of King David and Fair Bathsheba*
POETRY
Churchyard: *The Worthiness of Wales*
Fraunce: *The Lamentations of Amyntas* (transl. of Watson's Latin version of Tasso)
Gascoigne (*d.*1577): *The Pleasantest Works of George Gascoigne*
Grove: *History of Pelops and Hippodamia: Epigrams, Songs and Sonnets*
Turberville: *Tragical Tales*
Whetstone: *Sir Philip Sidney, His Honourable Life*

1588

Spanish Armada sent by Philip II of Spain defeated by English fleet under Howard of Effingham; Byrd: *Psalms, Sonnets and Songs*; *Y Beible Cyssegr-Lan* (Welsh Bible, Old and New Testaments translated by various hands); the Martin Marprelate Tracts (–1589): a series of seven anti-episcopal tracts written in the name of Martin Marprelate and his two sons, Martin Senior and Martin Junior, mixing theology with scurrilous and abusive satire; they were printed on a secret press moved about the country to avoid pursuit by the authorities; a number of anti-Martin replies were written, notably *An Almond for a Parrot*, probably by Thomas Nashe (1590).

PROSE
Bigges: *A Summary and True Discourse of Sir Francis Drake's West Indian Voyage*
Fraunce: *The Arcadian Rhetoric*
Greene: *Pandosto*; *Perimedes the Blacksmith*
DRAMA
Lodge: *The Wounds of Civil War, or Marius and Scilla*

DRAMA (*cont.*)
Lyly: *Endymion, the Man in the Moon*
Marlowe: *Tamburlaine the Great, Pt II*
POETRY
Munday: *A Banquet of Dainty Conceits*

1589

Accession of Henry IV of France (–1610); invention of hosiery-knitting machine by William Lee; Byrd: *Songs of Sundry Natures.*

PROSE
Greene: *Ciceronis Amor, Tullies Love*; *Greene's Arcadia, or Menaphon*; *The Spanish Masquerado*
Hakluyt: *The Principal Navigations, Voyages and Discoveries of the English Nation* (see 1598, 1600)
Nashe: *The Anatomy of Absurdity*
Puttenham: *The Art of English Poesy*

DRAMA
Greene: *Friar Bacon and Friar Bungay*
Lyly: *Midas*; *Mother Bombie*
Marlowe: *The Jew of Malta*
Munday: *John a Kent and John a Cumber*
Peele: *The Battle of Alcazar*

POETRY
Lodge: *Scillaes Metamorphosis* (*Glaucus and Scilla*)
Peele: *A Tale of Troy*

1590

Sea battles with the Spanish navy; construction of Hardwick Hall, Derbyshire, begun (compl. 1597); development of the compound microscope; Monteverdi takes up position at the court of Mantua (–1612): *Second Book of Madrigals.*

PROSE
Greene: *Greene's Mourning Garment*; *Greene's Never Too Late*; *The Royal Exchange*
Holland: *Treatise against Witchcraft*
Lodge: *Rosalynde*
Munday: *Amadis of Gaul* (transl., compl. in 4 pts by 1618)
Nashe: *The First Part of Pasquil's Apology*
Sidney (*d*.1586): *The Countess of Pembroke's Arcadia*
Webbe, Edward: *The Rare and Most Wonderful Things E.W. Has Seen*

DRAMA
Anon.: *King Leir*
Greene: *George a Greene, the Pinner of Wakefield*; *The Scottish History of James IV*; (with Lodge): *A Looking Glass for London and England*
Lyly: *Love's Metamorphosis*
Marlowe (with Nashe): *Dido, Queen of Carthage*
Peele: *The Old Wives' Tale*
Shakespeare Apocrypha: *Edward III*; *Fair Em, the Miller's Daughter*; *Mucedorus*
Wilson, Robert: *The Cobbler's Prophecy*

POETRY
(*c*.) Davies, Sir John, and Marlowe: *Epigrams and Elegies* (incl. transl. of Ovid)
Spenser: *The Faerie Queene* (bks i–iii, see 1596); *Muiopotmos, or The Fate of the Butterfly*
Watson: *Eclogue upon the Death of Sir Francis Walsingham*

DATES OF SHAKESPEARE'S PLAYS

In the table below the plays of Shakespeare are set out in the order that they appear in this chronology. The LIMITS column suggests likely earliest and latest dates for the writing and performance of the plays. The next column gives a suggested date for composition and performance of the plays (given the pressure on the companies of actors to come up with new material for their repertory, the plays are likely to have been staged soon after they were written). The final column (in brackets) suggests the tendency of more recent scholarly opinion with regard to the dating of some plays, as expressed in the new Oxford Shakespeare, edited by Stanley Wells and Gary Taylor, published in 1986. The editors of this exciting work of Shakespearian textual reorganisation repeatedly make clear the highly conjectural nature of all attempts at an exact chronology for the plays.

PLAY	LIMITS	WRITTEN/ PERFORMANCE	
Henry VI, Pt II	1590–2	1591	(1590–1)
Henry VI, Pt III	1590–2	1591	
Henry VI, Pt I	3 March	1592	
The Comedy of Errors	1590–4	1592	(1594)
Richard III	1591–7	1593	(1592–3)
The Two Gentlemen of Verona	1590–8	1593	(1590)
Titus Andronicus	23 January	1594	
The Taming of the Shrew	1594–8	1594	
Love's Labour's Lost	1588–97	1595	(1593–4)
Romeo and Juliet	1591–7	1595	(1594–5)
Richard II	1594–5	1595	
A Midsummer Night's Dream	1594–8	1595	(1594–5)
King John	1591–8	1596	(1595–6)
The Merchant of Venice	1594–7	1596	(1596–7)
Henry IV, Pt I	1596–8	1597	(1596)
Henry IV, Pt II	1597–8	1597	(1596–7)
Much Ado about Nothing	1598–1600	1598	(1598–9)
Love's Labour's Won (text lost)	1590–8	1598	
Henry V	1599	1599	
Julius Caesar	1598–1600	1599	
As You Like It	1598–1600	1599	(1600)
The Merry Wives of Windsor	1597–1602	1600	(1597)
Twelfth Night	1600–2	1600	(1601)
Hamlet	1599–1601	1601	(1600)
Troilus and Cressida	1601–3	1602	
All's Well That Ends Well	1601–3	1602	
Othello	1603–4	1604	(1603–4)
Measure for Measure	1603–4	1604	
King Lear	1605–6	1605	
Macbeth	1606–11	1606	
Timon of Athens	1606–8	1607	(1604)
Antony and Cleopatra	1606–8	1607	(1606)
Coriolanus	1605–10	1608	
Pericles	1606–8	1608	
Cymbeline	1608–11	1609	(1610–11)
The Winter's Tale	1610–11	1610	(1609–10)
The Tempest	1609–11	1611	(1610–11)
Cardenio (text lost)			(1613)
Henry VIII	June	1613	

1591

Elizabeth I founds Trinity College, Dublin; London merchant John Lancaster reaches the Spice Islands (East Indies); Vieta: *In Artem Analyticam Isagoge* ('Introduction to the Analytic Arts', on algebraic notation).

PROSE

Greene: *Greene's Farewell to Folly*; *A Notable Discovery of Cozenage* (pt i of *Cony Catching*); *The Second Part of Cony Catching* (*see* 1592)
Raleigh: *The Fight about the Azores*
Savile: *Histories of Tacitus* (transl.)
Southwell: *Mary Magdalen's Funeral Tears*

DRAMA

Anon.: *Arden of Faversham*; *Jack Straw*; *Locrine*; *The True Tragedy of Richard III*
Greene: *Orlando Furioso*
Peele: *Edward I*
Shakespeare: *Henry VI, Pts II and III*

POETRY

Breton: *Breton's Bower of Delights*
Drayton: *The Harmony of the Church*
Harington, Sir John: *Orlando Furioso in English Heroical Verse* (transl. of Ariosto)
Sidney (*d.*1586): *Astrophel and Stella*
Spenser: *Complaints*; *Daphnaida*

1592

Plague in London, leading to closing of theatres (–1594); literary quarrel between Greene, Nashe and Harvey over vilification of Greene (*d.*1592) in satirical pamphlets.

PROSE

Greene (*d.*1592): *A Disputation between a He Cony Catcher and a She Cony Catcher*; *Greene's Vision*; *A Groatsworth of Wit*; *A Quip for an Upstart Courtier*; *The Repentance of Greene: The Third Part of Cony Catching* (*see* 1591)
Harvey, Gabriel: *Four Letters and Certain Sonnets, Especially Touching Robert Greene*
Lodge: *Euphues's Shadow*
Nashe: *Pierce Penniless His Supplication to the Devil*; *Strange News of the Intercepting Certain Letters*
Rich: *The Adventures of Brusanus*
Stow: *Annals of England* (reissue of *The Chronicles of England*, *see* 1580)

DRAMA

Anon.: *A Knack to Know a Knave*; *Woodstock*
Greene (*d.*1592): *Selimus*; (with Chettle): *John of Bordeaux, or The Second Part of Friar Bungay*
Marlowe: *Doctor Faustus*; *Edward II*
Nashe: *Summer's Last Will and Testament*

DRAMA (*cont.*)

Shakespeare: *The Comedy of Errors*; *Henry VI, Pt I*
Warner: *Menaechmi* (transl. of Plautus)

POETRY

Breton: *Pilgrimage to Paradise*
Churchyard: *A Handful of Gladsome Verse Given to the Queen's Majesty*
Constable: *Diana*
Daniel: *The Complaint of Rosamund*; *Delia*
Sylvester: *La Semaine of Du Bartas* (transl., compl. in 4 instalments by 1599)

1593

Henry IV of France converts to Catholicism; in England, adult absentees from church to be imprisoned; execution of five Puritans for denying the Queen's supremacy; Markham: *A Discourse of Horsemanship*; Caravaggio: *The Young Bacchus* (*p*.).

PROSE

Chettle: *Kind Heart's Dream, Containing Five Apparitions, with Their Invectives against Abuses Reigning*

Gifford, George: *Dialogue Concerning Witches and Witchcraft*

Harvey: *A New Letter of Notable Contents*; *Pierce's Supererogation*

Hooker: *Of the Laws of Ecclesiastical Polity* (bks i–iv, bk v 1597)

Nashe: *Christ's Tears over Jerusalem*

Whetstone (*d.c.*1587): *Aurelia* (*Heptameron* of 1582, retitled)

DRAMA

Daniel: *Cleopatra*

Lyly: *The Woman in the Moon*

Marlowe: *The Massacre at Paris*

Shakespeare: *Richard III*; *The Two Gentlemen of Verona*

POETRY

Anon.: *Phoenix Nest*

Barnes: *Parthenophil and Parthenophe*

Churchyard: *Churchyard's Challenge*

Drayton: *Idea, the Shepherd's Garland*

POETRY (*cont.*)

Fletcher, Giles the elder: *Licea, or Poems of Love*

Lodge: *Phillis*

Marlowe: *Lucan's Pharsalia* (transl. of bk i)

Morley: *Canzonets*

Shakespeare: *Venus and Adonis*

Watson (*d.*1592): *Tears of Fancy*

1594

Giordano Bruno put on trial by the Inquisition for his support of Copernican theory of the universe (*see* 1600).

PROSE

Nashe: *The Terrors of the Night*; *The Unfortunate Traveller, or The Life of Jack Wilton*

DRAMA

Anon.: *A Knack to Know an Honest Man*

Bacon and others: *Gesta Grayorum*

Kyd: *Cornelia*

Lindsay (*d.*1555): *Squire Meldrum* (publ., earlier edns lost)

Shakespeare: *The Taming of the Shrew*; *Titus Andronicus*

POETRY

Barnfield: *The Affectionate Shepherd, Containing the Complaint of Daphnis for the Love of Ganymede*

Carew, Richard: *Godfrey of Bulloigne* (transl. of Tasso's *Jerusalem Delivered*, cantos i–v)

POETRY (*cont.*)

Chapman: *The Shadow of Night*

Daniel: *Delia and Rosamond Augmented*

Drayton: *Idea's Mirror*

Shakespeare: *The Rape of Lucrece*

Sylvester: *Monodia*

Willoby: *Willoby His Avisa*

1595

Tyrone's rebellion in Ireland begins (–1603); Raleigh sails to Guyana in search of El Dorado; Drake and Sir John Hawkins embark on expedition to the West Indies: both perish (Hawkins 1595, Drake 1596); Jesuit poet Southwell executed.

PROSE

Beddingfield: *Florentine History of Machiavelli* (transl.)

Chettle: *Piers Plainne's Seven Years Prenticeship*

(Montaigne (*d*.1592): *Essais*, final form, *see* 1580)

Sidney (*d*.1586): *An Apology for Poetry*

Southwell (*d*.1595): *Triumphs over Death*

DRAMA

Munday and others: *Sir Thomas More*

Shakespeare: *Love's Labours Lost*; *A Midsummer Night's Dream*; *Richard II*; *Romeo and Juliet*

POETRY

Barnes: *Divine Century of Spiritual Sonnets*

Barnfield: *Cynthia, with Certain Sonnets and The Legend of Cassandra*

Breton: *Mary Magdalen's Love*

Chapman: *Ovid's Banquet of Sense: A Coronet for Mistress Philosophy, and Other Poems*

Churchyard: *A Praise of Poetry*

POETRY (*cont.*)

Daniel: *The Civil Wars between the Houses of Lancaster and York* (compl. in 8 bks by 1609)

Drayton: *Endimion and Phoebe*

Edwards, Thomas: *Cephalus and Procris*

Lodge: *A Fig for Momus*

Southwell (*d*.1595): *Maeoniae, or Certain Poems*; *Saint Peter's Complaint*

Spenser: *Amoretti*; *Colin Clout's Come Home Again*; *Epithalamion*

1596

Rural unrest in Oxfordshire due to poor agrarian conditions; Earl of Essex storms Cadiz; Sir John Harington designs water-closet, installed in the Queen's Palace, Richmond (not to come into general use for 200 years).

PROSE

Harington, Sir John: *Anatomy of the Metamorphosed Ajax*; *An Apology or Rather a Recantation*; *Metamorphosis of Ajax*; *Ulysses upon Ajax*

Lodge: *A Margarite of America*; *Wit's Misery*

Nashe: *Have With You to Saffron Walden*

Raleigh: *The Discovery of the Empire of Guiana*

DRAMA

Chapman: *The Blind Beggar of Alexandria*

Greville: *Mustapha*

DRAMA (*cont.*)

Shakespeare: *King John*; *The Merchant of Venice*

POETRY

Davies, Sir John: *Orchestra*

Drayton: *Mortimeriados*; *The Tragical History of Robert, Duke of Normandy*

Middleton: *Wisdom of Solomon Paraphrased*

Spenser: *The Faerie Queene* (bks i–iii revised, plus bks iv–vi, *see* 1590); *Four Hymns*; *Prothalamion*

1597

Philip II of Spain's second Armada defeated by storms; Azores plundered by English raiders; potatoes (called, erroneously, Virginia potatoes) described in Gerarde's *Herbal*, having reached England via the Netherlands from Spain, where they had arrived from South America *c*.1580 (*see* 1670); Dowland: *First Book of Songs or Airs of Four Parts with Tableture for the Lute* (bk ii 1600, bk iii 1603); first opera, Peri's *Daphne*, performed in Florence (music lost).

PROSE
Bacon: *The Colours of Good and Evil* (essays much enlarged in edns of 1616 and 1625); *Essays*; *Meditationes Sacrae*
Breton: *Wit's Trenchmour*
(*c*.) Deloney: *The Gentle Craft*; *Jack of Newbery, the Famous and Worthy Clothier of England*
Hooker: *Of the Laws of Ecclesiastical Polity* (bk v, *see* 1593)
James VI of Scotland: *Demonology*

DRAMA
Chapman: *An Humorous Day's Mirth*
Jonson: *The Case Is Altered*
Shakespeare: *Henry IV, Pts I and II*

POETRY
Breton and others: *Arbour of Amorous Devices*
Drayton: *England's Heroical Epistles*
Hall, Joseph: *Virgidemiae* (bks i–iii, bks iv–vi 1598)

1598

Edict of Nantes allows right of worship to French Protestants; Tyrone's rebellion in Ireland continues with English defeat at Blackwater; Bodley begins rebuilding library at Oxford; first reference to game of cricket.

PROSE
Deloney: *The Six Worthy Yeomen of the West*
Hakluyt: *The Principal Navigations, Voyages and Discoveries of the English Nation* (second edn, enlarged, *see* 1589)
Meres: *Palladis Tamia*
Southwell (*d*.1595): *A Short Rule of Good Life*
Stow: *Survey of London*

DRAMA
Bernard: *Terence in English* (transl., publ.)
Chettle and Munday: *The Downfall and Death of Robert, Earl of Huntingdon* (*Robin Hood*)
Jonson: *Every Man in His Humour*
Shakespeare: *Much Ado about Nothing*

POETRY
Barnfield: *The Encomium of Lady Pecunia*

POETRY (*cont.*)
Chapman: *Seven Books of the Iliad*; *Achilles Shield: Other Seven Books of Homer* (both transl., compl. edn 1611)
Hall, Joseph: *Virgidemiae* (bks iv–vi, *see* 1597)
Marlowe (*d*.1593): *Hero and Leander*
Marston: *Metamorphosis of Pigmalion's Image, and Certain Satires*; *The Scourge of Villainy* (enlarged edn 1599)
Young: *Diana* (transl. of Montemayor)

1599

Earl of Essex disgraced for failing to crush Irish rebellion; erection of the Globe Theatre, Southwark (destroyed 1644).

PROSE
Hayward: *Life and Reign of King Henry IV*
James VI of Scotland: *Basilikon Doron*
Nashe: *Nashe's Lenten Stuff*
DRAMA
Dekker: *Old Fortunatus*; *The Shoemaker's Holiday*
Drayton and others: *Sir John Oldcastle*
Heywood, Thomas (?): *Edward IV, Pts I and II*
Jonson: *Every Man out of His Humour*
Marston: *Antonio and Mellida*; *Histriomastix, or The Player Whipped*
Shakespeare: *As You Like It*; *Henry V*; *Julius Caesar*

POETRY
Allott (ed.): *Wit's Theatre of the Little World*
Daniel: *Musophilus*; *Poetical Essays*
Davies, Sir John: *Hymns of Astraea*; *Nosce Teipsum*
Marston: *The Scourge of Villainy Corrected with New Satires* (*see* 1598)

1600

Mountjoy succeeds Earl of Essex in Ireland and subdues it by pillage and starvation; Elizabeth I grants charter to the East India Trading Company; Giordano Bruno burnt for heresy; population of England and Wales: 4.25 million; Scotland: 700,000; Ireland: 1.25 million; William Gilbert: *De Magnete* (study of magnetism); Dowland: *Second Book of Songs* (*see* 1597).

PROSE
Hakluyt: *The Principal Navigations, Voyages and Discoveries of the English Nation* (final version, *see* 1589)
DRAMA
Anon.: *Thomas Lord Cromwell* (Shakespeare Apocrypha)
Chettle (with Dekker and Haughton): *Patient Grissil*
Day, John (with Dekker and Haughton): *The Spanish Moor's Tragedy*
Greville: *Alaham*
Heywood, Thomas: *The Four Prentices of London*
Marston: *Antonio's Revenge*; *Jack Drum's Entertainment*
Shakespeare: *The Merry Wives of Windsor*; *Twelfth Night, or What You Will*
POETRY
Allott (ed.): *England's Parnassus*
Bodenham (ed.): *England's Helicon*

POETRY (*cont.*)
Breton: *Pasquil's Madcap and His Message*; *Pasquil's Foolscap, Sent to Such As Are Not Able to Conceive Aright His Madcap*; *Pasquil's Mistress, or The Worthy and Unworthy Woman*; *Pasquil's Pass and Passeth Not*
Fairfax: *Godfrey of Bulloigne* (transl. of Tasso's *Jerusalem Delivered*)
Tourneur: *The Transformed Metamorphosis*

1601

Earl of Essex raises an insurrection against Elizabeth I and is executed for treason; Parliament passes the Poor Law Act, making Justices of the Peace responsible for care of the poor in each parish; Ricci, Jesuit missionary, arrives at Peking; (*c.*) Hilliard writes *Treatise on the Art of Limning* (on portrait-painting, publ. 1912); Morley (ed.): *Madrigals: The Triumphs of Oriana*.

DRAMA

Dekker: *Satiromastix, or The Untrussing of the Humorous Poet*

Jonson: *Cynthia's Revels, or The Fountain of Self-Love*; *Poetaster, or The Arraignment*

Marston: *What You Will*

Shakespeare: *Hamlet*

POETRY

Breton: *A Divine Poem: The Ravished Soul and the Blessed Weeper*

POETRY (*cont.*)

Campion and Rosseter: *A Book of Airs*

Chester: *Love's Martyr* (incl. Shakespeare's 'The Phoenix and the Turtle')

Daniel: *Works Newly Augmented*

1602

Mountjoy defeats Spanish forces in Ireland; Bodleian Library, Oxford, opened.

PROSE

Breton: *A Post with a Mad Packet of Letters*

Campion: *Observations in the Art of English Poesie*

Lodge: *The Famous and Memorable Works of Josephus* (transl.)

Rowlands: *Greene's Ghost Haunting Cony Catchers*

DRAMA

Chapman: *The Gentleman Usher*; *May-Day*; *Sir Giles Goosecap*

Chettle: *Hoffman, or A Revenge for a Father*

DRAMA (*cont.*)

Davies, Sir John: *The Entertainment at Cecil House*

Heywood, Thomas: *How a Man May Choose a Good Wife from a Bad*

Middleton: *The Family of Love*

Shakespeare: *All's Well That Ends Well*; *Troilus and Cressida*

POETRY

Beaumont: *Salmacis and Hermaphroditus*

Davies, John: *Mirum in Modum: A Glimpse of God's Glory and the Soul's Shape*

1603

Death of Elizabeth I; accession of James I of England and VI of Scotland, the first Stuart king (–1625); Puritans demand the reform of the Church of England in the Millenary Petition to the King; plots by Cobham and Grey against James; Raleigh is implicated and imprisoned (–1616); plague in England; (*c.*) first English bank established; Dowland: *Third Book of Songs* (*see* 1597).

PROSE

Breton: *A Dialogue Full of Pith and Pleasure between Three Philosophers*

Daniel: *A Defence of Rhyme*

Dekker: *The Wonderful Year*

Florio: *Montaigne's Essays* (transl.)

Lodge: *A Treatise of the Plague*

DRAMA

Heywood, Thomas: *A Woman Killed with Kindness*

DRAMA (*cont.*)

Jonson: *The Entertainment of the Queen and Prince at Althorp*; *Sejanus His Fall*

POETRY

Daniel: *Poetical Epistles*

Davies, John: *Microcosmos*

Drayton: *The Barons' Wars*

1604

James I rejects Puritan petitions at the Hampton Court Conference; Catholic priests ordered to leave England; James's first Parliament asserts its rights and privileges, including demand for free elections and freedom from arrest during parliamentary sessions; first mention of chocolate and the tomato, in Grimstone's transl. of De Acosta's *The Natural and Moral History of the East and West Indies* (tomato not to become common in Britain until mid-eighteenth century).

PROSE
James I: *A Counterblast to Tobacco*
Middleton: *The Black Book*; *Father Hubbard's Tales*
DRAMA
Alexander: *Croesus*
Chapman: *All Fools*; *Bussy D'Ambois*; *Monsieur D'Olive*
Daniel: *Philotas*; *The Vision of the Twelve Goddesses* (masque)
Day, John: *Law Tricks, or Who Would Have Thought It*
Dekker: *The Magnificent Entertainment Given to King James*; (with Middleton): *The Honest Whore, Pt I*; (with Webster): *Westward Ho*; (with Webster and others): *Sir Thomas Wyatt*
Heywood, Thomas: *If You Know Not Me You Know Nobody, or The Troubles of Queen Elizabeth*; *The Wise Woman of Hogsdon*

DRAMA (*cont.*)
Jonson (and others): *The Coronation Triumph*
Marston: *The Dutch Courtesan*; *The Malcontent*
Shakespeare: *Measure for Measure*; *Othello*
POETRY
Alexander: *Aurora*
Breton: *The Passionate Shepherd*
Drayton: *The Owl*

1605

The Gunpowder Plot; Guy Fawkes and others captured; severe laws passed against Roman Catholics.

PROSE
Bacon: *The Advancement of Learning*
Breton: *An Old Man's Lesson, and a Young Man's Love*
(Cervantes: *Don Quixote*, pt i, pt ii 1615)
Hall, Joseph: *Mundus Alter et Idem* (Latin)
DRAMA
Chapman: *The Widow's Tears*; (with Jonson and Marston): *Eastward Ho*
Daniel: *The Queen's Arcadia*
Dekker: *The Honest Whore, Pt II*; (with Webster): *Northward Ho*
Jonson: *The Masque of Blackness* (*The Twelfth Night's Revels*) (scenery by Inigo Jones, first of a series of court masques produced in collaboration with Jones –1631)

DRAMA (*cont.*)
Marston: *Parasitaster, or The Fawn*; *The Wonder of Women, or Sophonisba*
Middleton: *A Trick to Catch the Old One*; *Your Five Gallants*
Shakespeare: *King Lear*
POETRY
Breton: *The Soul's Immortal Crown*
Daniel: *Certain Small Poems*
Davies, John: *Humours Heaven on Earth*
Drayton: *Poems*
Sylvester: *Du Bartas: His Divine Weeks and Works* (transl.)

1606

Execution of the Gunpowder Plotters (*see* 1605); Torres discovers straits between Australia and New Guinea; publication of the *Mercator-Hondius Atlas*.

PROSE
Dekker: *The Seven Deadly Sins of London*
DRAMA
Anon. (Tourneur or Middleton?): *The Revenger's Tragedy*
Beaumont (with Fletcher): *The Woman Hater*
Dekker: *The Whore of Babylon*
Jonson: *Hymenaei* (masque); *Volpone, or The Fox*
Middleton: *A Mad World, My Masters*; *Michaelmas Term*
Shakespeare: *Macbeth*

POETRY
Drayton: *Poems Lyric and Pastoral* (incl. 'To the Virginian Voyage' and 'The Ballad of Agincourt')

1607

English Parliament rejects union of England and Scotland, but common citizenship granted to English and Scottish people born after James I's accession; building begins of Hatfield House, Hertfordshire, for Robert Cecil (compl. 1612); Monteverdi: *Orfeo* (opera).

DRAMA
Alexander: *The Alexandraean Tragedy*; *Julius Caesar*
Barnes: *The Devil's Charter, or Pope Alexander VI*
Beaumont and Fletcher: *The Knight of the Burning Pestle*
Heywood, Thomas: *The Rape of Lucrece*
Shakespeare: *Antony and Cleopatra*; *Timon of Athens*

POETRY
Drayton: *The Legend of Great Cromwell* (later called *The Life and Death of Lord Cromwell*)

1608

Following defeat of rebellion in Ulster, land confiscated and given to Scottish and English settlers (–1610); Champlain founds Quebec; (*c.*) telescope probably invented in Holland; Rubens: *The Image of the Madonna Adored by Angels* (*The Vallicella Madonna*) (*p.*).

PROSE
Dekker: *The Bellman of London*; *Lanthorne and Candlelight* (pt ii of *The Bellman*, reprinted with revisions and additions, compl. 1632 as *English Villanies*)
Hall, Joseph: *Characters of Virtues and Vices*
DRAMA
Chapman: *The Conspiracy of Charles, Duke of Byron*

DRAMA (*cont.*)
Day, John: *Humour out of Breath*
Dekker: *The Roaring Girl, or Moll Cutpurse*
Fletcher: *The Faithful Shepherdess*
Jonson: *Two Royal Masques*
Rowley: *A Shoemaker a Gentleman*
Shakespeare: *Coriolanus*; *Pericles*

1609

Hudson explores river and bay named after him in Canada; Dutch introduce tea from China to Europe; Galileo modifies recently invented telescope for astronomical observation; Kepler: *Astronomia Nova* (demonstrates that the orbit of Mars is elliptical); Ravenscroft: *Pammelia: Music's Miscellany, or Mixed Variety of Pleasant Roundelays* (first collection of catches).

PROSE
Dekker: *The Gull's Hornbook*
Healey: *Discovery of a New World*
(transl. of Joseph Hall's *Mundus Alter et Idem*)
DRAMA
Beaumont (with Fletcher): *Philaster, or Love Lies a-Bleeding*
Field: *A Woman Is a Weathercock*
Fletcher (with Beaumont): *The Coxcomb*
Heywood, Thomas (with Rowley): *Fortune by Land and Sea*
Jonson: *Epicoene, or The Silent Woman*; *The Masque of Queens*
Shakespeare: *Cymbeline*
Tourneur: *The Atheist's Tragedy, or The Honest Man's Revenge*

POETRY
Chapman: *Euthymiae Raptus, or The Tears of Peace*
Daniel: *The Civil Wars between the Houses of Lancaster and York*
Heywood, Thomas: *Troia Britannica*
Shakespeare: *Sonnets*

1610

Failure of negotiations for the Great Contract between the Commons and James I, by which he would have received money annually in return for giving up certain feudal and financial rights; Henry IV of France assassinated; (*c.*) use of fork (for eating) spreads from Italy to England; Bodleian Library in Oxford to be sent a copy of every book by the Stationers' Company; *The Rheims and Douai Bible* (Old Testament, English transl. of Latin Vulgate, prepared by Roman Catholic scholars, *see* 1582); James grants Ben Jonson a pension of 100 marks a year, making him unofficially poet laureate (increased to £100 a year in 1629).

PROSE
Donne: *Pseudo-Martyr*
Selden: *The Duello, or Single Combat*
DRAMA
Chapman: *The Revenge of Bussy D'Ambois*
Fletcher (with Beaumont): *The Maid's Tragedy*
Heywood, Thomas: *The Fair Maid of the West, or A Girl Worth Gold*; *The Golden Age, or The Lives of Jupiter and Saturn*
Jonson: *The Alchemist*
Marston (with Barkstead): *The Insatiate Countess*
Shakespeare: *The Winter's Tale*
Webster: *The Devil's Law Case*

POETRY
Campion: *Two Books of Airs* (bks iii–iv 1612)
Fletcher, Giles the younger: *Christ's Victory and Triumph in Heaven and Earth, over and after Death*

1611

James I dissolves his first Parliament and introduces Order of Baronets as a means of raising money.

PROSE
The Authorised Version of the Bible
Coryate: *Coryate's Crudities Hastily Gobbled up in Five Months' Travels*
Donne: *Ignatius His Conclave*
DRAMA
Dekker: *If It Be Not Good, the Devil Is in It*; *Match Me in London*
Field: *Amends for Ladies*
Heywood, Thomas: *The Brazen Age*; *The Silver Age*
Jonson: *Catiline His Conspiracy*; *Love Freed from Ignorance and Folly* (masque); *Oberon, the Fairy Prince* (masque)

DRAMA (*cont.*)
Middleton: *A Chaste Maid in Cheapside*
Shakespeare: *The Tempest*
POETRY
Chapman: *The Iliad of Homer* (transl., compl. edn in 24 bks, *see* 1598)
Davies, John: *The Scourge of Folly*
Donne: *An Anatomy of the World: The First Anniversary*

1612

Last recorded burning of heretics in England; Orlando Gibbons: *Madrigals and Motets of Five Parts: Apt for Viols and Voices.*

PROSE
Davies, Sir John: *A Discovery of the True Causes Why Ireland Was Never Entirely Subdued until the Beginning of His Majesty's Happy Reign*
Hall, Joseph: *Contemplations* (compl. in 8 vols by 1626)
Heywood, Thomas: *An Apology for Actors*
DRAMA
Fletcher (with Beaumont): *The Captain*; (with Beaumont and Field): *Four Plays, or Moral Representations, in One*

DRAMA (*cont.*)
Heywood, Thomas: *The Iron Age, Pts I and II*
Jonson: *Love Restored* (masque)
Webster: *The White Devil*
POETRY
Campion: *Third and Fourth Book of Airs* (*see* 1610)
Donne: *The Second Anniversary: Of the Progress of the Soul*
Drayton: *Polyolbion* (pt i, pt ii 1622)

1613

Domestic water reservoir to supply London built at Clerkenwell.

PROSE
Purchas: *Purchas His Pilgrimage, or Relations of the World and the Religions Observed in All Ages*
DRAMA
Campion: *The Lords' Masque*
Fletcher: *Bonduca*; (with Beaumont): *The Scornful Lady*; (with others): *The Honest Man's Fortune*
Jonson: *The Irish Masque*
Middleton: *No Wit, No Help Like a Woman's*

DRAMA (*cont.*)
Shakespeare: *Henry VIII, or All Is True*; (with Fletcher, Shakespeare Apocrypha): *The Two Noble Kinsmen*
POETRY
Campion: *Songs of Mourning Bewailing the Untimely Death of Prince Henry*
(Góngora: *Soledades* ('Solitudes'), circulated in MS, publ. 1627)
Wither: *Abuses Stript and Whipt*

1614

James I's second Parliament called the Addled Parliament because it failed to pass a single act; the King in disagreement with the Commons over royal impositions; Napier: *Canonis Descriptio* (logarithm tables).

PROSE
Lodge: *The Works Both Moral and Natural of Seneca* (transl.)
Overbury (*d.*1613): *Characters* (many enlargements till sixteenth edn of 1638)
Raleigh: *History of the World*
DRAMA
Daniel: *Hymen's Triumph*
Fletcher: *Valentinian*
Jonson: *Bartholomew Fair*
Webster: *The Duchess of Malfi*

POETRY
Alexander: *Doomsday*
Chapman: *Homer's Odyssey* (transl., bks i–xii, compl. in 24 bks by 1615)

1615

Earl of Somerset falls from royal favour after the murder of Sir Thomas Overbury (1613); George Villiers becomes James I's favourite.

PROSE
(Cervantes: *Don Quixote*, pt ii, *see* 1605)
DRAMA
Fletcher, John: *Monsieur Thomas*
Fletcher, Phineas: *Sicelides* (a 'piscatory' or pastoral with fishermen)
Jonson: *The Golden Age Restored* (masque)
Middleton: *More Dissemblers Besides Women*; *The Witch*

POETRY
Harington, Sir John (*d.*1612): *Epigrams Both Pleasant and Serious, Never Before Published*
Wither: *Fidelia*; *The Shepherd's Hunting*

1616

Baffin discovers bay named after him; Galileo prohibited by Roman Church from teaching Copernican astronomy; Harvey lectures on the circulation of blood to the Royal College of Physicians.

PROSE
Breton: *The Good and the Bad, or Descriptions of the Worthies and Unworthies of This Age*
Coryate: *Greeting from the Court of the Great Mogul*
DRAMA
Fletcher (with Beaumont (*d.*1616)): *Love's Pilgrimage*
Jonson: *The Devil Is an Ass*; *Mercury Vindicated from the Alchemists at Court* (masque); *Works of Benjamin Jonson* (vol. i, plays collected and publ., vol. ii 1640, Second Folio 1692)

POETRY
Chapman: *Whole Works of Homer* (transl., *see* 1598, 1611, 1614)
Drummond: *Poems*

1617

Archduke Ferdinand of Styria elected King of Bohemia; his persecution of Protestants precipitates the Thirty Years War (*see* 1618);
Selden: *De Diis Syris* ('Concerning the Syrian Gods').

DRAMA
Fletcher: *The Mad Lover*
Jonson: *The Vision of Delight*
(masque)
Middleton (with Rowley): *A Fair
Quarrel*

POETRY
Drummond: *Forth Feasting*
Sylvester: *Tobacco Battered and Pipes
Shattered*

1618

James I attempts to introduce episcopalian reforms called the Five
Articles into the Church of Scotland; George Villiers, royal favourite, created Marquis of Buckingham; Raleigh's expedition to the
Orinoco in search of gold fails; on his return he is executed for
treason; Protestants in Bohemia revolt against Catholic Habsburg
authority in the Defenestration of Prague; start of the Thirty Years
War in Europe (–1648).

PROSE
Breton: *The Court and the Country*
Coryate (*d*.1617): *To His Friends in
England Sendeth Greeting: From
Agra*
Stow (*d*.1605): *A Summary of English
Chronicles* (final edn, *see* 1565)

DRAMA
Fletcher: *The Loyal Subject, or The
Faithful General*; (with Field and
Massinger): *The Knight of Malta*
Jonson: *Pleasure Reconciled to Virtue*
(masque)
Middleton: *Hengist, King of Kent,
or The Mayor of Quinborough*;
(with Rowley and Massinger): *The
Old Law, or A New Way to Please
You*

POETRY
Chapman: *The Georgics of Hesiod*
(transl.)
Harington, Sir John (*d*.1612): *The
Most Elegant and Witty Epigrams*
(enlarged version of 1615 edn)

1619

Archduke Ferdinand deposed as King of Bohemia, and made Holy
Roman Emperor (–1637); first publication (posthumous) of
Napier's second book on logarithms, which uses decimal point sys-
tematically; Inigo Jones starts building the Banqueting House,
Whitehall, in classical, Palladian style (compl. 1622); Schütz: *Psalms
of David* (choral music with instrumental accompaniment).

PROSE
Purchas: *Purchas His Pilgrim:
Microcosmos, or The History of
Man*

DRAMA
Fletcher: *The Humorous Lieutenant*
Massinger (with Field): *The Fatal
Dowry*
Rowley: *All's Lost by Lust*

DRAMA (*cont.*)
Shakespeare (*d*.1616): Quarto edns
publ. of *Henry V*; *Henry VI*; *King
Lear*; *The Merchant of Venice*; *The
Merry Wives of Windsor*; *A
Midsummer Night's Dream*;
Pericles

1620

A group of settlers, later to be called the Pilgrim Fathers, including Puritans of the Separatist Church, set sail in the *Mayflower* for the New World.

PROSE
Bacon: *Novum Organum* (Latin)
DRAMA
Dekker (with Massinger): *The Virgin Martyr*
Fletcher (with Massinger): *The False One*
Jonson: *News from the New World Discovered in the Moon* (masque)

POETRY
Dekker: *Dekker His Dream*
Quarles: *A Feast for Worms*
Sylvester (*d*.1618): *Sacred Works, Gathered into One Volume*

1621

Third Parliament of James I's reign (–1622); the Commons impeach Mompesson and Bacon for monopolies and corruption, and draw up a Protest to James concerning freedom of speech and parliamentary privileges; James tears up the Protest; attempts by the British to colonise Nova Scotia and Newfoundland; Oxford University Botanical Garden started; Scottish Parliament confirms charter for Edinburgh University, formerly the Tounis College (founded 1583); *Corante, or News from Italy, Germany, Hungary, Spain and France* (first English news-sheet, containing information from foreign papers).

PROSE
Burton: *The Anatomy of Melancholy* (final, revised edn 1676)
Hall, Joseph: *Works*
DRAMA
Dekker (with Ford and Rowley): *The Witch of Edmonton*
Fletcher: *The Wild Goose Chase*
Massinger: *The Duke of Milan*; *The Maid of Honour*; *A New Way to Pay Old Debts*; *The Woman's Plot*

DRAMA (*cont.*)
Middleton: *Anything for a Quiet Life*; *Women Beware Women*

1622

Dissolution of third Parliament of James I's reign; invention of the slide-rule; Sir Richard Hawkins: *Observations in His Voyage into the South Sea*.

PROSE
Bacon: *Historia Naturalis et Experimentalis* (Latin); *History of the Reign of Henry VII*
Peacham: *The Complete Gentleman*
DRAMA
Chapman: *Chabot, Admiral of France*
Fletcher (with Massinger): *The Spanish Curate*
Middleton (with Rowley): *The Changeling*

POETRY
Drayton: *The Second Part or a Continuance of Polyolbion* (*see* 1612)
Wither: *Fair Virtue*; *Juvenilia*

1623

Failure of visit by Prince Charles and Duke of Buckingham to Spain in order to woo the Infanta provokes breach with Spain; Statute of Monopolies forbids royal granting of monopoly rights, but allows 14-year exclusive rights for new inventions, the beginning of patent laws.

DRAMA
Jonson: *Time Vindicated to Himself and to His Honours* (masque)
Massinger: *The Noble Bondman*
Middleton (with Rowley): *The Spanish Gypsy*
Shakespeare (*d*.1616): The First Folio (publ., ed. Heminge and Condell, contains 36 plays, of which 20 had never been printed before, *Pericles* omitted; Second Folio 1632, Third Folio 1663, Fourth Folio 1685)

POETRY
Daniel (*d*.1619): *Whole Works*
Drummond: *Flowers of Sion, to Which Is Adjoined His Cypress Grove* (incl. prose)

1624

Fourth Parliament of James I's reign (–1625); England declares war on Spain; Virginia becomes Crown Colony; Hals: *The Laughing Cavalier* (*p*.).

PROSE
Donne: *Devotions upon Emergent Occasions*
Smith, John: *General History of Virginia*
DRAMA
Fletcher: *A Wife for a Month*
Jonson: *Neptune's Triumph for the Return of Albion* (masque)
Massinger: *The Parliament of Love*; *The Renegado, or The Gentleman of Venice*

DRAMA (*cont.*)
Middleton: *A Game at Chess*
Webster (with Thomas Heywood): *Appius and Virginia*

1625

Death of James I; accession of Charles I (–1649); marriage of Charles and Henrietta Maria of France; Parliament refuses Charles supplies for war with Spain, and allows him taxes on tonnage and poundage for one year only; Parliament dissolved; expedition to take Cadiz fails; plague in England; (*c*.) hackney coaches start plying for hire; first English settlement in Barbados; Norden: *An Intended Guide for Travellers* (early book of roads).

PROSE
Bacon: *Apophthegms New and Old*; *Essays* (final form, *see* 1597)
Purchas: *Hakluytes Posthumus, or Purchas His Pilgrims*
DRAMA
Fletcher (*d*.1625): *The Chances*; (with Massinger ?): *The Elder Brother*
Heywood, Thomas: *The English Traveller*

DRAMA (*cont.*)
Massinger: *Love's Cure, or The Martial Maid*
Rowley: *A New Wonder, or A Woman Never Vexed*
Webster (*d.c.*1625) (with Rowley): *A Cure for a Cuckold*

1626

Charles I's second Parliament insists on impeaching Duke of Buckingham; those responsible are sent to the Tower of London, but released after the Commons protest; Charles dissolves Parliament; Dutch found New Amsterdam on Manhattan Island.

PROSE
Breton (*d.c.*1626): *Fantasticks Serving for a Perpetual Prognostication*
Donne: *Five Sermons*

DRAMA
Dekker: *The Noble Spanish Soldier*
Hemming: *The Jew's Tragedy*
Jonson: *The Staple of News*
Massinger: *The Roman Actor*; *The Unnatural Combat*
Middleton: *The Triumphs of Health and Prosperity* (civic pageant)
Shirley: *The Maid's Revenge*; *The Wedding*

POETRY
Breton (*d.c.*1626): *Pasquil's Madcap*
Sandys: *Ovid's Metamorphoses* (transl.)

1627

Commercial disputes lead to war with France (–1630); Duke of Buckingham's expedition to La Rochelle fails; Kepler compiles his *Rudolphine Tables* (for calculating astronomical positions).

PROSE
Bacon (*d.*1626): *Sylva Sylvarum* (incl. 'New Atlantis')

DRAMA
Davenant: *The Cruel Brother*
Massinger: *The Great Duke of Florence*
Randolph: *The Conceited Pedlar*; *Plutophthalmia Plutogamia, or Hey for Honesty, Down with Knavery* (transl. of Aristophanes's *Plutus*)

POETRY
Drayton: *Nimphidia*; *The Quest of Cynthia*; *The Shepherd's Sirena*
Fletcher, Phineas: *Locustae: Vel Pietas Jesuitica* (*The Locusts, or The Apollyonists*)

1628

Third Parliament of Charles I's reign (–1629) forces him to accept the Petition of Right, preventing the King from imposing taxes without consent of Parliament, and defending the freedom of citizens against martial law and false imprisonment; Charles has to accept the Petition because of his financial difficulties; Duke of Buckingham assassinated; Huguenots of La Rochelle submit to Louis XIII; Harvey: *Exercitatio Anatomica de Motu Cordis et Sanguinis Animalibus* ('Essay on the Movement of the Heart and Blood in Animals'); Sir Kenelm Digby writing his journal (publ. as *Private Memoirs* 1827).

PROSE
Earle: *Micro-Cosmographie, or A Piece of the World Discovered, in Essays and Characters* (final augmented edn 1633)

DRAMA
Dekker: *Britannia's Honour* (civic pageant)

DRAMA (*cont.*)
Ford: *The Lover's Melancholy*
Shirley: *The Witty Fair One*

POETRY
Fletcher, Phineas: *Britain's Ida, Written by That Renowned Poet, Edmund Spenser*

1629

Tumult in the Commons as Eliot insists, against Charles I's orders, on reading resolutions attacking taxation and religious innovation; Parliament dissolved and ringleaders imprisoned; henceforth Charles rules without Parliament till 1640, advised by Wentworth and Bishop Laud, making use of the Star Chamber and the Courts to raise money, along with other semi-legal means; colony of Massachusetts founded; Richelieu incorporates company for trade in Canada (New France); Vermuyden contracted to drain Great Fens (compl. 1652).

PROSE
Andrewes (*d*.1626): *Ninety-Six Sermons*
Hobbes: *The Peloponnesian War of Thucydides* (transl.)
DRAMA
Brome: *The Northern Lass*
Davenant: *The Just Italian*; *The Tragedy of Albovine* (publ., never acted)
Ford: *The Broken Heart*
Jonson: *The New Inn, or The Light Heart*
Massinger: *The Picture*
Shirley: *The Grateful Servant*

POETRY
Chapman: *The Justification of a Strange Action of Nero: The Fifth Satire of Juvenal* (transl.)
(*c*.) Wither: *The Scholar's Purgatory*

1630

Without funds to continue war, peace is made with France and Spain; Dr Leighton fined, mutilated and imprisoned for life for his book *Sion's Plea against Prelacy* (1628); Gustavus Adolphus, King of Sweden, joins German Protestants to fight against the Catholic League.

DRAMA
Brome: *The City Wit, or The Woman Wears the Breeches*
Randolph: *Amyntas, or The Impossible Dowry*
POETRY
Drayton: *The Muses' Elysium*

POETRY (*cont.*)
Taylor: *All the Works of John Taylor the Water Poet*

1631

Inigo Jones designs Square of Covent Garden.

PROSE
Stow (*d*.1605): *Annals of England* (final edn, *see* 1565)
DRAMA
Brome: *The Queen's Exchange*
Davenport: *King John and Matilda*
Dekker: *The Wonder of a Kingdom*
Heywood, Thomas: *The Fair Maid of the West, Pt II*
Jonson: *Chloridia: Rites to Chloris and Her Nymphs* (masque)

DRAMA (*cont.*)
Massinger: *Believe As You List*; *The Emperor of the East*
Shirley: *Love's Cruelty*

1632

Eliot, one of the imprisoned Parliamentarians (*see* 1629), dies in the Tower of London; news-sheets suppressed because of anti-Spanish articles; Gustavus Adolphus of Sweden defeats Wallenstein, general of the imperial army, at Lützen, but is himself killed; Shah Jehan begins building the Taj Mahal (compl. 1648).

PROSE
Donne (*d*.1631): *Death's Duel*
DRAMA
Brome: *The Weeding of the Covent Garden, or The Middlesex Justice of Peace*
Ford: *Love's Sacrifice*; *'Tis Pity She's a Whore*
Jonson: *The Magnetic Lady, or Humours Reconciled*
Massinger: *The City Madam*

DRAMA (*cont.*)
Randolph: *The Jealous Lovers*
Shakespeare (*d*.1616): The Second Folio (publ., *see* 1623)
Shirley: *Changes, or Love in a Maze*; *Hyde Park*
Townshend: *Albion's Triumph* (masque)

1633

Wentworth appointed Lord Deputy in Ireland (–1639); Laud appointed Archbishop of Canterbury (–1645), and acts against Puritans in enforcing established Anglicanism; establishment of the oldest regular regiment in the British army, the Royal Scots; Galileo censured by the Inquisition for his adherence to Copernican theories.

PROSE
Prynne: *Histrio-Mastix: The Players' Scourge*
Spenser (*d*.1599): *A View of the Present State of Ireland*
DRAMA
Ford: *Perkin Warbeck*
Heywood, Thomas: *A Maidenhead Well Lost*
Jonson: *A Tale of a Tub*
Massinger: *The Guardian*
Shirley: *The Bird in a Cage*; *The Gamester*; *The Young Admiral*
POETRY
Cowley: *Poetical Blossoms* (second, enlarged edn 1637)

POETRY (*cont.*)
Donne (*d*.1631): *Poems*
Fletcher, Phineas: *The Purple Island* (incl. 'Piscatory Eclogues')
Greville (*d*.1628): *Certain Learned and Elegant Works*
Herbert (*d*.1633): *The Temple*
Quarles: *Divine Poems*

1634

Charles I imposes ship money tax on maritime counties and seaports, ostensibly for defence of the country, in fact to raise revenue; first settlement in Maryland; first performance of the Oberammergau Passion Play in Germany to celebrate the end of plague the previous year.

DRAMA
Brome (with Thomas Heywood): *The Late Lancashire Witches*
Carew, Thomas: *Coelum Britannicum* (masque)
Davenant: *Love and Honour*; *The Wits*

DRAMA (*cont.*)
Heywood, Thomas: *Love's Mistress, or The Queen's Masque* (masque)
Milton: *Comus* (masque)
Shirley: *The Opportunity*

1635

Extension of ship money to the whole country; royal posts made available to the public, leading to postal services between London and the rest of the country; Académie Française founded in Paris; Rubens installs ceiling painting at the Banqueting Hall, Whitehall.

DRAMA
Brome: *The Sparagus Garden*
(Corneille: *Médée*)
Davenant: *The Platonic Lovers*; *The Temple of Love* (masque)
Heywood, Thomas: *A Challenge for Beauty*
Marmion: *The Antiquary*

DRAMA (*cont.*)
Shirley: *The Lady of Pleasure*
POETRY
Heywood, Thomas: *The Hierarchy of the Blessed Angels*
Quarles: *Emblems*
Wither: *A Collection of Emblems*

1636

Foundation of Harvard College in America.

DRAMA
Davenant: *The Triumphs of the Prince D'Amour* (masque)

DRAMA (*cont.*)
Massinger: *The Bashful Lover*
Shirley: *The Duke's Mistress*

1637

Hampden fined for refusing to pay ship money; Charles I, advised by Archbishop Laud, attempts to introduce English Liturgy into Scotland, and meets angry opposition; Prynne fined, mutilated and imprisoned for *Histrio-Mastix* (1633), an attack on stage-plays which was thought to insult the Queen; Van Dyck: *Triple Portrait of Charles I* (*p.*, model for Bernini *sc.*).

PROSE
(Descartes: *Discourse on Method*)
Hobbes: *The Art of Rhetoric* (transl. of Aristotle)
DRAMA
Brome: *The English Moor*
(Corneille: *Le Cid*)
Milton: *A Masque Presented at Ludlow Castle* (*Comus*, publ., first performed 1634)

DRAMA (*cont.*)
Shirley: *The Royal Master*
POETRY
Alexander: *Recreations with the Muses*
Marmion: *Cupid and Psyche*

1638

Scots sign National Covenant against episcopacy, and prepare for war; Richelieu's allies defeat Habsburg imperial army at Rheinfelden; Taylor: *Carriers' Cosmography* (guide to stage coach and carrier services).

PROSE
Digby: *Conference with a Lady about Choice of Religion*
DRAMA
Brome: *The Antipodes*
Cowley: *Love's Riddle*; *Naufragium Joculare*
Davenant: *The Fair Favourite*; *The Unfortunate Lovers*
Shirley: *The Constant Maid, or Love Will Find Out a Way*

DRAMA (*cont.*)
Suckling: *Aglaura*; *The Goblins*
POETRY
Davenant: *Madagascar, and Other Poems*
Milton: 'Lycidas' (in *Obsequies in Memory of Mr Edward King*)
Quarles: *Hieroglyphics of the Life of Man*
Randolph (*d.*1635): *Poems*

1639

Charles I levies army against Scottish Covenanters; due to the unreliability of his army, he is forced to conclude the First Bishops' War at the Pacification of Berwick; General Assembly appointed to settle grievances; it condemns the English Prayer Book and abolishes episcopacy; (c.) tulip craze in Holland reaches its peak.

PROSE
Fuller: *The History of the Holy War*
DRAMA
Brome: *The Lovesick Court*; *A Mad Couple Well Matched*
Davenant: *The Spanish Lovers* (*The Distresses*)

DRAMA (*cont.*)
Shirley: *The Gentleman of Venice*; *The Politician*
Suckling: *Brennoralt, or The Discontented Colonel*

1640

Meeting of the Short Parliament, so named because of its swift dissolution by Charles I after it refuses him money and criticises his policy towards the Church; Scots invade England and defeat royal army near Newcastle; Charles concludes the Second Bishops' War at the Treaty of Ripon; lack of money forces Charles to call Parliament; Long Parliament commences (–1653); coke first made from coal (*see* 1709).

PROSE
Donne (*d.*1631): *Eighty Sermons* (incl. Walton's 'Life of Donne', *see* 1649)
Fuller: *Joseph's Party-Coloured Coat*
Hall, Joseph: *Episcopacy by Divine Right*
Quarles: *Enchyridion*
Selden: *Discourse Concerning the Power of Peers and Commons of Parliament*
DRAMA
Brome: *The Court Beggar*
Davenant: *Salmacida Spolia*

DRAMA (*cont.*)
Jonson (*d.*1637): *Works* (vol. ii of First Folio publ., incl. 'Timber, or Discoveries' (also called 'Explorata', prose work) *see* 1616)
Shirley: *The Arcadia*; *The Imposture*
POETRY
Beaumont (*d.*1616): *Poems*
Carew (*d.*1639): *Poems*

1641

Charles I's unpopular minister, Wentworth, Earl of Strafford, tried by Parliament and executed; Star Chamber and High Commission Court abolished, leading to freedom of the press, and release of Prynne and others; Grand Remonstrance passed by the Commons, listing Charles's unconstitutional acts; Commons pass resolution condemning church images and demanding strict observance of the sabbath; rebellion against English and Scottish colonists in Ireland; first publication of *Diurnal Occurrences in Parliament*; Evelyn begins his *Diary* (–1706).

PROSE
The Episcopacy Controversy: an exchange of pamphlets, for and against the role of bishops, between Joseph Hall, 'Smectymnuus' (several hands) and Milton (*see* 1642)
DRAMA
Brome: *A Jovial Crew*

DRAMA (*cont.*)
Denham: *The Sophy*
Quarles: *The Virgin Widow*
Shirley: *The Brothers*; *The Cardinal*
POETRY
Day, John (*d.*1640): *The Parliament of Bees*
Wither: *Hallelujah* (hymns)

1642

Charles I fails to arrest five Members of Parliament for their part in the Grand Remonstrance (*see* 1641) and for communicating with the Scots; he leaves London; Royalists and Parliamentarians prepare for civil war; indecisive battle at Edgehill; Tasman sights Tasmania and New Zealand; Pascal constructs simple digital calculating machine; Rembrandt: *The Night Watch* (*p.*); Monteverdi: *The Coronation of Poppea* (opera); theatres in England closed by the Puritans (–1660); dramatic activity continues in the form of masques and private performances.

PROSE
Milton: *An Apology against Smectymnuus*; *The Reason of Church-Government Urged against Prelacy*
Raleigh (*d*.1618): *The Prince, or Maxims of State*

DRAMA
Cowley: *The Guardian*
Shirley: *The Sisters*
POETRY
Denham: *Cooper's Hill*
More: *Psychozoia Platonica, or A Platonical Song of the Soul*

1643

Royalists and Parliamentarians in conflicts throughout England; Parliament makes a solemn League and Covenant with the Scots, and establishes Presbyterianism in England and Wales; Torricelli invents the barometer.

PROSE
Browne: *Religio Medici* (unauthorised version publ. 1642)
Digby: *Observations upon Religio Medici*

PROSE (*cont.*)
Milton: *The Doctrine and Discipline of Divorce*
Prynne: *The Sovereign Power of Parliaments*

1644

At Marston Moor, Cromwell's Ironsides defeat the Royalists under Prince Rupert, a turning point in the war; Tasman charts north-west coast of New Holland (Australia); Poussin: *The Seven Sacraments* (*p.*, second series, compl. 1648).

PROSE
Milton: *Areopagitica*; *Of Education*

PROSE (*cont.*)
Raleigh (*d*.1618): *Today a Man, Tomorrow None*

1645

Self-Denying Ordinance passed by Parliament to remove M.P.s from military command; Cromwell organises the New Model Army, which defeats Charles I at Naseby; Earl of Montrose, supporter of Charles, finally defeated by Covenanters at Philiphaugh; Archbishop Laud executed; Bernini working on the Cornaro Chapel, Rome, including *The Ecstasy of St Teresa* (*sc.*, compl. 1652).

PROSE
Digby: *Of the Immortality of Man's Soul*
Fuller: *Good Thoughts in Bad Times*
Milton: *Colasterion*; *Tetrachordon*
POETRY
Milton: *Poems* (incl. 'Christ's Nativity', 'L'Allegro', 'Il Penseroso', 'Sonnets' and others publ. earlier)

POETRY (*cont.*)
Waller: *The Works of Mr Edmund Waller Esq., Lately a Member of the Honourable House of Commons, in This Present Parliament*
Wither: *Vox Pacifica*

1646

Charles I surrenders to the Scots at Newark; breakdown of negotiations between King and Parliament; colonisation of the Bahamas begins; the Levellers proclaim sovereignty of the people and advocate abolition of the monarchy in *Remonstrance of Many Thousand Citizens*.

PROSE
Browne: *Pseudodoxia Epidemica, or Enquiries into Very Many Received Tenents and Commonly Presumed Truths* (also called *Vulgar Errors*)
Fuller: *Andronicus, or The Unfortunate Politician*
Taylor: *A Discourse Concerning Prayer*
DRAMA
Shirley: *The Triumph of Beauty* (masque, acted privately)

POETRY
Crashaw: *Steps to the Temple*
Shirley: *Poems*
Suckling (*d.*1642): *Fragmenta Aurea* (collected works)
Vaughan, Henry: *Poems*

1647

Charles I is handed over to the Parliamentary Commissioners by the Scots in return for £400,000; he is imprisoned in Carisbrooke Castle; Charles carries on intrigues with Scots, Independents and Presbyterians; Commons vote to disband the army; army moves into London; Lely: *The Children of Charles I* (*p.*); first known advertisement appears in *Perfect Occurrences of Every Day*.

PROSE
Fuller: *The Cause and Cure of a Wounded Conscience*; *Good Thoughts in Worse Times*
Hall, Joseph: *Hard Measures*
Hopkins: *The Discovery of Witches*
DRAMA
Beaumont (*d.*1616) and Fletcher (*d.*1625): *Comedies and Tragedies* (publ., ed. Shirley)

POETRY
Cleveland: *The Character of a London Diurnal, and Other Poems*
Cowley: *The Mistress*
More: *Philosophical Poems*

1648

Charles I persuades the Scots to invade England on his behalf, but Cromwell defeats them at Preston; in 'Pride's Purge' the Presbyterian majority are expelled from the Commons, leaving the 'Rump', who vote in favour of trying the King; in Europe, end of the Thirty Years War (*see* 1618) secured at the Peace of Westphalia; Glauber prepares hydrochloric acid from sulphuric acid and common salt.

PROSE
Stearne: *The Confirmation and Discovery of Witchcraft*
Taylor: *The Liberty of Prophesying*
POETRY
Denham: *Cato Major* (transl. of Cicero)
Hall, John: *Emblems*; *Satire against Presbytery*

POETRY (*cont.*)
Herrick: *Hesperides*
Wither: *Prosopopoeia Britannica*

1649

Charles I tried and executed; the Rump abolishes the House of Lords and the monarchy and proclaims England a Commonwealth; Levellers (extreme republicans) denounce conservative nature of the Commonwealth; they are suppressed by Cromwell and Fairfax; Royalist Protestants join Catholics and rebel in Ireland; Cromwell storms Drogheda and Wexford and slaughters many.

PROSE
Donne (d.1631): *Fifty Sermons (see 1640)*
Gauden (?): *Eikon Basilike: The Portrait of Truth's Majesty* (supposed thoughts of Charles I)
Milton: *Eikonoklastes*; *The Tenure of Kings and Magistrates*
Prynne: *A Historical Collection of the Ancient Parliaments of England*
POETRY
Dryden: *Upon the Death of the Lord Hastings*
Lovelace: *Lucasta*

POETRY (*cont.*)
R.B. (unknown ed.): *Lachrymae Musarum* (poems on the death of Lord Hastings by Dryden, Marvell, Herrick and Denham)

1650

Defeat and execution of Earl of Montrose after he rebels in favour of Charles II; Charles II lands in Scotland; Cromwell defeats the Scots at Dunbar and enters Edinburgh; first English coffee house opens, in Oxford; Von Guericke invents the air pump and initiates experiments with vacuums.

PROSE
Baxter: *The Saints' Everlasting Rest*
Hobbes: *De Corpore Politico, or The Elements of Law, Moral and Politic*; *Human Nature*
Taylor: *The Rule and Exercises of Holy Living*
POETRY
Bradstreet: *The Tenth Muse*
Vaughan, Henry: *Silex Scintillans*

POETRY (*cont.*)
Vaughan, Thomas: *Anthroposophia Theomagica*

1651

Scots crown Charles II king; he invades England but flees to France after defeat by Cromwell at Worcester; Navigation Act prohibits importation of goods by non-English vessels, aiming to give English ships monopoly of foreign trade; Louis XIV of France attains his majority.

PROSE
Donne (d.1631): *Essays in Divinity*
Hobbes: *Epistle to Davenant on Gondibert*; *Leviathan*
Laud (d.1645): *Sermons*
Taylor: *The Rule and Exercises of Holy Dying*
Walton: *The Life of Sir Henry Wotton*

POETRY
Cleveland: *Poems*
Davenant: *Gondibert*
Vaughan, Henry: *Olor Iscanus*

1652

War with Holland (–1654), caused by constant clashes of trading and colonial interests and rivalry at sea; Parliament passes Act of Pardon and Oblivion to reconcile Royalists; army petitions for new Parliament; Fronde insurrection in Paris; first coffee house in London opens; Dutch create colony at Cape of Good Hope; Winstanley: *The Law of Freedom, in a Platform, or True Magistracy Restored* (Digger pamphlet, attacking private ownership of land and advocating communism).

PROSE
Donne (*d*.1631): *Paradoxes, Problems, Essays, Characters*
Greville (*d*.1628): *The Life of the Renowned Sir Philip Sidney*
Hall, John: *Longinus on the Height of Eloquence* (transl.)
Herbert, George (*d*.1633): *Remains* (incl. 'A Priest to the Temple')
Vaughan, Henry: *The Mount of Olives, or Solitary Devotions* (transl. of Anselm)

POETRY
Benlowes: *Theophila, or Love's Sacrifice*

1653

Cromwell dissolves Parliament and institutes an Assembly of Nominees, the Barebones Parliament; the Instrument of Government is drawn up, regularising the office of Lord Protector and the summoning of Parliament; defeat of the Dutch off Portland; Wallis: *Grammatica Linguae Anglicanae* (language study, incl. treatise on formation of speech sounds); Ruysdael: *Two Water Mills and an Open Sluice* (*p*.).

PROSE
More: *An Antidote against Atheism*
Taylor: *Eniautos: Sermons for All the Sundays in the Year*
Urquhart: *The First Book of Mr Francis Rabelais, Doctor of Physic, Translated into English* (compl. in 5 bks by 1694, bk v transl. by Motteux)
Walton: *The Compleat Angler, or The Contemplative Man's Recreation* (second, enlarged edn 1655)
DRAMA
Flecknoe: *Love's Dominion* (closet drama)

DRAMA (*cont.*)
Shirley: *Cupid and Death* (masque)
POETRY
Newcastle: *Poems and Fancies*

1654

First Parliament meets under the Protectorate (–1655); Dutch agree to the Navigation Act after the Treaty of Westminster ends war (*see* 1652); Comenius: *Orbis Sensualium Pictus* ('The Visible World in Pictures', early illustrated children's book for Latin teaching, publ. in Nuremberg, first English edn 1659).

PROSE
Hobbes: *Of Liberty and Necessity*
Vaughan, Henry: *Flores Solitudinis*

1655

Cromwell divides the country into 11 military districts, each under a Major-General with almost absolute power to quell Royalist plots; first Protectorate Parliament is dissolved after opposing Cromwell and the Instrument (*see* 1653); Jews formally readmitted into England (after expulsion in 1290); capture by the English of Jamaica, the Caribbean base for buccaneers; Wallis: *Arithmetica Infinitorum* (introduces sign for infinity); (*c.*) Poussin: *Et in Arcadia Ego* (*p.*); publication of Cotgrave's two miscellanies: *The English Treasury of Literature and Language* and *Wits Interpreter: The English Parnassus*.

PROSE
Newcastle: *Philosophical and Physical Opinions*
Stanley: *The History of Philosophy* (all 4 vols by 1662)
Taylor: *The Golden Grove*
POETRY
Marvell: *First Anniversary of the Government under the Lord Protector*

POETRY (*cont.*)
Phillips: *Satire against Hypocrites*
Waller: *Panegyric to My Lord Protector*

1656

Cromwell summons second Protectorate Parliament (–1657); Spain declares war on England (–1659); Velasquez: *Las Meniñas* (*p.*); Rutland House 'Opera' opens in London.

PROSE
Bunyan: *Some Gospel Truths Opened*
Harrington: *Commonwealth of Oceana*
(Pascal: *Provincial Letters*)
DRAMA
Davenant: *The First Day's Entertainment at Rutland House*; *The Siege of Rhodes*
POETRY
Cowley: *Poems* (incl. 'Pindaric Odes' and 'Davideis')

POETRY (*cont.*)
Denham: *The Destruction of Troy* (transl. of Virgil)
Newcastle: *Nature's Pictures Drawn by Fancy's Pencil to the Life*

1657

Parliament draws up a constitution called the Humble Petition and Advice, giving Cromwell sovereign powers, but he rejects the title of King; appointment of Second House in Parliament; drinking chocolate first sold in London; tea first publicly sold, at Garway's coffee house; invention of the pendulum clock.

PROSE
Baxter: *A Call to the Unconverted*
Taylor: *A Discourse of Friendship*
DRAMA
Middleton (*d.*1627): *Women Beware Women* (publ. with other plays)
POETRY
Hall, John (*d.*1656): *Hierocles upon the Golden Verses of Pythagoras*

POETRY (*cont.*)
King: *Poems* (enlarged edn 1664)

1658

Third Protectorate Parliament meets and is dissolved by Cromwell because of intrigues between republicans in the Commons and the army; death of Cromwell; his son Richard declared Protector; Swedish bank devises the first banknote; Rembrandt: *Self-Portrait with a Stick* (*p.*).

PROSE
Browne: *The Garden of Cyrus*;
  Hydriotaphia, or Urn-Burial
Flecknoe: *Enigmatical Characters*
DRAMA
Chamberlayne: *Love's Victory*
Davenant: *The Cruelty of the
  Spaniards in Peru*
Shirley: *The Contention of Ajax and
  Ulysses for the Armour of Achilles*

POETRY
Waller: *The Passion of Dido for
  Aeneas*

1659

Richard Cromwell retires into private life after differences with the army; restoration of the Long Parliament (the Rump), which is dissolved by Lambert; Lambert rules through the Committee of Safety; George Monck, Cromwell's commander-in-chief in Scotland, supporting restoration of Parliament, marches from Scotland and is opposed by Lambert; Aurangzeb becomes Mogul Emperor of India (–1707).

PROSE
Baxter: *Holy Commonwealth*
Evelyn: *The Character of England*
Milton: *A Treatise of Civil Power in
  Ecclesiastical Causes*
POETRY
Chamberlayne: *Pharonnida*
Dryden: *Poem upon the Death of His
  Late Highness Oliver Lord
  Protector*
Lovelace (*d.*1657): *Posthume Poems*

POETRY (*cont.*)
Suckling (*d.*1642): *Last Remains*
Waller: *Upon the Late Storm and
  Death of His Highness*

1660

Monck enters London; Long Parliament dissolves itself; a Convention passes a resolution to restore the old form of government, while Charles II issues the Declaration of Breda, offering religious toleration and political amnesty; the Restoration: Charles returns to England and is restored to the throne (–1685); Act of Indemnity and Oblivion passed for all offences committed during the troubles; Royal Society founded (incorporated 1662); Robert Boyle: *New Experiments Physico-Mechanical, Touching the Spring of the Air and Its Effects*; Samuel Pepys begins his *Diary* (–1669); introduction of actresses on the English stage; King's and Duke's theatrical companies created by royal patent.

PROSE
Harrington: *Political Discourses*
Milton: *The Ready and Easy Way to
  Establish a Free Commonwealth*
Taylor: *Ductor Dubitantium*

DRAMA
Tatham: *The Rump, or The Mirror of
  the Late Times*
POETRY
Dryden: *Astraea Redux*

1661

Edward Hyde, Lord Chancellor and Charles II's chief minister, made Earl of Clarendon; Lambert, republican leader and Cromwell's major-general, imprisoned for life; Robert Boyle: *The Sceptical Chemist*; Versailles Palace started for Louis XIV (compl. 1787).

PROSE
Evelyn: *Fumifugium, or The Inconvenience of the Air and Smoke of London Dissipated*
Glanvill: *The Vanity of Dogmatising*
DRAMA
Cowley: *Cutter of Coleman Street*
Davenant: *Hamlet* (adaptation of Shakespeare)

DRAMA (*cont.*)
Flecknoe: *Erminia, or The Fair and Virtuous Lady*
POETRY
Dryden: *To His Sacred Majesty*
Waller: *St James's Park*; *To My Lady Morton*

1662

Charles II marries Catherine of Braganza; Act of Uniformity leads to ejection from their livings of Nonconformist ministers (about one fifth of the whole English clergy); *Poor Robin's Almanack* (first of a series of anonymous chapbooks, –1776).

PROSE
Revised version of *The Book of Common Prayer*
Anon: *The Noble Birth and Gallant Achievements of Robin Hood, Newly Collected by an Ingenious Antiquary*
Fuller (*d.*1661): *The History of the Worthies of England*

PROSE (*cont.*)
Hall, Joseph (*d.*1656): *Works*
POETRY
Butler: *Hudibras* (pt i, pt ii 1663, pt iii 1678)
Dryden: *To My Lord Chancellor*

1663

First Turnpike Act; Drury Lane Theatre opens; Robert Boyle: *Considerations Concerning the Usefulness of Experimental Philosophy*.

DRAMA
Dryden: *The Wild Gallant*
Shakespeare (*d.*1616): Third Folio (publ., contains *Pericles* and spurious plays, *see* 1623)

POETRY
Butler: *Hudibras* (pt ii, *see* 1662)
Cowley: *Verses upon Several Occasions*

1664

The Conventicle Act prevents Nonconformist ministers from forming their own congregations; trade rivalry causes further war with Holland (–1667); French West India Company formed to rival English Company; Stubbes: *The Indian Nectar: A Treatise on Chocolata*; Claude Lorraine: *Landscape with Psyche and the Palace of Love* (*p.*).

PROSE
Evelyn: *Sylva*
DRAMA
Davenant: *Macbeth* (adaptation of Shakespeare)
Dryden: *The Rival Ladies*
Etherege: *The Comical Revenge, or Love in a Tub*

POETRY
Cotton: *Scarronides, or The First Book of Virgil Travesty*
Waller: *Poems Written upon Several Occasions and to Several Persons, Never till Now Corrected and Published with the Approbation of the Author*

1665

Duke of York defeats the Dutch off Lowestoft; Five Mile Act continues legislation against Nonconformist clergy; Great Plague of London (–1666); Nell Gwyn acts part of Cydaria in Dryden's *The Indian Emperor*.

PROSE
Bunyan: *The Holy City*
Glanvill: *Scepsis Scientifica*
(La Rochefoucauld: *Maximes*)
Sprat: *Observations on Monsieur de Sorbier's Voyage into England*
Walton: *Life of Richard Hooker*
DRAMA
Dryden: *The Indian Emperor, or The Conquest of Mexico by the Spaniards*

POETRY
Herbert of Cherbury (*d*.1648): *Occasional Verses*
Marvell: *The Character of Holland*
Waller: *Upon Her Majesty's New Building at Somerset House*

1666

France joins Holland in war with England; Scottish Covenanters defeated at the battle of Pentland Hills; Great Fire of London, leading to reconstruction of St Paul's and 51 other London churches by Sir Christopher Wren; (*c*.) Vermeer: *Allegory on the Art of Painting* (*p*.); *London Gazette* established as government newspaper (first issued from Oxford 1665).

PROSE
Bunyan: *Grace Abounding to the Chief of Sinners*
Glanvill: *Philosophical Considerations Concerning Witches and Witchcraft*
DRAMA
(Molière: *Le Médecin malgré lui*; *Le Misanthrope*)

POETRY
Waller: *Instructions to a Painter*

1667

Dutch fleet raids Chatham, leading to peace at the Treaty of Breda; Clarendon, organiser of the Restoration Settlement, dismissed by Charles II, who forms a government by Cabinet, called the Cabal ministry (–1673).

PROSE
Laud (*d*.1645): *Sum of Devotions*
Sprat: *History of the Royal Society of London for the Improving of Natural Knowledge*
DRAMA
Davenant and Dryden: *The Tempest, or The Enchanted Island* (adaptation of Shakespeare)
Dryden: *Secret Love, or The Maiden Queen*; *Sir Martin Mar-All, or The Feigned Innocence*
(Molière: *Tartuffe*)
(Racine: *Andromaque*)

POETRY
Denham: *Instructions to a Painter*
Dryden: *Annus Mirabilis*
Marvell: *Clarendon's House-Warming*
Milton: *Paradise Lost* (in 10 bks, *see* 1674)

1668

Triple alliance formed between England, Holland and Sweden to protect the Netherlands from encroachment by Louis XIV of France.

PROSE
Dryden: *Essay of Dramatic Poesie*; *A Defence of an Essay of Dramatic Poesie*
Glanvill: *Plus Ultra*
More: *Divine Dialogues*
Wilkins: *Towards a Real Character and a Philosophical Language*
DRAMA
Dryden: *An Evening's Love, or The Mock Astrologer*
Etherege: *She Would If She Could*

DRAMA (*cont.*)
(Molière: *The Miser*)
Sedley: *The Mulberry Garden*
Shadwell: *The Sullen Lovers*
POETRY
Cowley (*d.*1667): *Works* (pt i, pt ii 1681)
Denham: *Poems and Translations* (other edns –1709)
(La Fontaine: *Fables*)

1669

Duke of York publicly acknowledges conversion to Roman Catholicism; one-day 'flying coach' service between London and Oxford inaugurated; first French trading station set up in India; Samuel Pepys ends *Diary* (*see* 1660).

PROSE
Burnet: *Conference between a Conformist and a Non-conformist*

DRAMA
Dryden: *Tyrannic Love, or The Royal Martyr*
Shadwell: *The Royal Shepherdess*

1670

Secret Treaty of Dover between Charles II and Louis XIV by which Charles agrees to help Louis annex Holland, and promises to declare his conversion to Roman Catholicism in return for a subsidy; Hudson's Bay Trading Company founded to compete in North America, especially in the fur trade; (*c.*) potatoes common food in England (*see* 1597); Vermeer: *The Lacemaker* (*p.*).

PROSE
Baxter: *The Life of Faith*
Milton: *History of Britain*
(Pascal (*d.*1662): *Pensées*)
Walton: *The Lives of Donne, Wotton, Hooker and Herbert*
DRAMA
Behn: *The Forced Marriage, or The Jealous Bridegroom*

DRAMA (*cont.*)
Dryden: *The Conquest of Granada, Pt I*
(Racine: *Bérénice*)
Shadwell: *The Humorists*
POETRY
Greville (*d.*1628): *Remains*

1671

English buccaneers under Morgan destroy Panama; French Senegal Company founded; Lely: *Francis Mercury Van Helmont* (*p.*).

PROSE
Bunyan: *Confession of My Faith*
DRAMA
Behn: *The Amorous Prince, or The Curious Husband*
Dryden: *The Conquest of Granada, Pt II* (*Almanzor and Almahade*)

DRAMA (*cont.*)
Milton: *Samson Agonistes* (publ.)
Villiers (and others): *The Rehearsal*
Wycherley: *Love in a Wood, or St James's Park*
POETRY
Milton: *Paradise Regained*

1672

Outbreak of Third Anglo-Dutch War (–1674); Charles II issues Declaration of Indulgence, suspending penal laws against Roman Catholics and Nonconformists; charter granted to the Royal African Company; Newton explains composition of white light.

PROSE
Marvell: *The Rehearsal Transprosed*
DRAMA
Dryden: *Amboyna, or The Cruelties of the Dutch to the English Merchants*; *The Assignation, or Love in a Nunnery*; *Marriage à la Mode*
Shadwell: *Epsom Wells*
Wycherley: *The Gentleman Dancing-Master*

POETRY
Phillips: *Maronides, or Virgil Travesty*

1673

Parliament forces Charles II to withdraw Declaration of Indulgence (*see* 1672); Test Act excludes Catholics from public office; Cabal ministry ends (*see* 1667).

DRAMA
Behn: *The Dutch Lover*
Davenant (*d*.1668): *Collected Works* (publ.)
Settle: *The Empress of Morocco*

POETRY
Milton: *Poems on Several Occasions* (revision of 1645 version)

1674

Third Dutch War ends (*see* 1672); war in Europe between France and triple alliance between the Emperor, the Netherlands and Spain (–1679); Cotton: *The Complete Gamester*.

PROSE
Rymer: *Reflections on Aristotle's Treatise of Poesie*
DRAMA
Lee: *Nero, Emperor of Rome*
(Racine: *Iphigénie*)
POETRY
(Boileau: *L'Art poétique*; *Le Lutrin*)

POETRY (*cont.*)
Hobbes: *Odyssey* (transl. of Homer)
Milton (*d*.1674): *Paradise Lost* (in 12 bks, *see* 1667)

1675

Ogilby: *Britannia, or an Illustration of the Kingdom of England and the Dominion of Wales by a Geographical and Historical Description of the Principal Roads Therein* (first road atlas); Roemer estimates the speed of light by astronomical methods; foundation of the Royal Observatory at Greenwich.

PROSE
Traherne (*d*.1674): *Christian Ethics*
DRAMA
Dryden: *Aureng-Zebe*
Lee: *Sophonisba, or Hannibal's Overthrow*
Otway: *Alcibiades*
Wycherley: *The Country Wife*

POETRY
Marvell: *Dialogue between Two Horses*
Rochester: *A Satire against Mankind*

1676

Charles II makes another secret treaty with Louis XIV (*see* 1670); end of war between settlers and Indians in New England.

PROSE

Cotton: dialogue between 'Piscator' and 'Viator' in Walton's *Compleat Angler* (fifth edn)

Glanvill: *Essays on Several Important Subjects*

DRAMA

Behn: *Abdelazer, or The Moor's Revenge*; *The Town Fop, or Sir Timothy Tawdrey*

D'Urfey: *Madam Fickle, or The Witty False One*

Etherege: *The Man of Mode, or Sir Fopling Flutter*

DRAMA (*cont.*)

Lee: *Gloriana, or The Court of Augustus Caesar*

Otway: *Don Carlos, Prince of Spain*

Shadwell: *The Virtuoso*

1677

Marriage of William III of Orange to Mary, daughter of James, Duke of York; Earl of Shaftesbury and Duke of Buckingham sent to the Tower of London (–1678) for questioning legality of prorogation of parliamentary session.

PROSE

(Spinoza (*d.*1677): *Ethics*)

DRAMA

Behn: *The Rover, or The Banished Cavaliers, Pt I*

Dryden: *All for Love, or The World Well Lost*

Lee: *The Rival Queens, or The Death of Alexander the Great*

Otway: *Titus and Berenice*

(Racine: *Phèdre*)

POETRY

Cleveland (*d.*1658): *Clevelandi Vindiciae*

Tate: *Poems*

Waller: *Of the Lady Mary*

1678

Titus Oates discloses a Popish plot, resulting in the persecution of Catholics; Louis XIV reveals secret treaty with Charles II (*see* 1676); Earl of Danby, involved in negotiating the treaty, impeached by the Commons and imprisoned in the Tower of London (–1684).

PROSE

Bunyan: *The Pilgrim's Progress* (pt i, pt ii 1684)

(La Fayette: *The Princess of Cleves*)

Rymer: *The Tragedies of the Last Age Considered*

DRAMA

Behn: *Sir Patient Fancy*

Dryden: *The Kind Keeper, or Mr Limberham*; (with Lee): *Oedipus*

Lee: *Mithridates, King of Pontus*

Otway: *Friendship in Fashion*

Shadwell: *A True Widow*

DRAMA (*cont.*)

Tate: *Brutus of Alba, or The Enchanted Lovers*

POETRY

Butler: *Hudibras* (pt iii, *see* 1662)

Marvell: *Advice to a Painter*

Vaughan, Henry: *Thalia Rediviva*

1679

Earl of Shaftesbury introduces Act of Habeas Corpus, to prevent illegal and indefinite imprisonment; Duke of Monmouth quells revolt of Scottish Covenanters; discovery of Niagara Falls by Hennepin; Dryden, wrongly supposed to be the author of a satire on Earl of Rochester, is attacked by hired men in Covent Garden.

PROSE

Burnet: *History of the Reformation of the Church of England* (compl. in 3 pts by 1682)

DRAMA

Beaumont (*d*.1616) and Fletcher (*d*.1625): *Fifty Comedies and Tragedies* (publ.)

Behn: *The Young King, or The Mistake*

DRAMA (*cont.*)

Dryden: *Troilus and Cressida, or Truth Found Too Late* (adaptation of Shakespeare)

Lee: *Caesar Borgia*

Otway: *Caius Marius* (adaptation of Shakespeare's *Romeo and Juliet*)

Shadwell: *The Woman Captain*

Tate: *The Loyal General*

POETRY

Oldham: *Garnet's Ghost*

1680

Crisis over the Exclusion Bill to exclude Charles II's brother, the Duke of York, from succession, on the grounds of his Catholicism; the Petitioners urge the King to call Parliament to pass the Bill which the Abhorrers oppose (these factions are later called 'Whigs' and 'Tories'); (*c.*) dodo becomes extinct; foundation of the Comédie Française in Paris.

PROSE

Bunyan: *The Life and Death of Mr Badman*

Burnet: *Some Passages of the Life and Death of the Earl of Rochester*

L'Estrange: *Select Colloquies of Erasmus* (transl.)

Temple: *Miscellanea* (see 1692, 1701)

DRAMA

Dryden: *The Spanish Friar, or The Double Discovery*

DRAMA (*cont.*)

Lee: *Theodosius, or The Force of Love*

Otway: *The Orphan, or The Unhappy Marriage*; *The Soldier's Fortune, Pt I*

Tate: *The Sicilian Usurper* (adaptation of Shakespeare's *Richard II*)

POETRY

Dryden: *Ovid's Epistles* (transl.)

Roscommon: *Horace's Art of Poetry* (transl.)

1681

Charles II dissolves two Parliaments in order to scotch the Exclusion Bill; Earl of Shaftesbury tried unsuccessfully for treason; Penn granted territory by Charles II in America.

PROSE

(Bossuet: *Discourse on Universal History*)

Glanvill (*d*.1680): *Sadducismus Triumphatus*

Hobbes (*d*.1679): *Behemoth*

DRAMA

Behn: *The False Count, or A New Way to Play an Old Game*; *The Rover, Pt II*

Lee: *The Princess of Cleve*

Tate: *King Lear* (adaptation of Shakespeare)

POETRY

Cotton: *The Wonders of The Peak*

Cowley (*d*.1667): *Collected Works* (pt ii, see 1668)

Dryden: *Absalom and Achitophel* (pt i, pt ii 1682)

Marvell (*d*.1678): *Miscellaneous Poems*

Oldham: *Satire against Virtue*; *Satires upon the Jesuits*

1682

Earl of Shaftesbury, apprehensive of arrest, flees the country; La Salle claims territory of Louisiana for France; Halley observes comet named after him, which he predicts will return in 1758; foundation of the Ashmolean Museum, Oxford.

PROSE
Bunyan: *The Holy War*
DRAMA
Behn: *The City Heiress, or Sir Timothy Treat-All*
Dryden (with Lee): *The Duke of Guise*
Otway: *Venice Preserved, or A Plot Discovered*

POETRY
Dryden: (with Tate) *Absalom and Achitophel* (pt ii, *see* 1681); *MacFlecknoe*; *The Medal*; *Religio Laici*
Waller: *Poems, with Several Additions Never Before Printed*

1683

Failure of the Rye House Plot to murder Charles II and Duke of York; execution of plotters, Russell and Sidney; in America, Penn makes peace treaty with Indians.

DRAMA
Lee: *Constantine the Great*
Otway: *The Atheist, or The Second Part of the Soldier's Fortune*

POETRY
Oldham (*d*.1683): *Poems and Translations*

1684

Duke of Monmouth, Charles II's illegitimate son, implicated in the Rye House Plot (*see* 1683), flees to Holland; the Bermudas become Crown Colony.

PROSE
Bunyan: *The Pilgrim's Progress* (pt ii, *see* 1678)
Burnet, Gilbert: *More's Utopia* (transl.)
Burnet, Thomas: *The Sacred Theory of the Earth* (vol. i, vol. ii 1690)

DRAMA
Tate: *A Duke and No Duke*
POETRY
Dryden (with others): *Miscellany Poems* (*see* 1685, 1693)
Roscommon: *An Essay on Translated Verse*

1685

Death of Charles II; accession of James II (–1688), Charles's Catholic brother; invasions and rebellions of Earl of Argyll in Scotland, and Duke of Monmouth in Dorset: both defeated; Judge Jeffreys tries and punishes Monmouth's followers; Louis XIV intensifies persecution of Huguenots by revoking the Treaty of Nantes (*see* 1598); Huguenots leave France in large numbers; French settle in Arkansas; Hemming introduces oil lamps in streets of London; (*c.*) wild boar extinct in Britain.

PROSE
Cotton: *Montaigne's Essays* (transl.)
Sprat: *A True Declaration of the Horrid Conspiracy*
DRAMA
Dryden: *Albion and Albanius* (opera)
Shakespeare (*d*.1616): Fourth Folio (publ., *see* 1623)

POETRY
Dryden: *Sylvae, or The Second Part of Poetical Miscellanies* (*see* 1684, 1693); *Threnodia Augustalis*
Rochester (*d*.1680): *Poems on Several Occasions, Written by a Late Person of Honour*
Waller: *Divine Poems*

1686

James II tries to repeal Test and Habeas Corpus Acts; he introduces Catholics into the Church and army; League of Augsburg unites the Empire, Spain, Sweden, Saxony and others against France; Lully: *Armide* (opera).

PROSE
Halifax: *Letter to a Dissenter*
DRAMA
Behn: *The Lucky Chance, or An Alderman's Bargain*
POETRY
Bunyan: *A Book for Boys and Girls*
Dryden: *To the Memory of Mrs Anne Killigrew*
Killigrew (*d.*1685): *Poems*

POETRY (*cont.*)
Waller: *Poems: Fifth Edition, with Several Additions Never Before Printed*

1687

James II issues Declaration of Indulgence for Liberty of Conscience, and continues to attempt to restore Catholicism and appoint Catholics to leading positions; Newton: *Philosophiae Naturalis Principia Mathematica* (laws of motion and dynamics); Talman starts rebuilding Chatsworth House, Derbyshire (compl. 1707).

DRAMA
Behn: *The Emperor of the Moon*
Sedley: *Bellamira, or The Mistress*
Tate: *The Island Princess*
POETRY
Cleveland (*d.*1658): *Works*
Dryden: *The Hind and the Panther*; *Song for St Cecilia's Day*

POETRY (*cont.*)
Prior and Montague: *The Hind and the Panther Transversed to the Story of the Country Mouse and the City Mouse*

1688

James II orders all churchmen to publicise the Second Declaration of Indulgence, suspending laws against Nonconformists and Catholics; seven bishops tried for their refusal and acquitted; the Bloodless Revolution; William of Orange invited to assist in the overthrow of James II; he lands in Torbay; James flees to France; accession of William III and Mary II (−1702, Mary dies 1694); Dampier sights Australia; Robert Boyle: *A Disquisition about the Final Causes of Things*.

PROSE
Behn: *Agnes de Castro, or The Force of Generous Love* (transl. of De Brilhac); *The Fair Jilt, or The History of Prince Tarquin and Miranda*; *Oroonoko, or The Royal Slave*
Halifax: *Character of a Trimmer*; *A Lady's New Year Gift, or Advice to a Daughter*
(La Bruyère: *Characters*)
DRAMA
Shadwell: *The Squire of Alsatia*

POETRY
Dryden: *Britannia Rediviva*

1689

Convention draws up a Declaration of Rights which is accepted by William and Mary; this becomes the Bill of Rights, to regularise the relationship between the monarch, private citizens and Parliament; Toleration Act gives freedom of worship, but not full citizenship, to Nonconformists; James II lands in Ireland; Irish Catholics besiege Protestants in Londonderry; Scots supporters of the rival Kings fight at the battle of Killiecrankie; Louis XIV declares war on England.

PROSE

Locke: *First Letter on Toleration* (*Second Letter* 1690, *Third Letter* 1692)
Selden (*d*.1654): *Table Talk*

DRAMA

Behn (*d*.1689): *The Widow Ranter, or The History of Bacon in Virginia*
Dryden: *Don Sebastian, King of Portugal*
Shadwell: *Bury Fair*
Tate: *Dido and Aeneas* (with music by Purcell, usually considered first English opera)

POETRY

Cotton (*d*.1687): *Poems on Several Occasions*
Marvell (*d*.1678): *Poems on Affairs of State*

1690

French victory at the battle of Beachy Head; William III defeats James II in Ireland at the battle of the Boyne; James flees to France; East India Company sets up trading post at Calcutta; Petty: *Political Arithmetic, or a Discourse Concerning the Value of Lands, People etc.* (comparative statistics); first publication of the *Worcester Postman* (early regular weekly provincial paper).

PROSE

Browne (*d*.1682): *A Letter to a Friend upon the Occasion of the Death of His Intimate Friend*
Locke: *An Essay Concerning Human Understanding*; *Second Letter on Toleration* (*see* 1689); *Two Treatises of Civil Government*

DRAMA

Dryden: *Amphitryon, or The Two Socias*
Shadwell: *The Amorous Bigot*; *The Scowrers*

1691

William III's commander-in-chief in Ireland, Godert de Ginkel, defeats Irish and French Jacobite army at Aughrim, and completes the conquest of Ireland by the capture of Limerick; Treaty of Limerick allows Jacobites to leave Ireland and promises religious toleration, which is never achieved, and is revoked by the Penal Code of 1695.

PROSE

Congreve: *Incognita*
Wood: *Athenae Oxonienses* (pt i, biographical dictionary of Oxford writers and bishops, pt ii 1692)

DRAMA

Dryden: *King Arthur, or The British Worthy* (opera with music by Purcell)

1692

Marlborough dismissed for suspected involvement in Jacobite plot; Louis XIV and James II attempt invasion of England, but their fleet is defeated at the battle of La Hogue; Massacre of Glencoe: the Campbells murder the Macdonalds, who had not taken the oath of allegiance to William III; Edward Lloyd's coffee house becomes centre of marine insurance; Coutts bank opens in London.

PROSE
Bentley: *A Confutation of Atheism from the Origin and Frame of the World* (compl. in 3 pts by 1693)
Bunyan (*d.*1688): *Works*
L'Estrange: *Fables of Aesop and Other Mythologists*
Locke: *Third Letter on Toleration* (*see* 1689)
Temple: *Miscellanea: The Second Part* (incl. essay on 'Ancient and Modern Learning'; this gave rise to controversy concerning the spurious epistles of Phalaris between Charles Boyle and Bentley and others, *see* 1680, 1701)
DRAMA
Dryden: *Cleomenes, the Spartan Hero*

DRAMA (*cont.*)
Jonson (*d.*1637): Second Folio (publ., *see* 1616)
Settle: *The Fairy Queen* (opera, adaptation of Shakespeare's *A Midsummer Night's Dream*)
Shadwell (*d.*1692): *The Volunteers, or The Stock Jobbers*
POETRY
Walsh: *Poems*

1693

National Debt commenced, originating in a loan to defray expenses of war with France; William III defeated by allies of France at Neerwinden.

PROSE
Dennis: *The Impartial Critic*
Locke: *Thoughts Concerning Education*
Rymer: *A Short View of Tragedy*
DRAMA
Congreve: *The Double Dealer*; *The Old Bachelor*

POETRY
Dryden: *Aeneid* (transl. of Virgil); *Examen Poeticum, Being the Third Part of Miscellany Poems* (*see* 1684–5); *The Satires of Juvenal and Persius* (transl. with others)

1694

Bank of England incorporated by Parliament to deal with all government money business, including raising money for war in Holland; Triennial Bill passed, limiting duration of Parliament to three years.

PROSE
Fox (*d.*1691): *Journal*
Wotton: *Reflections on Ancient and Modern Learning*
DRAMA
Settle: *The Ambitious Slave*
Southerne: *The Fatal Marriage, or The Innocent Adultery*

POETRY
Addison: *Fourth Georgic* (transl. of Virgil); *Ovid's Salmacis* (transl.); *Song for St Cecilia's Day* (contributions to Dryden's *Annual Miscellany*)
Dryden (ed.): *Annual Miscellany*; *To Congreve*

1695

William III recaptures Namur from the French; Bank of Scotland established.

PROSE
Dryden: *Du Fresnoy's De Arte Graphica* (transl.)
Locke: *The Reasonableness of Christianity*; *A Vindication of the Reasonableness of Christianity*
Temple: *Introduction to the History of England*
Tillotson (*d*.1694): *Works*

DRAMA
Anon.: *The Indian Queen* (with music by Purcell)
Congreve: *Love for Love*
Southerne: *Oroonoko*

POETRY
Addison: *A Poem to His Majesty*
Blackmore: *Prince Arthur*
Milton (*d*.1674): *Poetical Works* (first annotated edn)

1696

Plot to assassinate William III fails; new act regulates rights of the accused in trials for treason; French prepare to invade England; William campaigns against France in Holland; building begins of the first Eddystone lighthouse (compl. 1699); first insurance company (for property) in Britain, the Amicable Contributionship for the Insurance of Houses, later the Hand-in-Hand.

PROSE
Aubrey: *Miscellanies*
Baxter (*d*.1691): *Reliquiae Baxterianae*
Dennis: *Letters Written between Dryden, Wycherley, Congreve and Dennis*
Toland: *Christianity Not Mysterious*

DRAMA
Cibber: *Love's Last Shift, or The Fool in Fashion*; *Woman's Wit, or The Lady in Fashion*

DRAMA (*cont.*)
Vanbrugh: *Aesop, Pt I*; *The Relapse, or Virtue in Danger*

POETRY
Dryden: *Ode on Henry Purcell*

1697

Treaty of Ryswick signed between England and European nations, acknowledging William III as monarch and Anne as his heir; Grinling Gibbons carves stalls of St Paul's Cathedral.

PROSE
Bentley: *Dissertation upon the Epistles of Phalaris*
Dampier: *Voyages*
Defoe: *Essay upon Projects*
(Perrault: *Histoires ou Contes du temps passé* ('Tales of Long Ago'), fairy-tales)

DRAMA
Congreve: *The Mourning Bride*
Vanbrugh: *Aesop, Pt II*; *The Provoked Wife*

POETRY
Dryden: *Alexander's Feast, or The Power of Music*

1698

Charles II of Spain on the verge of dying without an heir; First Partition Treaty, agreed between England, France and Holland, divides the Spanish Empire between France, Bavaria and Austria; foundation of the Society for Promoting Christian Knowledge (S.P.C.K.), with the aim of teaching scriptures to children.

PROSE

Atterbury, Charles Boyle and others: *Dr Bentley's Dissertations upon the Epistles of Phalaris Examined*
Behn (*d.*1689): *Histories and Novels*
Collier: *A Short View of the Immorality and Profaneness of the English Stage* (leads to controversy involving Dennis, D'Urfey, Congreve, Dryden and Vanbrugh)
Milton (*d.*1674): *Collected Prose Works, English and Latin*

DRAMA

Dennis: *Rinaldo and Armida*
D'Urfey: *The Campaigners, or The Pleasant Adventures at Brussels*
Farquhar: *Love and a Bottle*
Vanbrugh: *The Country House* (transl. of Dancourt)

POETRY

Behn (*d.*1689): *Poetical Remains*

1699

Attempt by Scots to settle on the Isthmus of Darien fails; William III attacked for rewarding Dutch favourites; Vanbrugh designs Castle Howard, Yorkshire (compl. 1726).

PROSE

Burnet: *Exposition of the Thirty-Nine Articles*
(Fénelon: *Télémaque*)

DRAMA

Cibber: *Richard III* (adaptation of Shakespeare); *Xerxes*
Dennis: *Iphigenia*

DRAMA (*cont.*)

Farquhar: *The Constant Couple, or A Trip to the Jubilee*

POETRY

Garth: *The Dispensary*

1700

Second Partition Treaty signed, dividing the Spanish Empire (*see* 1698); death of Charles II of Spain; Philip of Anjou, grandson of Louis XIV, accedes to the Spanish throne in contravention of the Treaty; Peter the Great issues laws regulating clothes worn by Russians to help effect westernisation of Russia; population of England and Wales: 5.75 million; Scotland: 1 million; Ireland: 2.5 million; London: 675,000; Glasgow: 35,000; Moore: *Vox Stellarum* (later known as *Old Moore's Almanac*).

PROSE

Halifax (*d.*1695): *Miscellanies*

DRAMA

Cibber: *Love Makes a Man, or The Fop's Fortune*
Congreve: *The Way of the World*

POETRY

(*c.*) Anon: *Robin Hood's Garland, Containing His Merry Exploits, and the Several Fights Which He, Little John and Will Scarlet Had upon Several Occasions*

POETRY (*cont.*)

Dryden (*d.*1700): *Fables*
Tate: *Panacea: A Poem on Tea*

1701

Act of Settlement secures Protestant Hanoverian succession; James II dies in France; Grand Alliance formed between England, Holland and Austria to support claims of Archduke Charles to the Spanish throne; Louis XIV recognises James Francis Edward (the Old Pretender) as rightful King of England; preparations for war against France; Jethro Tull invents horse-drawn seed-driller; foundation of the University of Yale in America.

PROSE
Dennis: *The Advancement and Reformation of Modern Poetry*
Steele: *The Christian Hero*
Swift: *Contests in Athens and Rome*
Temple (*d*.1699): *Miscellanea: The Third Part* (*see* 1680, 1692)
DRAMA
Rowe: *Tamerlane*

DRAMA (*cont.*)
Steele: *The Funeral, or Grief à la Mode*
POETRY
Defoe: *A True Born Englishman*

1702

Death of William III; accession of Queen Anne (–1714), during whose reign Whigs and Tories steadily polarise over issues concerning the Church, foreign policy and the royal prerogative; start of the War of the Spanish Succession (–1713); Buckingham House, London, begun (compl. 1705); Kneller starts painting portraits of the Kit-Cat Club (compl. 1717); first daily newspaper in London issued, *The Daily Courant* (–1735).

PROSE
Clarendon (*d*.1674): *The History of the Rebellion and Civil Wars* (compl. in 3 vols by 1704)
Defoe: *The Shortest Way with Dissenters*

DRAMA
Vanbrugh: *The False Friend*

1703

England and Portugal forge alliance in the Methuen Treaties, securing supply of wines in exchange for cloth; Peter the Great founds St Petersburg; Hickes: *Thesaurus of the Ancient Northern Languages* (vol. i, vol. ii 1705); Defoe imprisoned for his *The Shortest Way with Dissenters* (1702).

DRAMA
Rowe: *The Fair Penitent*
POETRY
Addison: *Letter from Italy to Lord Halifax*

POETRY (*cont.*)
Defoe: *A Hymn to the Pillory*

1704

Duke of Marlborough defeats French and Bavarians at the battle of Blenheim; British capture Gibraltar; Newton: *Opticks*; Defoe: *The Review* (periodical, thrice weekly –1713).

PROSE
Dennis: *The Grounds of Criticism in Poetry*
Swift: *The Battle of the Books*; *A Tale of a Tub*

DRAMA
Cibber: *The Careless Husband*
Dennis: *Liberty Asserted*
Steele: *The Lying Lover*

1705

Meeting of Commissioners to discuss union of Scotland and England; Vanbrugh designs Blenheim Palace for Duke of Marlborough.

PROSE
Addison: *Remarks on Italy*
DRAMA
Rowe: *Ulysses*
Steele: *The Tender Husband*
Vanbrugh: *The Confederacy*

POETRY
Addison: *The Campaign*
Mandeville: *The Grumbling Hive*
Philips, John: *Blenheim*; *The Splendid Shilling: An Imitation of Milton* (unauthorised version 1701)

1706

Allies under Duke of Marlborough victorious at Ramillies; Beau Nash raises £18,000 for the repair of roads in Bath, part of his efforts to make the city a centre of fashion.

PROSE
Defoe: *The Apparition of Mrs Veal*
DRAMA
Farquhar: *The Recruiting Officer*
Vanbrugh: *The Mistake*

POETRY
Defoe: *Jure Divino*
Watson (ed.): *Choice Collection of Scottish Poems* (compl. in 3 vols by 1711)
Watts: *Horae Lyricae*

1707

Act of Union ends separate Scottish Parliament, giving Scots representation in English Parliament and allowing free trade with England.

DRAMA
Addison: *Rosamund: An Opera*
Farquhar (*d*.1707): *The Beaux' Stratagem*

POETRY
Watts: *Hymns and Spiritual Songs*

1708

Walpole made Secretary of War; Old Pretender visits Scotland; early excavations of Roman site at Herculaneum, near Naples.

PROSE
Shaftesbury: *Letter Concerning Enthusiasm*
Swift: *Esquire Bickerstaff's Most Strange and Wonderful Predictions for the Year 1708* (*Bickerstaff Papers*)

POETRY
Philips, John: *Cider*

1709

Darby produces coke furnace for smelting iron ore (*see* 1640); first piano built, in Florence; Steele starts *The Tatler* (periodical –1711).

PROSE
Berkeley: *A New Theory of Vision*
Defoe: *The History of the Union of Great Britain*
DRAMA
Rowe (ed.): *The Works of Mr William Shakespeare* (publ., compl. in 6 vols by 1710)

POETRY
Pope: *Pastorals*
Prior: *Poems on Several Occasions*

1710

Fall of the pro-war Whig ministry; Sir Christopher Wren completes St Paul's Cathedral, London; first English Copyright Act establishes authors as recipients of copyright law, but allows rights to pass in time into public domain; Leibniz: *Théodicée* (philosophical work).

PROSE
Berkeley: *Treatise on the Principles of Human Knowledge*
Shaftesbury: *Advice to an Author*
Swift: *Meditation upon a Broomstick*

POETRY
Philips, Ambrose: *Pastorals*

1711

Duke of Marlborough accused of peculation and dismissed; formation of the English South Sea Trading Company; Queen Anne initiates the Ascot races; Addison (ed.): *The Spectator* (periodical –1712).

PROSE
Dennis: *On the Genius and Writings of Shakespeare*
Gay: *The Present State of Wit*
Shaftesbury: *Characteristics of Men, Manners, Opinions, Times*
Swift: *An Argument against Abolishing Christianity*; *Conduct of the Allies*

POETRY
Pope: *An Essay on Criticism*

1712

Secret negotiations result in truce between Britain and France; last execution for witchcraft in England; Newcomen constructs steam-powered water pump; Corelli: *Concerti Grossi* (form of concerto popular throughout much of the century).

PROSE
Arbuthnot: *History of John Bull*
Swift: *Proposal for Correcting the English Language*
DRAMA
Gay: *The Mohocks*

POETRY
Blackmore: *The Creation: A Philosophical Poem*
Pope: *The Rape of the Lock* (in 2 cantos, *see* 1714)

1713

Treaty of Utrecht ends War of the Spanish Succession (*see* 1702), disallows unity of France and Spain, and gives Britain and Austria territorial and political rights, including the sole right for Britain to import slaves into America (the Asiento), held by Britain's African Company till 1750; Steele (ed.): *The Guardian* (periodical, January–September).

DRAMA
Addison: *Cato*
POETRY
Gay: *Rural Sports*
Parnell: *An Essay on the Different Styles of Poetry*
Pope: *Ode for Music (on St Cecilia's Day)*; *Windsor-Forest*

POETRY (*cont.*)
Tickell: *On the Prospect of Peace*
Winchilsea: *Miscellany Poems*

1714

Death of Queen Anne; accession of George I, first Hanoverian king (–1727); Schism Act forbids non-members of the Church of England to teach; Fahrenheit invents mercury thermometer with scale.

PROSE

Mandeville: *The Fable of the Bees, or Private Vices, Public Benefits*
Shaftesbury: 'A Letter Concerning the Art or Science of Design' (in second edn of *Characteristics*)

DRAMA

Rowe: *The Tragedy of Jane Shore*

POETRY

Gay: *The Shepherd's Week*
Pope: *The Rape of the Lock* (in 5 cantos, *see* 1712)

1715

Tory leader Bolingbroke flees the country to join the Old Pretender; Whigs assume power; Walpole made Chancellor of the Exchequer (–1717); Jacobite rebellion in the North defeated at Preston and Sherrifmuir; death of Louis XIV of France; accession of Louis XV (–1774); first Liverpool Dock opened; Stradivarius creates the Alard, a famous violin; Handel: *Water Music* (concertos); Alessandro Scarlatti: *Il Tigrane* (opera).

PROSE

Defoe: *The Family Instructor* (vol. i, vol. ii 1718)
(Le Sage: *Gil Blas*)

DRAMA

Addison: *The Drummer, or The Haunted House*
Rowe: *Lady Jane Grey*

POETRY

Pope: *The Iliad* (transl. of Homer, compl. in 6 vols by 1720); *The Temple of Fame*
Tickell: *The First Book of Homer's Iliad* (transl.)
Watts: *Divine Songs for the Use of Children*

1716

Septennial Act prolongs Parliaments to seven-year duration; Hawksmoor starts building St Mary Woolnoth (compl. 1727), one of his six London churches.

PROSE

Shaftesbury (*d*.1713): *Several Letters Written by a Noble Lord to a Young Man at the University*

POETRY

Gay: *Trivia, or The Art of Walking the Streets of London*

1717

Triple Alliance of Britain, France and Holland against Spain and to uphold the Treaty of Utrecht (1713); Walpole resigns from office; Freemasonry initiated in London.

PROSE

Ashmole (*d*.1692): *Memoirs*

DRAMA

Gay, Pope and Arbuthnot: *Three Hours after Marriage*

POETRY

Garth (ed.): *Ovid's Metamorphoses, Translated by the Most Eminent Hands* (incl. Addison, Congreve, Dryden, Gay and Tate)

POETRY (*cont.*)

Pope: *Works* (vol. i, incl. 'Verses to the Memory of an Unfortunate Lady' and 'Eloisa to Abelard', vol. ii 1735)

1718

Austria joins the Allies against Spain; Admiral Byng destroys the Spanish fleet off Cape Passaro; Schism Act repealed (*see* 1714); Lady Mary Wortley Montagu popularises inoculation against smallpox in Britain (*see* 1798); Watteau: *Fête in a Park* (*p.*).

DRAMA
Cibber: *The Non-Juror*
Savage: *Love in a Veil*
POETRY
Prior: *Poems*

POETRY (*cont.*)
Ramsay (ed.): *Christ's Kirk on the Green*
Rowe (*d.*1718): *Lucan's Pharsalia* (transl.)

1719

The Old Pretender persuades the Spanish to support his claims to the English throne, but their attempt at invasion of Scotland fails; France at war with Spain (–1720); Westminster Hospital founded.

PROSE
Defoe: *Robinson Crusoe*; *Further Adventures of Robinson Crusoe*
DRAMA
Young: *Busiris*

POETRY
D'Urfey: *Wit and Mirth, or Pills to Purge Melancholy*
Watts: *Psalms of David* (transl.)

1720

Walpole returns to Government; peace in Europe, ending wars between France and Spain, and between Prussia and Sweden; 'South Sea Bubble': collapse of the South Sea Company makes the Government take over the National Debt.

PROSE
Defoe: *Adventures of Captain Singleton*; *Memoirs of a Cavalier*
Swift: *Proposal for the Universal Use of Irish Manufactures*

POETRY
Gay: *Collected Poems*
Pope: *Verses to Lady Mary Wortley Montagu*
Ramsay: *Poems*

1721

Walpole appointed Chancellor of the Exchequer and First Lord of the Treasury (–1742), becoming the first British 'Prime Minister'; Russia, steadily gaining power in Europe, wins territory in the Baltic from Sweden at the Treaty of Nystad; J.S. Bach: six *Brandenburg Concertos*.

PROSE
Addison (*d.*1719): *Works*
(Montesquieu: *Persian Letters*)
Swift: *Letter to a Young Gentleman Lately Entered into Holy Orders*

DRAMA
Young: *The Revenge*

1722

Atterbury, Bishop of Rochester, imprisoned in Tower of London for complicity in attempts to restore the Stuarts; foundation of hospital in Southwark by Thomas Guy, bookseller; Gibbs starts building church of St Martin-in-the-Fields, London (compl. 1726).

PROSE
Defoe: *The History of Colonel Jack*; *Journal of the Plague Year*; *Moll Flanders*
DRAMA
Steele: *The Conscious Lovers*

POETRY
Parnell (*d.*1718): *Poems on Several Occasions*

1723

Uproar in Ireland at minting of Wood's Halfpence, copper coinage issued by a licensed English iron master; Workhouse Test Act empowers parishes to establish workhouses and states that anyone refusing to enter the workhouse should not be entitled to relief.

PROSE
Burnet (*d*.1715): *Bishop Burnet's History of His Own Time* (pt i, pt ii 1734)
Law: *Remarks on the Fable of the Bees*
Mandeville: 'Essay on Charity and Search into the Nature of Society' (in *The Fable of the Bees*, second edn)

1724

Foundation of Longmans, oldest British publishers still extant; Swift attacks Wood's Halfpence in *The Drapier's Letters*, causing withdrawal of the coinage in 1725.

PROSE
Defoe: *The Fortunate Mistress, or A History of the Life of the Lady Roxana*; *A Tour Thro' the Whole Island of Great Britain* (compl. in 3 vols by 1726)
Johnson, Charles: *General History of the Most Notorious Pirates*
Mandeville: *A Modest Defence of Public Stews*

DRAMA
Savage: *Sir Thomas Overbury*
POETRY
Mallet: *William and Margaret*
Ramsay (ed.): *The Ever Green*; (ed.): *The Tea Table Miscellany* (compl. in 3 vols by 1727)

1725

Britain organises the Treaty of Hanover against Spain and Austria; death of Peter the Great of Russia, who is succeeded by his widow Catherine (–1727); (*c*.) gin-drinking becomes widespread (by 1735 there were *c*.7,000 unlicensed gin shops in London); Vivaldi: *The Four Seasons* (violin concertos).

DRAMA
Pope (ed.): *Plays of Shakespeare* (publ.)
Ramsay: *The Gentle Shepherd*

POETRY
Pope: *Odyssey* (transl. of Homer, compl. in 6 vols by 1726)

1726

Famine in Ireland (–1729); General Wade's military road construction begun in Scotland, to aid in the pacification and disarming of the Highland clans; Edinburgh's first circulating library opened; Voltaire in England (–1729).

PROSE
Dennis: *The Stage Defended*
Law: *Christian Perfection*; *The Unlawfulness of Stage Entertainments*
Swift: *Gulliver's Travels*
POETRY
Carey: *Namby Pamby*

POETRY (*cont.*)
Swift: *Cadenus and Vanessa*
Thomson: *Winter* (*see* 1730)

1727

Death of George I; accession of George II (–1760); Gibraltar blockaded by Spain; Hales: *Vegetable Staticks* (study of plant nutrition and physiology).

PROSE
Defoe: *The History and Reality of Apparitions*; *A System of Magic*
Pope, Swift and others: *Miscellanies* (compl. in 4 vols by 1735)

POETRY
Dyer: *Grongar Hill*
Gay: *Fables* (first series, second series 1738)
Thomson: *Summer* (*see* 1730); *To the Memory of Sir Isaac Newton*

1728

Bering discovers straits between Asia and America; Wood the elder begins Queen Square, Bath, with Palladian façade (compl. 1736); Gibbs: *Book of Architecture* (influential study, probably inspiring the White House in Washington); Ephraim Chambers publishes *Cyclopaedia*.

PROSE
Defoe: *Captain Carleton*
Law: *A Serious Call to Devout and Holy Life*
Swift: *A Short View of the State of Ireland*
DRAMA
Cibber: *The Provoked Husband, or A Journey to London*
Fielding: *Love in Several Masques*
Gay: *The Beggar's Opera*

POETRY
Pope: *The Dunciad: An Heroic Poem in Three Books* (*see* 1729, 1742–3)
Ramsay: *Poems*
Savage: *The Bastard*
Thomson: *Spring* (*see* 1730)
Young: *Love of Fame: The Universal Passion, in Seven Characteristic Satires*; *Ocean: An Ode*

1729

Treaty of Seville negotiated by Walpole to settle differences with Spain; J.S.Bach: *St Matthew Passion* (oratorio).

PROSE
Swift: *A Modest Proposal for Preventing the Children of Poor People from Being a Burden to Their Parents*
DRAMA
Gay: *Polly* (publ.)
POETRY
Carey: *Poems on Several Occasions*

POETRY (*cont.*)
Pope: *The Dunciad Variorum, with the Prolegomena of Scriblerus* (bks i–iii, with notes, indices and appendix, *see* 1728, 1742–3)
Savage: *The Wanderer*
Thomson: *Britannia*

1730

John and Charles Wesley start Methodist Society in Oxford; 'Turnip' Townshend introduces four-yearly rotation of crops; Ged obtains licence to print Bibles using stereotype plates, but printers hinder the development of the invention.

PROSE
Bolingbroke: 'Remarks upon History' (in *The Craftsman*)
Tindal: *Christianity As Old As the Creation*
DRAMA
Fielding: *The Author's Farce*; *Tom Thumb* (revised as *The Tragedy of Tragedies* 1731)

DRAMA (*cont.*)
Thomson: *Sophonisba*
POETRY
Duck: *Poems*
Thomson: *The Seasons* (contains 'Winter' (1726), 'Summer' (1727), 'Spring' (1728), 'Autumn', also 'Britannia' and 'To the Memory of Sir Isaac Newton', revised version 1744)

1731

Hadley demonstrates his navigational octant, an improved quadrant and forerunner of the sextant; *The Gentleman's Magazine* started (monthly –1914, original of the term 'magazine' for this kind of publication).

PROSE
Law: *The Case of Reason*
(Prévost: *Manon Lescaut*)
DRAMA
Lillo: *The London Merchant,*
or The History of George
Barnwell

POETRY
Pope: *Of Taste: An Epistle to the Earl*
of Burlington

1732

Royal charter granted for foundation of Georgia in North America; original Covent Garden Opera House opened in London; first publication of *The London Magazine* (–1785).

PROSE
Watts: *A Short View of the Whole*
Scripture History
DRAMA
Fielding: *The Modern Husband*
(Voltaire: *Zaïre*)

POETRY
Pope: *Of the Use of Riches: An*
Epistle to Lord Bathurst

1733

Walpole introduces Excise Bill, imposing duties on wine and tobacco, but violent opposition causes its withdrawal; Kay's flying shuttle loom patented; Hales: *A Friendly Admonition to the Drinkers of Brandy.*

DRAMA
Fielding: *The Miser, Taken from*
Plautus and Molière
POETRY
Pope: *An Essay on Man* (compl. in 4
pts by 1734); *The First Satire of*
Horace (transl.); *Of the Knowledge*
and Characters of Men: An Epistle
to Viscount Cobham

1734

War between France and Austria in Italy (–1738); first issue of *Lloyd's List*, the shipping register; Dilettanti Society founded, to aid persons making the Grand Tour and systematise their archaeological and artistic discoveries; building begins of Holkham Hall, Norfolk (Palladian mansion, compl. 1761); Charles Johnson: *General History of the Lives and Adventures of the Most Famous Highwaymen.*

PROSE
Atterbury (*d.*1732): *Sermons*
Sale: *The Koran* (transl.)
Watts: *Reliquiae Juveniles:*
Miscellaneous Thoughts in Prose
and Verse
DRAMA
Gay: *The Distressed Wife*

POETRY
Pope: *An Epistle to Dr Arbuthnot*;
The Second Satire of Horace
(transl.)

1735

William Pitt made M.P. for Old Sarum, a notorious 'Rotten Borough'; Linnaeus: *Systema Naturae* (systematisation of natural phenomena); Rameau: *Les Indes galantes* (*ballet héroique*); (*c.*) Hogarth: *A Rake's Progress* (series of paintings and engravings); John Wesley starts his *Journal* (–1790, extracts publ. 1739–91, compl. in 4 vols 1827).

PROSE
Bolingbroke: *Dissertation upon Parties*
Johnson: *A Voyage to Abyssinia*
Lyttelton: *Letter from a Persian in England*
Swift: *Collected Works*
DRAMA
Lillo: *The Christian Hero*

POETRY
Pope: *Of the Characters of Women*; *Works* (vol. ii, *see* 1717)
Somerville: *The Chace*
Thomson: *Liberty* (compl. in 5 pts by 1736)

1736

Riots in Edinburgh; Captain Porteous fires on mob, and is sentenced to death, but then reprieved; finally he is dragged from prison and lynched; india-rubber described by French scientists returning from South America.

PROSE
Butler: *Analogy of Religion*
Warburton: *The Alliance between Church and State*
DRAMA
Fielding: *Pasquin*

POETRY
Pope: *Works* (with explanatory notes, compl. in 6 vols by 1737)
Swift: *The Legion Club*

1737

Frederick, Prince of Wales becomes focus for opposition to the Government; Parliament decrees that the Lord Chamberlain license plays; Cruden: *Biblical Concordance*; Lady Mary Montagu: *The Nonsense of Common Sense* (weekly newspaper –1738).

DRAMA
Lillo: *Fatal Curiosity*
POETRY
Green (*d.*1737): *The Spleen*
Pope: *The First Epistle of the First Book of Horace Imitated*

POETRY (*cont.*)
Shenstone: *Poems on Various Occasions* (incl. 'The Schoolmistress')
Wesley, John: *Psalms and Hymns*

1738

Pope Clement XII's bull, *In Eminenti*, attacks Freemasonry; Domenico Scarlatti: *Essercizi per gravicembalo* (harpsichord music, incl. *Cat's Fugue*).

PROSE
Watts: *The World to Come*
POETRY
Gay (*d.*1732): *Fables* (second series, *see* 1727)
Johnson: *London: A Poem in Imitation of the Third Satire of Juvenal*

POETRY (*cont.*)
Pope: *Epilogue to the Satires*; *Poems and Imitations of Horace*

1739

Outbreak of the War of Jenkins's Ear with Spain (–1748), caused by trading conflicts in the West Indies and alleged violence to British sailors; John Wesley starts developing Methodist Societies in London; execution of Dick Turpin, highwayman.

PROSE
Hume: *Treatise of Human Nature* (compl. in 3 vols by 1740)
POETRY
Swift: *Verses on the Death of Dr Swift*

POETRY (*cont.*)
Wesley, John and Charles: *Hymns and Sacred Poems*

1740

Opposition to Walpole grows, following lack of British success in the War of Jenkins's Ear (*see* 1739); accession of Frederick II (the Great) of Prussia (–1786); War of the Austrian Succession begins (–1748).

PROSE
Cibber: *An Apology for the Life of Mr Colley Cibber, Comedian*
Richardson: *Pamela, or Virtue Rewarded* (compl. edn in 4 vols 1742)
Whitefield: *A Short Account of God's Dealings with George Whitefield*

DRAMA
Thomson and Mallet: *Alfred* (masque, incl. 'Ode in Honour of Great Britain'; with music by Arne, this becomes 'Rule Britannia')
POETRY
Dyer: *The Ruins of Rome*
Prior (*d.*1721): *Complete Works*

1741

Bering discovers Alaska; Garrick's first appearance on the London stage.

PROSE
Arbuthnot (*d.*1735), Pope, Gay and others: *Memoirs of Martinus Scriblerus*
Fielding: *Shamela*
Hume: *Essays Moral and Political*
Richardson: *Letters Written to and for Particular Friends, Directing the Requisite Style and Forms to be Observed in Writing Familiar Letters*
Watts: *Improvement of the Mind*

POETRY
Shenstone: *The Judgement of Hercules*

1742

Resignation of Walpole; invention of centigrade temperature scale; first performance, in Dublin, of Handel's oratorio *The Messiah*.

PROSE
Fielding: *Joseph Andrews*
POETRY
Collins: *Persian Eclogues*
Pope: *The New Dunciad As It Was in the Year 1741* (bk iv, *see* 1728–9, 1743)
Shenstone: *The Schoolmistress*

POETRY (*cont.*)
Young: *The Complaint, or Night Thoughts on Life, Death and Immortality* (compl. with all 9 'nights' by 1745)

1743   Britain drawn into the War of the Austrian Succession, upholding (with Hanover) Maria Theresa against France, Prussia and Bavaria; George II defeats the French at the battle of Dettingen, last battle in which a king of England took the field; Hogarth: *Marriage à la Mode* (series of paintings and engravings, compl. 1745).

PROSE
Fielding: *Miscellanies* (incl. *Jonathan Wild*)
POETRY
Blair, Robert: *The Grave*
Collins: *Verses on Hanmer's Shakespeare*

POETRY (*cont.*)
Pope: *The Dunciad* (final form, in 4 bks, *see* 1728–9, 1742)

1744   French invasion fleet, commanded by Charles Edward, son of the Old Pretender, scattered by storms; Anson returns home after circumnavigating the globe.

PROSE
Johnson: *Life of Richard Savage*
POETRY
Akenside: *The Pleasures of Imagination*
Armstrong: *The Art of Preserving Health*
Thomson: *The Seasons* (revised version, *see* 1730)
Warton, Joseph: *The Enthusiast*

POETRY (*cont.*)
Wesley, John and Charles: *A Collection of Psalms and Hymns*

1745   English defeated by the French at Fontenoy; Jacobite rebellion (the 'Forty-Five'); after defeating the royal army at the battle of Preston Pans, Highland troops march south as far as Derby, where Charles Edward loses heart and retreats; Von Kleist invents the Leyden jar for storing static electricity.

PROSE
Johnson: *Observations on Macbeth*
Swift (*d.*1745): *Directions to Servants*
DRAMA
Thomson: *Tancred and Sigismunda*
POETRY
Akenside: *Odes on Several Subjects*

POETRY (*cont.*)
Young: *The Consolation: Night the Ninth and Last* (*see* 1742)

1746   Duke of Cumberland routs Charles Edward at Culloden; he earns the nickname 'Butcher' for the ruthlessness with which he suppresses the clans; foundation of Princeton University in America; Hogarth: *Garrick as Richard III* (*p.*).

PROSE
(Diderot: *Pensées philosophiques*)
POETRY
Collins: *Odes on Several Descriptive and Allegorical Subjects* (incl. 'Ode to Evening')

POETRY (*cont.*)
Warton, Joseph: *Odes on Various Subjects*

1747

Highland chiefs deprived of their hereditary jurisdiction over clans, and forbidden to carry arms or wear the tartan; discovery of sugar in beet; Glasse: *The Art of Cookery Made Plain and Easy.*

PROSE
Johnson: *Plan of a Dictionary of the English Language*
Richardson: *Clarissa Harlowe* (compl. in 7 vols by 1748, *see* 1751)
Whitefield: *The Full Account of God's Dealings with George Whitefield*

DRAMA
Garrick: *Miss in Her Teens*

POETRY
Gray: *Ode on a Distant Prospect of Eton College*

POETRY (*cont.*)
Montagu, Lady Mary: *Town Eclogues*
Warton, Thomas: *The Pleasures of Melancholy*

1748

Treaty of Aix-la-Chapelle ends the War of the Austrian Succession (*see* 1740); the Young Pretender expelled from France; first machines for carding wool; Commissioned Officers in Royal Navy adopt distinctive blue uniform; excavations at Pompeii begin.

PROSE
Anson: *Voyage around the World*
Hume: *Philosophical Essays Concerning Human Understanding*
Smollett: *The Adventures of Roderick Random*

POETRY
Dodsley (ed.): *A Collection of Poems* (vols i–iii, incl. new and revised work by Collins and Gray, compl. in 6 vols by 1758)

POETRY (*cont.*)
Hamilton: *Poems on Several Occasions*
Thomson (*d.*1748): *The Castle of Indolence*

1749

Foundation of Halifax, Nova Scotia; Swedenborg: *Arcana Celesta* (mystical philosophy, compl. in 8 vols by 1756).

PROSE
Bolingbroke: *Letters on the Spirit of Patriotism*; *On the Idea of a Patriot King*; *On the State of the Parties at the Accession of George I*
Fielding: *The History of Tom Jones, a Foundling*
Hartley: *Observations on Man*
Smollett: *Gil Blas* (transl. of Le Sage)

DRAMA
Johnson: *Irene: A Tragedy*
Smollett: *The Regicide, or James the First of Scotland*

POETRY
Collins: *On the Death of Thomson*

POETRY (*cont.*)
Johnson: *The Vanity of Human Wishes: The Tenth Satire of Juvenal Imitated*
Warton, Thomas: *The Triumph of Isis*

1750

Britain gives up Asiento rights to sell slaves in America (*see* 1713); France and Britain in confrontation over mutual boundaries in North America; population of England and Wales: 6 million; Scotland: 1.25 million; Ireland: 3 million; Tiepolo starts rococo frescoes of the Kaisersaal in Würzburg (compl. 1753); Horace Walpole designs Strawberry Hill in Gothic style.

PROSE
Cleland: *Memoirs of Fanny Hill*
(abridged version of *Memoirs of a
Woman of Pleasure*, publ. 1749)
Johnson (ed.): *The Rambler* (bi-
weekly –1752)
DRAMA
Fielding: *The Intriguing
Chambermaid*

POETRY
Thomson (*d*.1748): *Poems on Several
Occasions*

1751

Clive captures Arcot from the French, leading to the gradual ascendancy of British power in India; foundation of the Worcester porcelain works; Gin Act curbs consumption of gin by prohibiting unlicensed gin shops; publication of first vol. of the French *Encyclopédie* (compl. in 35 vols by 1780).

PROSE
Arbuthnot (*d*.1735): *Miscellaneous
Works*
Dodsley: *The Economy of Human
Life, Translated from an Indian
Manuscript, Written by an Ancient
Brahmin*
Fielding: *Amelia*; *An Enquiry
into the Causes of the Late Increase
of Robbers*
Hume: *Enquiry Concerning
Principles of Morals*
Kames: *Essays on the Principles of
Morality and Natural Religion*
Richardson: *Letters and Passages
Restored from the Original
Manuscript of the History of
Clarissa* (*see* 1747)

PROSE (*cont.*)
Smollett: *The Adventures of Peregrine
Pickle*
POETRY
Gray: *Elegy Written in a Country
Churchyard*

1752

Franklin invents lightning conductor; adoption of the Gregorian calendar in Britain (*see* 1582): 11 'lost days' cause riots; Pringle: *Observations on Diseases of the Army*; Smellie: *Treatise on the Theory and Practice of Midwifery*.

PROSE
Bolingbroke (*d*.1751): *Letters on the
Study and Use of History*;
*Reflections Concerning Innate
Moral Principles*
Hume: *Political Discourses*
Law: *The Way to Divine Knowledge*

POETRY
Smart: *Poems on Several Occasions*
(incl. 'The Hop-Garden')

1753

Parliament grants charter for establishment of the British Museum (*see* 1759); Linnaeus: *Species Plantarum* (botanical classification).

PROSE
Richardson: *The History of Sir Charles Grandison* (compl. in 7 vols by 1754)
Smollett: *The Adventures of Ferdinand, Count Fathom*

POETRY
Gray: *Hymn to Adversity*
Wesley, Charles and John: *Hymns and Spiritual Songs*

1754

Colonial struggle between Britain and France, called the Great War for the Empire, begins in North America (–1763); Lind: *A Treatise on the Scurvy*; Chippendale: *The Gentleman and Cabinet Maker's Director*; Canaletto: *Old Walton Bridge over the Thames* (*p.*).

PROSE
(Condillac: *Traité des sensations*)
Hume: *History of England* (vol. i, vol. ii 1757, final version in 2 vols 1762)

PROSE (*cont.*)
Warton, Thomas: *Observations on the Faerie Queene of Spenser*

1755

Earthquake in Lisbon kills *c.*30,000; Winckelmann: *On the Imitation of Greek Works* (influential German neoclassical art history, English transl. 1765); Dr Johnson writes letter to Lord Chesterfield concerning patronage (publ. 1790).

PROSE
Amory: *Memoirs of Several Ladies of Great Britain*
Fielding (*d.*1754): *Journal of a Voyage to Lisbon*
Johnson: *A Dictionary of the English Language*
Smollett: *Don Quixote* (transl. of Cervantes)

POETRY
Doddridge (*d.*1751): *Hymns*

1756

Start of the Seven Years War (–1763), during which Prussia emerges as a European power and Britain and France clash over colonial interests; Britain allies with Frederick the Great of Prussia against France, Austria, Russia, Sweden and Saxony; in Calcutta, the Nawab of Bengal's incarceration of 146 British prisoners leads to the notorious Black Hole tragedy: only 23 survive.

PROSE
Amory: *The Life of John Buncle Esq.* (vol. i, vol. ii 1766)
Burke: *A Philosophical Enquiry into the Origin of Our Ideas of the Sublime and the Beautiful*; *A Vindication of Natural Society*
Johnson: *Proposals for Printing the Dramatic Works of Shakespeare*

PROSE (*cont.*)
Smollett: *Compendium of Authentic and Entertaining Voyages*
Warton, Joseph: *An Essay on the Genius and Writings of Pope* (final version in 2 vols 1782)

DRAMA
Home: *Douglas*

1757

Pitt directs war as Secretary of State, with Newcastle as P.M. (–1761); Admiral Byng, having failed in 1756 to recapture Minorca from the French, executed 'to encourage the others', as Voltaire put it; in India, Clive secures Bengal by defeating the Nawab at Plassey; first British canal built, at Sankey, Lancashire.

PROSE

Hume: *Four Dissertations* (incl. 'The Natural History of Religion')
Smollett: *A Complete History of England* (compl. in 4 vols by 1758)

POETRY

Collins: *Oriental Eclogues*
Dyer (*d.*1757): *The Fleece*
Gray: *Odes by Mr Gray* (contains 'The Progress of Poetry' and 'The Bard')

1758

British land victories against the French in North America, and sea victories in the Mediterranean; Highland regiments serve in the war for the first time; Johnson begins *The Idler* (weekly essays –1760).

PROSE

Goldsmith: *Memoirs of a Protestant Condemned to the Galleys of France* (transl. of Marteilhe)
Hume: *Enquiry Concerning Human Understanding*
Swift (*d.*1745): *The History of the Four Last Years of the Queen*

POETRY

Akenside: *Ode to the Country Gentlemen of England*
Parnell (*d.*1718): *Posthumous Works*
Walpole: *Fugitive Pieces in Verse and Prose*

1759

Quebec captured by Wolfe; establishment of the Carron ironworks for making 'carronades' (short naval guns of large calibre); British Museum opens at Montagu House (*see* 1753); Kew Botanical Gardens founded; Harrison completes his chronometer, designed to determine longitude (essential for accurate navigation), which eventually wins a government prize.

PROSE

Gerard: *An Essay on Taste*
Goldsmith: *An Enquiry into the Present State of Polite Learning in Europe*
Hurd: *Moral and Political Dialogues*
Johnson: *Rasselas, Prince of Abyssinia*

PROSE (*cont.*)

Sterne: *A Political Romance* (later known as *The History of a Good Warm Watch-Coat*)
(Voltaire: *Candide*)
Young: *Conjectures on Original Composition*

1760

Death of George II; accession of George III (–1820); defeat of French colonial aspiration in India after battle at Wandiwash; capture of Montreal by the British; (*c.*) piano-making in Britain begins.

PROSE

(Diderot: *La Religieuse*)
Lyttelton: *Dialogues of the Dead*
Sterne: *The Life and Opinions of Tristram Shandy* (compl. in 9 vols by 1767)

POETRY

Macpherson: *Fragments of Ancient Poetry Collected in the Highlands of Scotland, and Translated from the Gallic or Erse Language*

1761

After failing to persuade the rest of the Government to declare war on France's ally Spain, Pitt resigns; opening of the Bridgewater Canal between Manchester and Worsley, cutting cost of coal in Manchester by half; Victor: *The History of the Theatres of London and Dublin* (compl. in 3 vols by 1771).

PROSE
Gibbon: *Essai sur l'étude de la littérature*
Johnson: *Life of Roger Ascham*
(Rousseau: *The New Héloïse*)

POETRY
Churchill: *The Rosciad*
Macpherson: *Fingal: An Ancient Epic Poem, Together with Other Poems by 'Ossian'*

1762

Bute, a favourite of George III, becomes P.M. (–1763); Britain declares war on Spain; accession of Catherine the Great of Russia (–1796), during whose reign the power and extent of Russia is vastly increased by wars with Sweden and Turkey and the partition of Poland; Black describes latent heat of steam; Zoffany: *Garrick in 'The Farmer's Return'* (*p.*); Gluck: *Orpheus and Euridice* (opera); Wilkes and Churchill start the *North Briton* (periodical –1763).

PROSE
Goldsmith: *The Citizen of the World, or Letters from a Chinese Philosopher Residing in London to His Friends in the East* (serialised as 'Chinese Letters' in *The Public Examiner* 1760–1)
Hurd: *Letters on Chivalry and Romance*
Kames: *Elements of Criticism*
(Rousseau: *Émile, or Education*; *The Social Contract*)
Smollett: *Sir Lancelot Greaves*

POETRY
Churchill: *The Ghost* (final version 1763)

1763

Grenville takes over from Bute as P.M. (–1765); Seven Years War (*see* 1756) ended by the Peace of Paris, redefining British, French and Spanish colonial territories, to Britain's advantage; Wilkes imprisoned for attacking the Government in the *North Briton*; Dr Johnson and Boswell meet.

PROSE
Blair, Hugh: *Critical Dissertation on the Poems of Ossian*
Johnson: *On the Life and Writings of Collins*
Montagu, Lady Mary (*d.*1762): *Letters*
POETRY
Churchill: *An Epistle to William Hogarth*; *The Prophecy of Famine: A Scots Pastoral*
Macpherson: *Temora: An Ancient Epic Poem, Together with Other Poems by 'Ossian'*

POETRY (*cont.*)
Percy: *Five Pieces of Runic Poetry*
Smart: *A Song to David*

1764

Invention of the Spinning Jenny, allowing one person to spin several threads and leading eventually to mechanisation of the spinning process, till now a cottage industry; Angelica Kauffmann: *Portrait of Winckelmann* (*p.*).

PROSE
Goldsmith: *The History of England in a Series of Letters from a Nobleman to His Son*
POETRY
Churchill (*d.*1764): *The Candidate*; *The Duellist*; *Gotham*; *The Times*
Evans: *Some Specimens of the Poetry of the Ancient Welsh Bards* (transl.)
Goldsmith: *The Traveller*

POETRY (*cont.*)
Shenstone (*d.*1763): *Works in Verse and Prose*
Warton, Thomas (ed.): *The Oxford Sausage*

1765

Grenville antagonises the North American Colonists by attempting to impose on them a Stamp Act to help meet war and defence expenses; 'Capability' Brown landscapes grounds of Blenheim Palace; Queen Charlotte patronises Wedgwood's cream-coloured china, called thereafter Queen's Ware; (*c.*) preeminence of the Hambledon Cricket Club.

PROSE
Fuseli: *Painting and Sculpture of the Greeks* (transl. of Winckelmann, *see* 1755)
Goldsmith: *Essays*
Lyttelton: *Four New Dialogues of the Dead*
Walpole: *The Castle of Otranto*

DRAMA
Johnson (ed.): *The Works of William Shakespeare*
POETRY
Collins (*d.*1759): *Poetical Works*
Percy: *Reliques of Ancient English Poetry*
Smart: *The Psalms of David* (transl.)

1766

American opposition to the Stamp Act (*see* 1765) leads to its repeal; Pitt rejoins ministry as Earl of Chatham (–1768); General Warrants made illegal after the Wilkes case (*see* 1763); Cavendish analyses composition of air and identifies hydrogen; Stubbs: *Anatomy of the Horse* (illustrated study); Fragonard: *The Swing* (*p.*); Rousseau in England (–1767).

PROSE
Goldsmith: *The Vicar of Wakefield*
(Lessing: *Laokoön*)
Smollett: *Travels through France and Italy*

PROSE (*cont.*)
Swift (*d.*1745): *Letters* (compl. in 4 vols by 1768)
POETRY
Anstey: *The New Bath Guide*

1767

New Revenue Act imposes duties on imports to America (including tea) to help pay for the government of the colonies; Priestley: *The History and Present State of Electricity*; Wood the younger starts building the Royal Crescent, Bath (compl. 1774).

PROSE
Lyttelton: *The History of Henry II*
POETRY
Goldsmith: *Poems for Young Ladies*

POETRY (*cont.*)
Wesley, Charles and John: *Hymns for the Use of Families*

1768

Resignation of Earl of Chatham as P.M.; Cook starts his first voyage to the Antipodes (with Banks, the botanist, –1771); Adam brothers design Adelphi Terrace in neo-classical style (Thames-side houses, now largely destroyed); foundation of the Royal Academy of Arts with Reynolds as first President; Joseph Wright of Derby: *Experiment with an Air Pump* (*p.*); first edn of *Encyclopaedia Britannica* (ed. Smellie, in instalments –1771).

PROSE
Boswell: *An Account of Corsica, the Journal of a Tour to That Island, and Memoirs of Pascal Paoli*
Sterne (*d.*1768): *A Sentimental Journey*
Walpole: *Historic Doubts on the Life and Reign of Richard III*
DRAMA
Goldsmith: *The Good Natured Man*
Walpole: *The Mysterious Mother*

POETRY
Gray: *Poems by Mr Gray*
Macintyre: *Orain Ghaidhealach* (Gaelic songs, incl. 'Praise of Ben Dorain')
Montagu, Lady Mary (*d.*1762): *Poetical Works*

1769

Cugnot constructs steam-powered carriage; Reynolds: *A Discourse Delivered at the Opening of the Royal Academy* (further discourses on art –1791); publication of *The New Peerage or Present State of the Nobility of England* (vol. ii Scotland, vol. iii Ireland); the Letters of 'Junius', attacking the Government, appear in *The Public Advertiser* (–1772).

PROSE
Burke: *Observations on a Late State of the Nation*
Montagu, Elizabeth: *An Essay on the Writings and Genius of Shakespeare*
Smollett: *The Adventures of an Atom*
DRAMA
Home: *The Fatal Discovery*

POETRY
Chatterton: *Elinoure and Juga*
Gray: *Installation Ode*

1770

Lord North becomes P.M. (–1782); repeal of American import duties except on tea; in Massachusetts, skirmish between British troops and crowd, the 'Boston Massacre'; Spaniards expel British settlers from the Falkland Islands; Cook discovers Botany Bay, Australia; Bruce traces source of the Blue Nile; Hargreaves patents improved Spinning Jenny (*see* 1764).

PROSE
Beattie: *An Essay on the Nature and Immutability of Truth, in Opposition to Sophistry and Scepticism*
Burke: *Thoughts on the Cause of the Present Discontents*
Percy: *Northern Antiquities*
Young, Arthur: *A Six Months' Tour through the North of England*

POETRY
Goldsmith: *The Deserted Village*

1771

Last attempt to prevent reporting of parliamentary debates; Arkwright builds first water-powered spinning mill; Hunter: *Treatise on the Natural History of the Human Teeth* (vol. i, vol. ii 1778); Gainsborough: *The Harvest Wagon* (*p.*); Zoffany: *Life School at the Royal Academy with Portraits of Leading Artists Including Reynolds* (*p.*); Bougainville: *Voyage round the World*.

PROSE
Goldsmith: *A History of England*
Mackenzie: *The Man of Feeling*
Smollett (*d.*1771): *The Expedition of Humphry Clinker*
Wesley, John: *Collected Prose Works* (compl. in 32 vols by 1774)

POETRY
Beattie: *The Minstrel, or The Progress of Genius* (bk i, bk ii 1774)

1772

Cook's second voyage of discovery to the Antipodes begins (–1775); Rutherford discovers nitrogen; Haydn: Symphony No. 45 (*Farewell*).

PROSE
Hurd: *An Introduction to the Study of Prophecies Concerning the Christian Church, and in Particular Concerning the Church of Papal Rome*

POETRY
Akenside (*d.*1770): *Poems*
Chatterton (*d.*1770): *The Execution of Sir Charles Bawdin*
Jones, William: *Poems from Asiatic Languages*

1773

Lord North brings political activities of the East India Company under government control, and establishes Warren Hastings as Governor of Bengal; the 'Boston Tea Party', a protest by Bostonians against the duty on tea; assay offices for gold and silver opened in Birmingham and Sheffield; Adam: *Works in Architecture*; Hawkesworth: *An Account of Voyages in the Southern Hemisphere* (incl. an account of Cook's voyage).

PROSE
Mackenzie: *The Man of the World*
Sterne (*d.*1768): *Letters from Yorrick to Eliza*
DRAMA
Goldsmith: *She Stoops to Conquer*

POETRY
Barbauld: *Poems*
Fergusson: *Auld Reikie: A Poem*; *Poems*

1774

First Congress of the Colonies at Philadelphia opposes British colonial policy, and issues a 'Declaration of Rights'; Priestley: *Experiments and Observations on Different Kinds of Air* (compl. in 3 vols by 1777); Walpole: *Description of Strawberry Hill* (Gothic revival architecture, *see* 1750); Reynolds: *Dr Beattie* (*The Triumph of Time*) (*p.*).

PROSE
Barbauld: *Early Lessons for Children*
Burke: *Speech on American Taxation*
Chesterfield (*d.*1773): *Letters to His Natural Son*
(Goethe: *The Sorrows of Young Werther*)

PROSE (*cont.*)
Gerard: *Essay on Genius*
Goldsmith (*d.*1774): *A History of the Earth and Animated Nature*
Johnson: *The Patriot*
Warton, Thomas: *A History of English Poetry* (compl. in 3 vols by 1781)

1775

Outbreak of the War of American Independence (–1783); battles at Lexington and Bunker's Hill; Watt and Boulton start producing commercial steam engines; Sarah Siddons first appears on the London stage.

PROSE
Burke: *Speech on Resolutions for Conciliation with the Colonies*
Johnson: *A Journey to the Western Islands of Scotland*
Sterne (*d*.1768): *Letters to His Friends on Various Occasions*
Woolman (*d*.1772): *Journal*

DRAMA
(Beaumarchais: *The Barber of Seville*)
Garrick: *Bon Ton, or Life above Stairs*
Sheridan: *The Rivals*

POETRY
Crabbe: *Inebriety*
Gray (*d*.1771): *Poems*
Savage (*d*.1743): *Collected Works*

1776

American Colonists issue on 4 July a Declaration of Independence from Britain; the British are forced out of Boston; Wilkinson uses a steam engine to operate bellows in a blast furnace for smelting iron; Smith: *An Inquiry into the Nature and Causes of the Wealth of Nations*; Chambers begins Somerset House in Palladian style, in imitation of former building by Inigo Jones (compl. 1835); Charles Burney: *A General History of Music* (compl. in 4 vols by 1789); last appearance of Garrick on the stage.

PROSE
Gibbon: *The Decline and Fall of the Roman Empire* (compl. in 6 vols by 1788)
Paine: *Common Sense*

DRAMA
Cowley, Hannah: *The Runaway*

1777

The British defeat the American Colonists at Brandywine, but surrender at Saratoga, which proves to be a turning point of the war in favour of the Colonists; Stars and Stripes (originally 13) adopted as the Colonists' flag; Cook: *Voyage towards the South Pole and round the World in 1772–5*.

PROSE
Burke: *Letter to the Sheriffs of Bristol*
Mackenzie: *Julia de Roubigné*
More: *Essays on Various Subjects, Principally Designed for Young Ladies*
Morgann: *Essay on the Character of Falstaff*
Reeve: *The Champion of Virtue: A Gothic Story* (renamed *The Old English Baron* 1778)

DRAMA
More: *Percy: A Tragedy*
Sheridan: *The School for Scandal*

POETRY
Chatterton (*d*.1770): *Poems, Supposed to Have Been Written by Thomas Rowley in the Fifteenth Century* (ed. Tyrwhitt)
Warton, Thomas: *Poems*

1778

France allies with the American Colonists; North attempts unsuccessfully to conciliate the Colonists; Britain declares war on France; Cook lands in Hawaii, where he is murdered (1779).

PROSE
Burney: *Evelina, or The History of a Young Lady's Entry into the World*

1779

Spain joins France against Britain; Gibraltar is besieged (–1782); completion of first cast-iron bridge in the world, across the Severn near Coalbrookdale; Gluck: *Iphigenia in Tauris* (opera); Mackenzie: *The Mirror* (periodical –1780).

PROSE
Hume (*d*.1776): *Dialogues Concerning Natural Religion*
Johnson: *The Works of the English Poets, with Prefaces, Biographical and Critical* (compl. in 68 vols, incl. 10 vols of Prefaces, by 1781, Prefaces then publ. as *Lives of the Poets*)
DRAMA
Cowley, Hannah: *Albina*
More: *The Fatal Falsehood*

DRAMA (*cont.*)
Sheridan: *The Critic, or A Tragedy Rehearsed*
POETRY
Cowper (with Newton): *Olney Hymns*
Fergusson (*d*.1774): *Poems on Various Subjects*

1780

Several European nations, resisting British attempts to search shipping, join the alliance called the Armed Neutrality; Rodney defeats the Spanish fleet off Cape St Vincent; 'No Popery' Gordon Riots in London; (*c*.) invention of the circular saw; (*c*.) introduction of willow pattern on plates; first Derby horse race.

PROSE
Burke: *Speech on a Plan for the Better Security of the Independence of Parliament and Economic Reform*
Davies, Thomas: *Memoirs of the Life of David Garrick*
Paine: *Public Good*

DRAMA
Cowley, Hannah: *The Belle's Stratagem*
POETRY
Crabbe: *The Candidate*
(Wieland: *Oberon*)

1781

Washington forces surrender of British troops under Cornwallis at Yorktown; William Pitt the younger enters Parliament; Joseph II, Emperor of Austria, publishes Edict of Toleration for Protestants and Orthodox Christians, one of his many social and religious reforms, including abolishing serfdom; (*c*.) organisation of first Building Society, in Birmingham; Herschel discovers Uranus; Fuseli: *The Nightmare* (*p*.).

PROSE
Barbauld: *Hymns in Prose for Children*
(Kant: *Critique of Pure Reason*)

POETRY
Crabbe: *The Library*

1782

Pitt the younger appointed Chancellor of the Exchequer; Rodney defeats the French at the battle of the Saints off Dominica, restoring British naval supremacy; siege of Gibraltar relieved (*see* 1779).

PROSE
Burney: *Cecilia*
(Laclos: *Les Liaisons dangereuses*)
(Rousseau: *Confessions*, compl. in 4 pts by 1789)

POETRY
Cowper: *John Gilpin's Ride*; *Poems*
'Peter Pindar': *Lyric Odes to the Royal Academicians*

1783

The Treaty of Versailles signed between Britain, France, Spain and the United States; the independence of the American colonies is recognised; invention of machine printing of fabric; Montgolfier brothers make first balloon ascent.

PROSE
Beattie: *Dissertations Moral and Critical*
Beckford: *Dreams, Waking Thoughts and Incidents, in a Series of Letters from Various Parts of Europe* (*see* 1834)
Blair, Hugh: *Lectures on Rhetoric and Belles-Lettres*

PROSE (*cont.*)
Day, Thomas: *The History of Sandford and Merton: A Work Intended for the Use of Children* (compl. in 3 vols by 1789)

POETRY
Blake: *Poetical Sketches*
Crabbe: *The Village*

1784

Pitt the younger's Government of India Act puts the East India Company under the control of six Privy Councillors; scheduled mail coach service begins between London, Bath and Bristol; building of Brighton Pavilion begins (compl. 1827); Arthur Young starts *The Annals of Agriculture* (–1809); Cook (*d*.1779): *A Voyage to the Pacific Ocean in the Years 1776–80*; Raeburn: *The Reverend Robert Walker Skating* (*p.*); Reynolds: *Mrs Siddons as the Tragic Muse* (*p.*).

PROSE
Burke: *Speech on Mr Fox's India Bill*

DRAMA
(Beaumarchais: *The Marriage of Figaro*)

1785

Defeat of Pitt's attempts to reform Parliament; Cartwright patents power-loom; first Channel crossing by balloon; Mackenzie: *The Lounger* (periodical –1787).

PROSE
Boswell: *A Tour of the Hebrides*
Burke: *Speech on the Nabob of Arcot's Debts*
Johnson (*d*.1784): *Prayers and Meditations*
Paley: *The Principles of Moral and Political Philosophy*
Raspe: *Baron Munchausen's Travels*
Reeve: *The Progress of Romance through Times, Centuries and Manners*

PROSE (*cont.*)
Smith, Charlotte: *Manon Lescaut* (transl. of Prévost)
Walpole: *An Essay on Modern Gardening*

POETRY
Cowper: *The Task: A Poem in Six Books*
Crabbe: *The Newspaper*
Johnson (*d*.1784): *Poetical Works*
'Peter Pindar': *The Lousiad: An Heroic-Comic Poem* (compl. in 5 cantos by 1795)

1786

Cornwallis reforms legal, administrative and police systems in Bengal; Mont Blanc climbed for the first time; Taylor: *An Essay Intended to Establish a Standard for an Universal System of Stenography*; Mozart: *The Marriage of Figaro* (opera).

PROSE
Beckford: *Vathek: An Arabian Tale*
Burke: *Articles of Charge against Warren Hastings*
Piozzi (Mrs Thrale): *Anecdotes of Samuel Johnson*
Tooke: *The Diversions of Purley* (vol. i, vol. ii 1805)
Trimmer: *Fabulous Histories* (later called *The History of the Robins*)

POETRY
Burns: *Poems Chiefly in Scottish Dialect*
Rogers: *Ode to Superstition, and Other Poems*

1787

In France, Calonne's proposals for financial reform are rejected by Notables; Federal Government established in U.S.A.; Sierra Leone founded as settlement for freed slaves; foundation of the Marylebone Cricket Club; publication of the *Paston Letters* (compl. in 4 vols by 1789, *see* 1420).

PROSE
Beattie: *Scoticisms, Arranged in Alphabetical Order, Designed to Correct Improprieties of Speech and Writing*
Johnson (*d.*1784): *Works*
Paine: *Prospects on the Rubicon*
(Saint-Pierre: *Paul et Virginie*)
Wollstonecraft: *Thoughts on the Education of Daughters*

DRAMA
Holcroft: *Seduction*
(Schiller: *Don Carlos*)

1788

Regency crisis after George III's first attack of madness; Warren Hastings impeached on charges of oppression and corruption in India (–1795); bread riots in France; convict settlement founded in New South Wales, Australia; *The Times* started; Hepplewhite: *The Cabinet Makers' and Upholsterers' Guide*; Mozart: Symphony No. 41 (*Jupiter*).

PROSE
More: *Thoughts on the Importance of the Manners of the Great to the General Society*
Smith, Charlotte: *Emmeline*
POETRY
Collins (*d.*1759): *Ode on the Popular Superstitions of the Highlands*
'Peter Pindar': *The Poetical Works of Peter Pindar Esq.*
Wesley, Charles and John: *A Collection of Psalms and Hymns*

POETRY (*cont.*)
for the Lord's Day (Methodist Liturgy)

1789

Outbreak of the French Revolution; States-General meets (the first since 1614); the Third Estate declares itself a National Assembly, issues a Declaration of the Rights of Man, and overthrows the government; the Bastille falls to the revolutionaries; Louis XVI arrested and detained; first National Election in U.S.A.: George Washington becomes the first President (–1797); mutiny on the *Bounty*; Klaproth discovers uranium; Lavoisier: *Elementary Treatise on Chemistry*; White: *The Natural History of Selborne*.

PROSE
Bentham: *An Introduction to the Principles of Morals and Legislation*
Gilpin: *Observations on the Highlands of Scotland*
Phillip: *The Voyage of Governor Phillip to Botany Bay*
Radcliffe: *The Castles of Athlin and Dunbayne*
Smith, Charlotte: *Ethelinde, or The Recluse of the Lake*

PROSE (*cont.*)
Wollstonecraft (ed.): *The Female Reader: Miscellaneous Pieces for the Improvement of Young Women*
POETRY
Blake: *The Book of Thel*; *Songs of Innocence*
Bowles: *Sonnets Written Chiefly on Picturesque Spots, During a Tour*

1790

First steam-powered rolling mill in Britain; Forth–Clyde canal opened; Leblanc develops process for industrial production of soda; Bewick: *General History of Quadrupeds* (wood-engravings); (*c.*) waltz introduced into Britain; Lawrence: *Queen Charlotte* (*p.*).

PROSE
Burke: *Reflections on the Revolution in France*
Paley: *Horae Paulinae, or The Truth of the Scripture History of St Paul*
Porson: *Letters to Mr Archdeacon Travis, in Answer to His Defence of the Three Heavenly Witnesses*

PROSE (*cont.*)
Radcliffe: *A Sicilian Romance*
Smollett (*d.*1771): *Miscellaneous Works*
Williams, Helen: *Letters Written in France, Containing Anecdotes Relative to the Revolution*

1791

Church and King rioting in Birmingham against supporters of the French Revolution (including Priestley); in France, Louis XVI accepts the new Constitution, then attempts flight, but is taken prisoner; Galvani publishes results of experiments with electricity on frogs' legs; Ordnance Survey established in Britain; Mozart: *The Magic Flute* (opera).

PROSE
Bentham: *Panopticon*
Boswell: *The Life of Johnson*
Burke: *Appeal from the New to the Old Whigs*; *Letter to a Member of the National Assembly*
D'Israeli, Isaac: *Curiosities of Literature* (compl. in 6 vols by 1834)
Inchbald: *A Simple Story*
Paine: *The Rights of Man* (pt i, pt ii 1792)
Radcliffe: *The Romance of the Forest*

POETRY
Burns: *Tam o'Shanter*
Cowper: *Iliad and Odyssey* (transl. of Homer)
Darwin, Erasmus: *The Botanic Garden: A Poem In Two Parts* (pt i 'The Economy of Vegetation', pt ii 'The Loves of the Plants')
Warton, Thomas (*d.*1790): *Poems on Various Subjects*

1792

France is declared a Republic; September massacre of Royalists; the guillotine erected; Austria and Prussia invade France; in Britain, Wilberforce's motion for gradual abolition of the slave trade is passed by the Commons but held up by the Lords; in Redruth, Cornwall, the first home is lit by coal-gas.

PROSE
Bage: *Man As He Is*
Burke: *Collected Works* (compl. in 8 vols by 1827)
Gilpin: *Essays on Picturesque Beauty*
Goldsmith (*d.*1774): *Miscellaneous Works*
Holcroft: *Anna St Ives*
Trimmer: *Reflections upon the Education of Children in Charity Schools*
Wollstonecraft: *A Vindication of the Rights of Woman*
Young, Arthur: *Travels in France*

DRAMA
Holcroft: *The Road to Ruin*
POETRY
Blake: *Song of Liberty*
Rogers: *The Pleasures of Memory, with Other Poems*

1793

France declares war on Britain; Aliens Act restricts liberty of foreigners in Britain; execution of Louis XVI; Girondists ousted by Jacobins; Danton, Marat (murdered in July) and Robespierre govern through the Committee of Public Safety; the Reign of Terror: several thousands put to death all over France; Revolutionary Army formed; David: *Death of Marat* (*p.*).

PROSE
Godwin: *An Enquiry Concerning Political Justice*
Smith, Charlotte: *The Old Manor House*
Whitehead: *Life of John Wesley* (vol. i, vol. ii 1796)
DRAMA
Inchbald: *Every One Has His Fault*

POETRY
Blake: *America*; *The Gates of Paradise*; (*c.*) *The Marriage of Heaven and Hell*; *Vision of the Daughters of Albion*
Burns: *Poems*; *Songs*
Wordsworth: *Descriptive Sketches*; *An Evening Walk*

1794

Pitt, fearful of Revolutionary sympathies, suspends Habeas Corpus and curbs the freedom of the press; war with France continues; Lord Howe defeats the French fleet off Brest; Danton and Robespierre guillotined; the chemist Lavoisier executed on a false charge; Whitney invents cotton gin for extracting cotton seed.

PROSE
Darwin, Erasmus: *Zoonomia* (vol. i, vol. ii 1796)
Godwin: *Caleb Williams*
Holcroft: *Hugh Trevor*
Paine: *The Age of Reason* (compl. in 3 pts by 1811)
Paley: *View of the Evidences of Christianity*
Radcliffe: *The Mysteries of Udolpho*

DRAMA
Southey (with Coleridge): *The Fall of Robespierre*
POETRY
Blake: *The Book of Urizen*; *Europe*; *Songs of Innocence and Experience*
Coleridge: *Monody on the Death of Chatterton*

1795

Holland, Luxembourg and Belgium capitulate to France; government of France by the Directory (–1799); Napoleon defeats insurrection in Paris with a 'whiff of grapeshot'; in Britain, Pitt introduces Treasonable Practices and Seditious Meetings Bills; introduction of Speenhamland system of poor relief; Mungo Park begins his first exploration of West Africa (–1797); (*c.*) first settlements in New Zealand; invention of jar for preserving foods; Bramah patents hydraulic pump; France adopts metric system; White (*d.*1793): *A Naturalist's Calendar*; Haydn: Symphony No. 104 (*London*).

PROSE
(De Sade: *Philosophy in the Boudoir*)
D'Israeli, Isaac: *The Literary Character*
Edgeworth: *Letters for Literary Ladies*
Murray: *English Grammar*
Paine: *First Principles of Government*
Williams, Helen: *Letters Containing a Sketch of the Politics of France*

POETRY
Blake: *The Book of Ahania*; *The Book of Los*; *The Song of Los*
Chatterton (*d.*1770): *Poetical Works*
La.·lor: *Poems*

1796

Britain fails to negotiate peace with the Directory in France; French invasion of Ireland fails; Spain declares war on Britain; Napoleon begins campaign against Austria in Italy; Beckford starts construction of Fonthill Abbey in Gothic style (compl. *c.*1800); Coleridge (ed.): *The Watchman* (periodical, 10 nos only).

PROSE
Bage: *Hermsprong, or Man As He Is Not*
Burke: *Letter on a Regicide Peace*
Burney: *Camilla, or A Picture of Youth*
Edgeworth: *The Parent's Assistant, or Stories for Children*
Gibbon (*d.*1794): *Miscellaneous Works, with Memoir by Himself*
Inchbald: *Nature and Art*
Lewis: *The Monk*

PROSE (*cont.*)
Wollstonecraft: *Letters Written during a Short Residence in Sweden, Norway and Denmark*

POETRY
Coleridge: *Poems on Various Subjects*
Southey: *Joan of Arc*

1797

Naval mutinies at Spithead and the Nore suppressed; British naval victories over the French at Cape St Vincent and over the Dutch at Camperdown; Napoleon defeats Austria and establishes French authority over Austrian-occupied north Italy; publication of Young's *Night Thoughts* with illustrations by Blake.

PROSE
Burke (*d.*1797): *Thoughts on the French Affairs*
Godwin: *The Enquirer*
(Hölderlin: *Hyperion*, vol. i, vol. ii 1799)
Radcliffe: *The Italian*
Southey: *Letters Written in Spain and Portugal*

DRAMA
Lewis: *The Castle Spectre*; *The Minister* (publ.)

POETRY
Southey: *Poems*

1798

Suppression of Irish rebellion of Wolfe Tone; Napoleon invades Egypt; Nelson defeats French fleet at the battle of Aboukir Bay; French troops continue campaign in Italy, setting up republics in Rome and Naples; invention of lithography; Jenner publicises his successful vaccination treatment against smallpox (*see* 1718); Malthus: *An Essay on the Principle of Population As It Affects the Future of Society.*

PROSE
Edgeworth: *Practical Education*
Godwin: *Memoirs of the Author of a
  Vindication of the Rights of Woman*
  (Mary Wollstonecraft)
Lamb: *A Tale of Rosamund Gray and
  Old Blind Margaret*
Sheridan: *Collected Speeches*
Wakefield: *Reflections on the Present
  Condition of the Female Sex*
POETRY
Coleridge: *Fears in Solitude*; *France:
  An Ode*; *Frost at Midnight*
Cowper: *Two Poems*

POETRY (*cont.*)
Landor: *Gebir*
Rogers: *Epistle to a Friend*
Wordsworth and Coleridge: *Lyrical
  Ballads* (incl. 'Tintern Abbey' and
  'The Ancient Mariner', *see* 1800,
  1802)

1799

Combination Laws suppress trade unionism; Pitt introduces income tax as a war measure, and negotiates a coalition against France; Napoleon overthrows the Directory and establishes the Consulate; Rosetta Stone discovered in Egypt, leading to deciphering of Egyptian hieroglyphics (*see* 1822); Goya: *The Caprices* (etchings); Park: *Travels in the Interior of Africa in 1795–7.*

PROSE
Godwin: *St Leon*
DRAMA
Sheridan: *Pizarro*

POETRY
Campbell: *The Pleasures of Hope*
Lewis: *Tales of Terror*

1800

Pitt passes bill for the union of Great Britain and Ireland, uniting Parliaments; Napoleon defeats Austria at Marengo and Hohenlinden and reconquers Italy; Alessandro Volta makes the first electric battery; carriage road begun over the Alps at the Simplon Pass (compl. 1806); population of England and Wales: 9.25 million; Scotland: 1.25 million; Ireland: 5.25 million; London: 864,000; U.S.A.: 5.3 million; New York: 60,500; David: *Portrait of Madame Récamier* (*p.*).

PROSE
Edgeworth: *Castle Rackrent*
DRAMA
(Schiller: *Maria Stuart*)
POETRY
Bloomfield: *The Farmer's Boy*
Burns (*d.*1796): *Works, with Life,
  New Poems, and Correspondence*
Coleridge: *Poems* (in *Annual
  Anthology*)

POETRY (*cont.*)
Moore: *Odes of Anacreon* (transl.)
Wordsworth and Coleridge: *Lyrical
  Ballads* (2-vol. edn, incl. new
  poems and Preface, *see* 1798, 1802)

1801

Addington P.M. (–1804) after Pitt resigns over George III's refusal to allow Catholic emancipation; British naval victory over the Danes at Copenhagen; Jefferson elected President of U.S.A. (–1809); Union Jack becomes flag of the United Kingdom; first population censuses; Strutt: *Sports and Pastimes of the People of England*; Haydn: *The Seasons* (oratorio).

PROSE
Edgeworth: *Belinda*; *Moral Tales for Young People*
Lewis (ed.): *Tales of Wonder*
POETRY
Bowles: *The Sorrows of Switzerland*
Burns (*d.*1796): *Poems Ascribed to Robert Burns*
Hogg: *Scottish Pastorals, Poems and Songs*

POETRY (*cont.*)
Moore: *Poems by Thomas Little*
Southey: *Thalaba the Destroyer*

1802

Napoleon becomes President of the Italian Republic, and is made First Consul of France for life; Peace of Amiens between England and France; Health and Morals of Apprentices Act passed to protect factory workers; Telford begins constructing roads in the Scottish Highlands; MacArthur introduces sheep into Australia; Ritter discovers ultra-violet rays; Cobbett starts the *Weekly Political Register* (–1835); Whig *Edinburgh Review* started (–1929).

PROSE
Paley: *Natural Theology*
DRAMA
Holcroft: *A Tale of Mystery*
POETRY
Bloomfield: *Rural Tales*
Landor: *Poetry by the Author of Gebir*
Scott (ed.): *Minstrelsy of the Scottish Border* (vols i–ii, vol. iii 1803)

POETRY (*cont.*)
Wordsworth and Coleridge: *Lyrical Ballads* (third edn, with new Preface, *see* 1798, 1800)

1803

Renewed war with France (–1815); rebellion and execution of Emmet, Irish patriot; shrapnel shell adopted by the British army (first used 1804); Trevithick builds first successful railway steam engine; Turner: *Calais Pier* (*p.*); Beethoven: Symphony No. 3 (*Eroica*); Jeffrey becomes editor of *The Edinburgh Review* (–1829).

PROSE
Cowper (*d.*1800): 'Letters' (in *Life and Posthumous Writings*, ed. Hayley)
Montagu, Lady Mary (*d.*1762): *Works, Including Letters*
POETRY
Chatterton (*d.*1770): *Collected Works*
Darwin, Erasmus (*d.*1802): *The Temple of Nature*

POETRY (*cont.*)
Southey: *Amadis of Gaul* (transl.)

1804

Napoleon crowned Emperor (–1815); younger Pitt P.M. (–1806); preparations along the English coast against possible French invasion; Hobart, Tasmania founded; Royal Horticultural Society presents first flower show; British and Foreign Bible Society founded; foundation of the English Water Colour Society; Bewick: *A History of British Birds* (engravings).

PROSE
Edgeworth: *A Modern Griselda*; *Popular Tales*
Richardson (*d.*1761): *Correspondence* (ed. with 'Life' by Mrs Barbauld)
Smith, Charlotte: *Conversations Introducing Poetry*

POETRY
Blake: *Jerusalem*; *Milton: A Poem* (?1808)

POETRY (*cont.*)
Taylor, Ann and Jane: *Original Poems for Infant Minds*

1805

Sea battle of Trafalgar against the French; Napoleon crowns himself King of Italy, and defeats Russian and Austrian forces at Austerlitz; Mungo Park starts second expedition to the Niger (–1806); discovery of morphine; in Manchester, a cotton mill is lit by gas; (*c.*) Blake: *The Spiritual Form of Pitt Guiding Behemoth* (*p.*).

PROSE
(Chateaubriand: *René*)
Godwin: *Fleetwood*
Hazlitt: *An Essay on the Principles of Human Action*
Johnson (*d.*1784): *Account of His Own Life*
Walpole (*d.*1797): *Reminiscences*

POETRY
Campbell: *Collected Poems*
Scott: *The Lay of the Last Minstrel*

POETRY (*cont.*)
Southey: *Madoc*
Wordsworth completes a major draft of his autobiographical poem, publ. in 1850 as *The Prelude*

1806

Napoleon continues conquest of Europe; his Berlin Decrees attempt to destroy Britain's foreign trade; Dartmoor prison built to hold French prisoners of war; Beaufort designs scale for wind strength; opening of the East India Docks in London.

PROSE
Edgeworth: *Leonora*; *Letters*
Hazlitt: *Free Thoughts on Public Affairs*

DRAMA
Lamb: *Mr H.*

POETRY
Bloomfield: *Wild Flowers*
Byron: *Fugitive Pieces*
Moore: *Epistles, Odes, and Other Poems*
Scott: *Ballads and Lyrical Pieces*

POETRY (*cont.*)
Taylor, Ann and Jane: *Rhymes for the Nursery* (incl. 'Twinkle, twinkle, little star')

1807

France, Russia and Prussia come to terms at Tilsit; abolition of the slave trade in British possessions; emancipation of Prussian serfs; first successful paddle steamer built, in U.S.A.

PROSE
Lamb, Charles and Mary: *Tales from Shakespeare*
Maturin: *Fatal Revenge*

POETRY
Byron: *Hours of Idleness*; *Poems on Various Occasions*
Crabbe: *Poems* (incl. 'The Parish Register')
Hogg: *The Mountain Bard*
Moore: *Irish Melodies*
Tannahill: *Poems and Songs*

POETRY (*cont.*)
Wordsworth: *Poems in Two Volumes* (incl. 'Ode to Duty' and 'Intimations of Immortality')

1808

Peninsular War between France and Britain in Spain begins (–1814); U.S.A. prohibits import of slaves from Africa; Canova: *Pauline Bonaparte Borghese as Venus Victrix* (*sc.*); Leigh Hunt (ed.): *The Examiner* (periodical –1821).

PROSE
Lewis: *Romantic Tales*
Smith, Sydney: *The Letters of Peter Plymley to My Brother Abraham Who Lives in the Country*
Southey (with Frere): *The Chronicle of the Cid* (transl.)

DRAMA
(Goethe: *Faust, Pt I*)

POETRY
Hemans: *England and Spain*; *Poems*
Moore: *Corruption and Intolerance*
Scott: *Marmion*

1809

British victory at Talavera in Spain; Napoleon as King of Italy abolishes the temporal power of the Papacy and is excommunicated by Pope Pius VII; he occupies Vienna; Pall Mall, London, lit by gas; Birkbeck helps found the London Institute for the Diffusion of Science, Medicine and the Arts; Beethoven: Piano Concerto No. 5 (*The Emperor*); Coleridge edits *The Friend*; anti-Whig *Quarterly Review* starts (ed. by Gifford –1824).

PROSE
Blake: *A Descriptive Catalogue of Pictures, Poetical and Historical Inventions*
Edgeworth: *Tales of Fashionable Life* (first series, second series 1812)
Montagu, Elizabeth (*d.*1800): *Letters* (compl. in 4 vols by 1813)
More: *Coelebs in Search of a Wife*
Wordsworth: *Concerning the Relations of Great Britain, Spain and Portugal as Affected by the Convention of Cintra*

POETRY
Byron: *English Bards and Scotch Reviewers*; *Imitations and Translations from the Classics, with Original Poems*
Campbell: *Gertrude of Wyoming, and Other Poems*
Lamb, Charles and Mary: *Poetry for Children*

1810

Napoleon annexes Holland; British goods burnt in France; invention of method of preserving food in cans; Dalton: *A New System of Chemical Philosophy*; Blake: *The Canterbury Pilgrims* (engraving); Goya: *The Disasters of War* (etchings, compl. 1814, publ. in full 1863).

PROSE
The British Novelists (50 vols, selected by Mrs Barbauld)
Southey: *The History of Brazil* (compl. in 3 vols by 1819)
POETRY
Crabbe: *The Borough*
Cunningham: *Remains of Nithsdale and Galloway Song*

POETRY (*cont.*)
Hogg: *The Forest Minstrel*
Rogers: *The Voyage of Columbus*
Scott: *The Lady of the Lake*
Shelley, P.B., and Elizabeth: *Original Poetry by Victor and Cazire*
Southey: *The Curse of Kehama*
Taylor, Ann and Jane: *Hymns for Infant Minds*

1811

Napoleon violates the Treaty of Tilsit (*see* 1807), thus alienating Russia; George III's insanity worsens; Prince of Wales becomes Regent (–1820); Luddite rioters near Nottingham start machine breaking; foundation of the Krupp ironworks at Essen.

PROSE
Austen: *Sense and Sensibility* (all Jane Austen's novels published anonymously during her lifetime)
(Goethe: *Dichtung und Wahrheit* ('Poetry and Truth'), compl. in 4 vols by 1832)
Shelley: *The Necessity of Atheism*

DRAMA
(Kleist (*d*.1811): *Prinz Friedrich von Homburg*)
POETRY
Bloomfield: *The Banks of the Wye*
Scott: *The Vision of Don Roderick*
Shelley: *A Poetical Essay on the Existing State of Things*

1812

P.M. Percival assassinated; Napoleon invades Russia and wins narrow victory over the Russians at Borodino; winter forces him to retreat and decimates his army; Luddite riots spread through the Midlands and north of England; Bell's steamship *Comet* on the Clyde; final shipment of the Elgin Marbles arrives in London (removal from Athens started 1802).

PROSE
D'Israeli, Isaac: *Calamities of Authors, Including Some Inquiries Respecting Their Moral and Literary Characters*
Edgeworth: *Tales of Fashionable Life* (second series, *see* 1809)
(Grimm Brothers: *Fairy Tales*, first 3 vols by 1813)
Maturin: *The Milesian Chief*
Nichols: *Literary Anecdotes of the Eighteenth Century* (compl. in 9 vols by 1815)
Shelley: *An Address to the Irish People*; *Declaration of Rights*; *Proposals for an Association of Philanthropists for Ireland*

PROSE (*cont.*)
Southey and Coleridge: *Omniana*
DRAMA
Landor: *Count Julian: A Tragedy* (publ.)
POETRY
Byron: *Childe Harold* (cantos i–ii, with 20 other poems, canto iii 1816, canto iv 1818)
Crabbe: *Tales in Verse*
Hemans: *Domestic Affections, and Other Poems*
Wilson: *The Isle of Palms, and Other Poems*

1813

Napoleon, after several victories, is defeated by the Allies (including Austria) at the battle of Leipzig; Wellington drives the French from Spain; at York, 17 men executed for Luddism; Leigh Hunt imprisoned (–1815) for attacking the Prince Regent in *The Examiner*.

PROSE
Aubrey (*d.*1697): *Brief Lives*
Austen: *Pride and Prejudice*
Hobhouse: *A Journey through Albania and Other Provinces of Turkey*
Owen: *A New View of Society*
Shelley: *A Vindication of Natural Diet*
Southey: *The Life of Nelson*
DRAMA
Coleridge: *Remorse*
POETRY
Byron: *The Bride of Abydos*; *The Giaour*
Cunningham: *Collected Works*; *Songs Chiefly in the Rural Dialect of Scotland*
Hogg: *The Queen's Wake*
Mitford: *Narrative Poems on the Female Character* (only vol. i publ.)
Montgomery: *The World before the Flood*
Moore: *Intercepted Letters, or The Two-Penny Postbag*

POETRY (*cont.*)
Scott: *The Bridal of Triermain*; *Rokeby*
Shelley: *Queen Mab*
Smith, James and 'Horatio': *Horace in London*

1814

Allies invade France; Napoleon abdicates and retires to Elba; provisional government in France restores the monarchy; First Treaty of Paris between the Allies and France, followed by the Congress of Vienna (–1815); Stephenson constructs efficient steam locomotive.

PROSE
Austen: *Mansfield Park*
Burney: *The Wanderer*
D'Israeli, Isaac: *Quarrels of Authors*
Edgeworth: *Patronage*
Scott: *Waverley* (publ. anonymously)
Shelley: *Refutation of Deism*
POETRY
Byron: *The Corsair*; *Lara*; *Ode to Napoleon*
Cary: *Dante's Divine Comedy* (transl., publ. in pts since 1805)
Hunt: *Feast of the Poets*
Rogers: *Jacqueline*
Southey: *Odes to the Prince Regent, the Emperor of Russia and the King of Prussia*; *Roderick, the Last of the Goths*

POETRY (*cont.*)
Wordsworth: *The Excursion, Being a Portion of the Recluse* (contains 'Essay upon Epitaphs')

1815 Napoleon escapes from Elba and marches on Paris; within three weeks he is Emperor again, but is defeated by Wellington at Waterloo; he abdicates, and is banished to St Helena; Second Treaty of Paris amongst European nations; British Parliament passes Corn Law, preventing import of corn till price reaches 80 shillings per quarter; William Smith: *Geologic Map of England and Wales with Part of Scotland*; Nash begins building Brighton Pavilion in pseudo-oriental style (compl. 1823).

PROSE
Scott: *Guy Mannering*
POETRY
Byron: *Collected Works*; *Hebrew Melodies*
Cowper (*d*.1800): *Poems*
Hogg: *The Pilgrims of the Sun*
Hunt: *The Descent of Liberty: A Masque*
Moore: *National Airs*
Scott: *The Field of Waterloo*; *The Lord of the Isles*
Tannahill (*d*.1810): *Poems and Songs, Chiefly in the Scottish Dialect*

POETRY (*cont.*)
Wordsworth: *Poems, Including Lyrical Ballads, Miscellaneous Pieces and Preface*; *The White Doe of Rylstone*

1816 Heavy taxation, stagnant trade and a bad harvest cause riots in several places in Britain; invention of the stethoscope; Rossini: *The Barber of Seville* (comic opera).

PROSE
Austen: *Emma*
Coleridge: *The Statesman's Manual: A Lay Sermon*
(Constant: *Adolphe*)
Cowper (*d*.1800): *Memoirs of Early Life, Written by Himself*
Holcroft (*d*.1809): *Memoirs*
Peacock: *Headlong Hall*
Scott: *The Antiquary*; *Tales of My Landlord* (incl. *The Black Dwarf* and *Old Mortality*)
Wordsworth: *A Letter to a Friend of Burns*
DRAMA
Maturin: *Bertram, or The Castle of St Aldobrand*
POETRY
Byron: *Childe Harold* (canto iii, *see* 1812); *Monody on the Death of Sheridan*; *Poems on His Domestic Circumstances*; *The Prisoner of Chillon, and Other Poems*; *The Siege of Corinth*
Coleridge: *Christabel, Kubla Khan and The Pains of Sleep*

POETRY (*cont.*)
Hogg: *Madoc of the Moor*; *The Poetic Mirror*
Moore: *On the Death of Sheridan*; *Sacred Songs*
Shelley: *Alastor, and Other Poems*
Southey: *The Lay of the Laureate*; *A Poet's Pilgrimage to Waterloo*
Wilson: *The City of the Plague, and Other Poems*

1817 Civil unrest continues; Prince Regent attacked; suspension of Habeas Corpus; march of the Manchester 'Blanketeers' towards London; Derbyshire insurrection quelled; Ricardo: *Principles of Political Economy and Taxation*; *Blackwood's Magazine* started (–1980).

PROSE

Chesterfield (*d.*1773): *Letters to A.C. Stanhope on the Education of His Godson*

Cobbett: *English Grammar*

Coleridge: *Biographia Literaria*

Edgeworth: *Harington*; *Ormond*

Godwin: *Mandeville*

Hazlitt: *Characters of Shakespeare's Plays*

Hogg: *The Brownie of Bodsbeck*; *Dramatic Tales*

Lockhart and Wilson: 'The Cockney School of Poets' (an attack on Leigh Hunt, Keats and others in *Blackwood's Magazine*)

Mill, James: *History of British India*

Scott: *Rob Roy*

Shelley: *Address to the People on the Death of Princess Charlotte*

DRAMA

Edgeworth: *Comic Dramas* (publ.)

Maturin: *Manuel* (publ.)

Southey: *Wat Tyler* (publ.)

POETRY

Byron: *The Lament of Tasso*; *Manfred: A Dramatic Poem*

Coleridge: *Sybilline Leaves*

Frere: *Prospectus and Specimen on an Intended National Work by William and Robert Whistlecraft Intended to Comprise the Most Interesting Particulars Relating to King Arthur and His Round Table* (cantos i–ii, hereafter *The Monks and the Giants, see* 1818)

Hemans: *Modern Greece*

Keats: *Poems*

Moore: *Lalla Rookh*

Shelley: *Laon and Cythna, or The Revolution of the Golden City* (publ. as *The Revolt of Islam* 1818)

1818 Repeal of act suspending Habeas Corpus (*see* 1817); overwhelming defeat of Burdett's motion for universal suffrage and annual Parliaments; first iron passenger ship on the Clyde, Wilson's *Vulcan*; Institute of Civil Engineers established; Bowdler: *The Family Shakespeare* (censored for family reading).

PROSE

Austen (*d.*1817): *Northanger Abbey*; *Persuasion* (publ. together)

Egan: *Boxiana* (compl. in 4 vols by 1824)

Evelyn (*d.*1706): *Diary, 1641–1706*

Ferrier: *Marriage*

Hazlitt: *Lectures on the English Poets*; *A Review of the English Stage*

Lamb: *Collected Works*

Maturin: *Women, or Pour et Contre*

Peacock: *Nightmare Abbey*

Scott: *Tales of My Landlord* (second series, contains *The Heart of Midlothian*)

Shelley, Mary: *Frankenstein, or The Modern Prometheus*

POETRY

Byron: *Beppo*; *Childe Harold* (canto iv, *see* 1812)

Frere: *The Monks and the Giants* (all 4 cantos, *see* 1817)

Hunt: *Foliage*

Keats: *Endymion*

Moore: *The Fudge Family in Paris*

Shelley: *The Revolt of Islam* (originally *Laon and Cythna, see* 1817)

1819

Peterloo Massacre at Manchester: mounted yeomanry and soldiers charge a crowd assembled to hear speeches on political reform; Parliament passes the Six Acts, repressive measures to prevent sedition; Factory Act forbids employment of children under nine in cotton mills; foundation of settlement at Singapore by Raffles; first Macadam roads laid; S.S. *Savannah* crosses the Atlantic in 26 days; Géricault: *The Raft of the 'Medusa'* (*p.*); Schubert: Piano Quintet (*The Trout*).

PROSE
Hazlitt: *Lectures on the English Comic Writers*; *Political Essays, with Sketches of Public Characters*
Lockhart: *Peter's Letters to His Kinsfolk*
(Schopenhauer: *The World As Will and Idea*)
Scott: *Ivanhoe*; *Tales of My Landlord* (third series, incl. *The Bride of Lammermoor*)
DRAMA
Maturin: *Fredolfo*
Shelley: *The Cenci* (publ.)
POETRY
Byron: *Don Juan* (cantos i–ii, cantos iii–v 1821, cantos vi–xiv 1823, cantos xv–xvi 1824); *Mazeppa*
Crabbe: *Tales of the Hall*

POETRY (*cont.*)
Field: *First Fruits of Australian Poetry*
Hunt: *Hero and Leander, and Bacchus and Ariadne*
Keats: 'Ode to the Nightingale' (in *Annals of the Fine Arts*)
Macaulay: *Pompeii*
Rogers: *Human Life*
Shelley: *Rosalind and Helen, and Other Poems*
Wordsworth: *Peter Bell*; *The Waggoner* (both incl. sonnets)

1820

Death of George III; accession of Prince Regent as George IV (–1830); failure of the Cato Street Conspiracy, a plot to murder the Cabinet; George IV's attempt to dissolve his marriage to the popular Queen Caroline fails; Frederick Accum: *A Treatise on Adulterations of Food* (protest at bad food); foundation of the Royal Astronomical Society; Ingres: *The Vow of Louis XIII* (*p.*); *London Magazine* started (–1829).

PROSE
Galt: *The Ayrshire Legatees*
Godwin: *Of Population, in Answer to Mr Malthus*
Hogg: *Winter Evening Tales*
Lamb: 'Essays of Elia' (in *London Magazine*, see 1823)
Malthus: *Principles of Political Economy*
Maturin: *Melmoth the Wanderer*
Peacock: *The Four Ages of Poetry*
Scott: *The Abbot*; *The Monastery*
Southey: *The Life of John Wesley*
POETRY
Browning, E.B.: *The Battle of Marathon*
Clare: *Poems, Descriptive of Rural Life*

POETRY (*cont.*)
Crabbe: *Collected Works*
Hemans: *The Sceptic*
Keats: *Lamia, Isabella, Eve of St Agnes, Hyperion, and Other Poems*
Scott: *Miscellaneous Poems, Collected*
Shelley: *Oedipus Tyrannus*; *Prometheus Unbound, and Other Poems*
Wordsworth: *The River Duddon: A Series of Sonnets*; *Vaudracour and Julia, and Other Poems*

1821

Greece begins revolt against the Turks (–1829); Faraday expounds principles of the electric motor; James Mill: *Elements of Political Economy*; Constable: *The Hay Wain* (*p.*).

PROSE
Cobbett: *Twelve Sermons*
Cooper: *The Spy*
De Quincey: 'The Confessions of an English Opium-Eater' (in *London Magazine*)
Egan: *Life in London* (see 1828)
Galt: *Annals of the Parish*
Hazlitt: *Lectures on Elizabethan Drama*
Scott: *Kenilworth*
Southey: 'The Life of Cromwell' (in *Quarterly Review*)

DRAMA
Byron: *Cain: A Mystery*; *Sardanapalus: A Tragedy*; *The Two Foscari: A Tragedy* (all publ.); *Marino Faliero*
Smith, 'Horatio': *Amarynthus the Nympholept*

POETRY
Beddoes: *The Improvisatore, with Other Poems*

POETRY (*cont.*)
Byron: *Don Juan* (cantos iii–v, see 1819)
Clare: *The Village Minstrel, and Other Poems*
Scott: *An Account of George IV's Coronation*
Shelley: *Adonais*; *Epipsychidion*
Southey: *Carmen Triumphale*; *A Vision of Judgement*

1822

Foreign Secretary Castlereagh commits suicide; Champollion deciphers Egyptian hieroglyphics, using the Rosetta Stone (*see* 1799); completion of the Caledonian Canal; Daguerre's *Diorama* opens in Paris (scenic pictures viewed under special lights to create an illusion of three-dimensional reality); Martin: *The Destruction of Herculaneum* (*p.*).

PROSE
Bentham: *The Influence of Natural Religion upon Temporal Happiness*
Galt: *The Provost*; *Sir Andrew Wylie*
Lockhart: *Adam Blair*
Peacock: *Maid Marian*
Scott: *The Fortunes of Nigel*; *Peveril of the Peak*; *The Pirate*
Walpole (*d.*1797): *Memoirs of the Last Ten Years of the Reign of George II*
Wilson: *Lights and Shadows of Scottish Life*; (with others): 'Noctes Ambrosianae' (in *Blackwood's Magazine* –1835)

DRAMA
Beddoes: *The Bride's Tragedy* (publ.)

POETRY
Bloomfield: *May Day with the Muses*
Byron: *The Vision of Judgement*

POETRY (*cont.*)
Hemans: *Welsh Melodies*
Rogers: *Italy* (final version, with illustrations after Stothard and Turner, 1830)
Shelley: *Hellas*
Wordsworth: *Ecclesiastical Sketches*; *Memorials of a Tour on the Continent*

1823

President Monroe proclaims doctrine that any attempt by a foreign power to extend its influence in the Americas will be considered as dangerous to peace; in Britain, heavy duties on foreign trade are moderated by Huskisson's Reciprocities of Duties Act; Peel begins series of penal reforms; Mechanics Institutes founded in London and Glasgow (providing education for artisans); Macintosh develops rubberised material bearing his name (manufactured 1824); medical journal, *The Lancet*, started; Beethoven: Symphony No. 9 (*Choral*).

PROSE
Carlyle: 'The Life of Schiller' (serialised in *London Magazine* –1824)
Cooper: *The Pioneers*
Galt: *The Entail*
Hazlitt: *Liber Amoris*
Lamb: *Essays of Elia* (collected, *see* 1820)
Martineau: *Devotional Exercises for the Use of Young Persons*
Scott: *Quentin Durward*
Southey: *History of the Peninsular War* (compl. in 3 vols by 1832)
DRAMA
Byron: *Werner: A Tragedy* (publ.)

POETRY
Byron: *The Age of Bronze*; *Don Juan* (cantos vi–xiv, *see* 1819); *The Island*
Shelley (*d*.1822): *Poetical Pieces*

1824

Repeal of Combinations Act (*see* 1799) allows workers to unionise; foundation of the Royal Society for the Prevention of Cruelty to Animals; foundation of the National Gallery in London; Byron dies at Missolonghi in Greece, during war of independence against Turkey.

PROSE
Bentham: *The Book of Fallacies*
Carlyle: *Goethe's Wilhelm Meister's Apprenticeship* (transl.)
Ferrier: *Inheritance*
Godwin: *The History of the Commonwealth of England* (compl. in 4 vols by 1828)
Hazlitt: *Sketches of the Principal Picture-Galleries of England*
Hogg: *The Confessions of a Justified Sinner*
Landor: *Imaginary Conversations of Literary Men and Statesmen* (vols i–ii, vols iii–iv 1828, vol. v 1829)
Maturin (*d*.1824): *The Albigenses: A Romance*
Medwin: *A Journal of Conversations with Lord Byron*
Mitford: *Our Village: Sketches of Rural Life, Character and Scenery* (compl. in 6 vols by 1832)
Scott: *Redgauntlet*; *St Ronan's Well*

POETRY
Byron (*d*.1824): *Don Juan* (cantos xv–xvi, *see* 1819)
Campbell: *Theodoric, and Other Poems*
Shelley (*d*.1822): *Posthumous Poems* (ed. Mary Shelley)

1825

Commercial crisis after boom year; Robert Owen sets up New Harmony experimental cooperative community in Indiana, U.S.A. (–1829); opening of the first passenger railway, between Stockton and Darlington; 'tinplate canister' patented, improving quality of canned foods; Nash starts reconstruction of Buckingham House as royal palace (compl. 1830); foundation of the Society for the Diffusion of Useful Knowledge.

PROSE
Byron (d.1824): *Correspondence*
Coleridge: *Aids to Reflection*
Hazlitt: *The Spirit of the Age*
Moore: *The Life of Sheridan*
Pepys (d.1703): *Diary* (many subsequent edns with additional material)
Scott: *The Betrothed*; *The Talisman*
Wilson: *The Foresters*

POETRY
Cunningham: *Songs of Scotland*
Hemans: *The Forest Sanctuary* (1829 edn incl. 'Casabianca')
Hood and Reynolds: *Odes and Addresses to Great People*
Moore: *Evenings in Greece*
Southey: *A Tale of Paraguay*

1826

University College, London, founded; Niepce takes the first photograph; 'Shoreham Period' of Samuel Palmer, visionary landscape painter.

PROSE
Bowdler (d.1825): *Gibbon's Decline and Fall, with Omissions of Passages of Irreligious or Immoral Tendency*
Cooper: *The Last of the Mohicans*
Disraeli: *Vivian Grey* (publ. anonymously, compl. in 5 vols by 1827)
Galt: *The Last of the Lairds*
Hazlitt: *Journey through France and Italy*; *The Plain Speaker*

PROSE (*cont.*)
Scott: *Woodstock*
Shelley, Mary: *The Last Man*
Smith, 'Horatio': *Brambletye House, or Cavaliers and Roundheads*
POETRY
Browning, E.B.: *An Essay on Mind, with Other Poems*
Hogg: *Queen Hynde*
Hood: *Whims and Oddities* (first series, second series 1827)

1827

In the course of the Greek war of independence, Egyptian and Turkish fleets are destroyed at the battle of Navarino Bay; Niepce makes photographs on a metal plate; sulphur matches invented; Schubert: *Die Winterreise* (song-cycle); Audubon: *Birds of America* (issued serially –1838).

PROSE
Carlyle: *German Romance*
De Quincey: 'On Murder Considered as One of the Fine Arts' (in *Blackwood's Magazine*)
(Manzoni: *I promessi sposi* ('The Betrothed'))
Scott: *Chronicles of the Canongate* (first series, second series 1828); *The Life of Napoleon Bonaparte*; *Miscellaneous Prose Works* (6 vols, edn in 9 vols 1827–34, edn in 30 vols 1834–71)

POETRY
Clare: *The Shepherd's Calendar*
Hood: *The Plea of the Midsummer Fairies*; *Whims and Oddities* (second series, *see* 1826)
Keble: *The Christian Year*
Tennyson, Alfred and Charles: *Poems by Two Brothers*

1828

Wellington becomes P.M. (–1830), with Peel as his Home Secretary; repeal of Test and Corporation Acts, which had kept Catholics and Nonconformists from important office; O'Connell elected to Parliament, but, as a Catholic, unable to take up his seat; Schubert: Symphony No. 9 (*Great C Major*); Webster: *American Dictionary of the English Language.*

PROSE
(Casanova (*d.*1798): *Mémoires*, compl. in 12 vols by 1838)
Disraeli: *The Voyage of Captain Popanilla*
Egan: *Finish to the Adventures of Tom, Jerry and Logic* (conclusion of *Life in London, see* 1821; illustrations by Cruikshank)
Hazlitt: *The Life of Napoleon Bonaparte* (compl. in 4 vols by 1832, revised edn 1852)
Hunt: *Lord Byron and Some of His Contemporaries*
Landor: *Imaginary Conversations of Literary Men and Statesmen* (vols iii–iv, *see* 1824)
Lockhart: *The Life of Robert Burns*
Lytton: *Pelham*

PROSE (*cont.*)
Scott: *Chronicles of the Canongate* (second series, contains *The Fair Maid of Perth, see* 1827); *Tales of a Grandfather* (first series, second series 1829, third and fourth series 1830)
POETRY
Hemans: *Records of Woman, with Other Poems*
Moore: *Odes upon Cash, Corn, Catholics*

1829

Wellington and Peel force the Catholic Emancipation Bill through Parliament; O'Connell (*see* 1828) re-elected and takes up his seat; Peel establishes Metropolitan Police Force; Fremantle starts colonisation of western Australia; Stephenson builds the *Rocket* railway engine; Braille evolves reading system for the blind; publication of Baedeker's first guide book (to Koblenz); Delacroix: *Death of Sardanapalus* (*p.*); Rossini: *William Tell* (opera); Milman: *The History of the Jews.*

PROSE
Carlyle: 'Signs of the Times' (publ. anonymously in *The Edinburgh Review*)
Cunningham: *The Lives of the Most Eminent British Painters, Sculptors and Architects* (first edn, compl. in 6 vols by 1833)
Landor: *Imaginary Conversations of Literary Men and Statesmen* (vol. v, *see* 1824)
Lytton: *The Disowned*
Mill, James: *Analysis of the Human Mind*
Scott: *Tales of a Grandfather* (second series, *see* 1828)
Southey: *Sir Thomas More*
Taylor, Isaac: *Natural History of Enthusiasm*

DRAMA
Jerrold: *Black-Eyed Susan*
POETRY
Hogg: *The Shepherd's Calendar*
Hood: 'The Dream of Eugene Aram' (in *The Gem*); *The Epping Hunt*
Tennyson: *Timbuctoo*

1830

Death of George IV; accession of William IV (–1837); Wellington's government resigns after his unpopular refusal to support reform of Parliament; agricultural labourers riot; 'July Revolution' in Paris; Louis-Philippe becomes the 'citizen king' (–1848); Huskisson killed by train at opening of the Manchester–Liverpool railway; foundation of the Royal Geographic Society; (c.) horse-drawn omnibuses operate in London; Sir Charles Lyell: *Principles of Geology* (compl. in 3 vols by 1833); Berlioz: *Symphonie fantastique*.

PROSE
Carleton: *Traits and Stories of the Irish Peasantry* (first series, second series 1833)
Cobbett: *Advice to Young Men*; *Rural Rides*
Coleridge: *On the Constitution of Church and State*
Godwin: *Cloudesley: A Tale*
Lytton: *Paul Clifford*
Marryat: *The King's Own*
Moore (ed.): *Letters and Journals of Lord Byron*

PROSE (*cont.*)
Scott: 'Letters on Demonology and Witchcraft' (in *Murray's Family Library*); *Tales of a Grandfather* (third and fourth series, *see* 1828)
DRAMA
Byron (*d.*1824): *Werner*
Jerrold: *The Mutiny at the Nore*; *Sally in Our Alley*
POETRY
Hemans: *Songs of the Affections*
Moore: *Legendary Ballads*
Tennyson: *Poems, Chiefly Lyrical*

1831

Whigs initiate First and Second Reform Bills; both rejected by Parliament, resulting in fierce riots in Derby, Nottingham and Bristol; formation of the National Union of the Working Classes; cholera outbreak in England (–1833); Gloucester–Cheltenham steam-coach service runs four trips daily.

PROSE
Disraeli: *The Young Duke*
Ferrier: *Destiny*
Peacock: *Crotchet Castle*
(Stendhal: *Scarlet and Black*)
Trelawny: *The Adventures of a Younger Son*

POETRY
Elliott: *Corn-Law Rhymes*
Hogg: *Songs*
Poe: *Poems*

1832

Reform Bill eventually passed; disenfranchisement of 'rotten boroughs' and redistribution of seats and right of voting; Royal Commission into the English Poor Law (–1834); still for the production of alcoholic drinks perfected by Coffey; Mendelssohn: Overture *The Hebrides* (*Fingal's Cave*).

PROSE
Burney, F. (ed.): *Memoirs of Dr Burney*
Disraeli: *Contarini Fleming: A Psychological Autobiography*
Lytton: *Eugene Aram*
Scott: *Tales of My Landlord* (fourth series, contains *Count Robert of Paris* and *Castle Dangerous*)
Trollope, Frances: *Domestic Manners of the Americans*
DRAMA
Jerrold: *The Rent Day*

POETRY
Byron (*d.*1824): *Works, with Letters and Journals, and His Life by Thomas Moore* (compl. in 17 vols by 1833)
Hunt: *Poetical Works* (*see* 1844)
Shelley (*d.*1822): *The Masque of Anarchy*
Tennyson: *Poems* (incl. 'The Lady of Shalott', 'The Lotos Eaters', etc.)

1833

First reformed Parliament meets, with Whig majority and the Tories (who come to be called 'Conservatives') led by Peel; slavery abolished in all British Dominions; Education Grant Act gives money for elementary education; Factory Act fixes maximum working week for children, to be enforced by inspectors: 48 hours for those aged 9–13 and 68 hours for those aged 13–18; anthracite used for iron smelting; Oxford Movement, favouring pre-Reformation Catholic tradition in Anglicanism, starts with Keble's sermon on 'National Apostasy'.

PROSE

Carlyle: 'Sartor Resartus' (in *Fraser's Magazine* –1834; publ. in 1 vol.: Boston 1835, London 1838)
Disraeli: *The Wondrous Tale of Alroy, and the Rise of Iskander*
Keble, Newman, Pusey and others: *Tracts for the Times* (90 nos –1841)
Lamb: *Last Essays of Elia*
Lytton: *England and the English*; *Godolphin*
Moore: *Travels of an Irish Gentleman in Search of a Religion*
Shelley (*d.*1822): *Shelley Papers, with a Memoir by Thomas Medwin*

POETRY

Browning, E.B.: *Prometheus Bound* (transl. of Aeschylus)
Browning, R.: *Pauline: A Fragment of a Confession*

1834

New Poor Law Act establishes Union workhouses; Irish Church question causes resignation of Grey as P.M.; Peel follows Melbourne as P.M. (–1835); the Tolpuddle Martyrs, six agricultural labourers who tried to form a union, are transported to Australia; Houses of Parliament destroyed by fire (*see* 1836); two-wheeled Hansom cab patented; harvesting machine invented in U.S.A. (*see* 1836).

PROSE

Ainsworth: *Rookwood*
(Balzac: *Old Goriot*)
Beckford: *Italy, with Sketches of Spain and Portugal* (additions to 1783 edn)
Blessington: *Conversations of Lord Byron*
Hallam (*d.*1833): *Remains in Verse and Prose by A.H.H.*
Hogg: *Familiar Anecdotes of Sir Walter Scott*
Lytton: *The Last Days of Pompeii*
Marryat: *Jacob Faithful* (serialised 1833–4); *Peter Simple* (serialised 1832–3)
Southey: *The Doctor* (compl. in 7 vols by 1847)

DRAMA

Byron (*d.*1824): *Sardanapalus: A Tragedy*

POETRY

Burns (*d.*1796): *Collected Poems* (ed. Cunningham)
Crabbe (*d.*1832): *Poetical Works*

1835

Melbourne returns as P.M. (–1841); Municipal Reform Act regularises elections and finances of town councils in England and Wales; Great Western Railway begun; Samuel Colt patents the revolver; Donizetti: *Lucia di Lammermoor* (opera, based on Scott's *The Bride of Lammermoor* (1819)); Schumann: *Carnaval* (piano music).

PROSE

(Andersen: *Tales, Told for Children,* other collections 1843, 1847, 1852)

Beckford: *Recollections of an Excursion to the Monasteries of Alcobaça and Batalha*

Coleridge (*d.*1834): *Specimens of Table Talk*

Dickens: *Sketches by Boz* (first series, second series 1836)

Lytton: *Rienzi*

Mitford: *Belford Regis, or Sketches of a Country Town*

Shelley, Mary: *Lodore*

POETRY

Browning, R.: *Paracelsus*

Clare: *The Rural Muse*

Darley: *Nepenthe*

Hunt: *Captain Sword and Captain Pen*

POETRY (*cont.*)

Moore: *The Fudges in England*

Wordsworth: *Yarrow Revisited, and Other Poems*

1836

Act for registration of births, deaths and marriages; Adelaide becomes capital of South Australia; full charter for London University; horse-drawn 'combination harvester-thresher' in use in Michigan, U.S.A.; Pugin designs decorations for the new Houses of Parliament in neo-Gothic style (architecture by Barry, begun 1840, compl. 1852).

PROSE

Coleridge (*d.*1834): *Literary Remains* (prose and verse, compl. in 4 vols by 1838)

Dickens: *Sketches by Boz* (second series, *see* 1835)

Hazlitt (*d.*1830): *Literary Remains, with Memoir by His Son*

Landon: *Traits and Trials of Early Life*

Landor: *Pericles and Aspasia* (prose and verse)

Marryat: *Japhet in Search of a Father* (serialised 1834–6); *Mr Midshipman Easy*

DRAMA

(Büchner: *Woyzeck*)

(Gogol: *The Inspector General*)

Lytton: *The Duchesse de la Vallière*

POETRY

Froude, Keble, Newman and others: *Lyra Apostolica*

1837

Death of William IV; accession of Queen Victoria (–1901); insurrection in Canada led by Mackenzie and Papineau; last use of the pillory in England; Cook and Wheatstone patent the electric telegraph and develop its use on the railways; Morse develops the telegraph in U.S.A.; Pitman: *Stenographic Sound-Hand* (shorthand system).

PROSE
Carlyle: *The French Revolution*; *Lectures on German Literature*
Dickens: *The Pickwick Papers* (serialised 1836–7)
Disraeli: *Henrietta Temple*; *Venetia*
Lamb (*d.*1834): *Letters, with Life by Talfourd*
Landon: *Ethel Churchill, or The Two Brides*
Landor: *Literary Hours, by Various Friends*
Lockhart: *The Life of Sir Walter Scott* (compl. in 7 vols by 1838)
Lytton: *Ernest Maltravers*
Ruskin: 'The Poetry of Architecture' (serialised in *Architectural Magazine* –1838)
Thackeray: 'The Professor' (in *Bentley's Miscellany*)

PROSE (*cont.*)
Trollope, Frances: *The Vicar of Wrexhill*
DRAMA
Browning, R.: *Strafford*
(Hugo: *Ruy Blas*)

1838

Chartist movement, demanding political reform, begins in Glasgow; formation of the Anti-Corn-Law League in Manchester; Lord Durham reports on the Canadian situation (*see* 1837); steamship service across the Atlantic: S.S. *Great Western* does the journey in under 15 days; opening of the London–Birmingham railway.

PROSE
Bentham (*d.*1832): *Collected Works* (ed. Bowring, compl. in 11 vols by 1843)
Carlyle: *Lectures on the History of Literature*
Dickens: *Memoirs of Joseph Grimaldi*; *Oliver Twist* (serialised in *Bentley's Miscellany* 1837–8); *Sketches of Young Gentlemen*
Lytton: *Alice, or The Mysteries*
Surtees: *Jorrocks's Jaunts and Jollities*
Thackeray: *The Yellowplush Papers* (serialised in *Fraser's Magazine* 1837–8)
Trollope, Frances: *The Widow Barnaby*
DRAMA
Boucicault: *A Legend of the Devil's Dyke*
Lytton: *The Lady of Lyons*

POETRY
Browning, E.B.: *The Seraphim, and Other Poems*
Hood: *Hood's Own, or Laughter from Year to Year* (miscellany)
Milnes: *Poems of Many Years*
Tupper: *Proverbial Philosophy* (first series, fourth, final series 1876)
Wordsworth: *Sonnets, with a Few Additional Ones Now First Printed*

1839 Melbourne returns to office (–1841); Chartists have their petition rejected by Parliament; riots in Birmingham and Newport, Monmouthshire; opium war with China (–1842), caused by Chinese attempts to stop smuggling of opium, in which many British merchants are involved; Goodyear invents process of india-rubber vulcanisation; steam-hammer invented by Nasmyth; Darwin: *The Voyage of H.M.S. Beagle*; Turner: *The Fighting Téméraire* (*p.*); Chopin: *Twenty-Four Preludes* (piano music).

PROSE
Carleton: *Fardorougha the Miser, or The Convicts of Lisnamona*
Carlyle: *Chartism*
Dickens: *Nicholas Nickleby* (serialised 1838–9)
Hazlitt (*d.*1830): *Sketches and Essays, Collected by His Son*
Marryat: *The Phantom Ship* (serialised in *New Monthly Magazine* 1837)
Martineau: *Deerbrook*
(Stendhal: *The Charterhouse of Parma*)

PROSE (*cont.*)
Thackeray: 'Catherine' (serialised in *Fraser's Magazine* –1840); 'Stubb's Calendar, or The Fatal Boots' (in *Cruikshank's Comic Annual*)
DRAMA
Landor: *Andrea of Hungary*; *Giovanna of Naples* (publ.)
Lytton: *Richelieu, or The Conspiracy*
POETRY
Bailey: *Festus*
Hemans (*d.*1835): *Collected Works*
Moore: *Alciphron*
Shelley (*d.*1822): *Poetical Works* (ed. Mary Shelley)

1840 Quadruple alliance of Russia, Britain, Prussia and Austria offer Egypt to Mehemet Ali as hereditary possession in return for surrender of his earlier conquests; union of Upper and Lower Canada; at the Treaty of Waitangi, Maori chiefs surrender sovereignty of New Zealand to Britain; marriage of Queen Victoria and Prince Albert; Rowland Hill introduces the penny postage service and starts reform of the Post Office; transportation of convicts to New South Wales ceases; Auckland, New Zealand, founded; (*c.*) can-can introduced in Paris; (*c.*) Saxe invents the saxophone.

PROSE
Ainsworth: *The Tower of London*
Carlyle: *Critical and Miscellaneous Essays*
Coleridge (*d.*1834): *Confessions of an Inquiring Spirit*
Dickens: *Sketches of Young Couples*
D'Israeli, Isaac: *Amenities of Literature*
Poe: *Tales of the Grotesque and Arabesque*
Shelley (*d.*1822): *Essays, Letters from Abroad, Translations and Fragments*
Thackeray: *Character Sketches*; *An Essay on the Genius of George Cruikshank*; *A Paris Sketch Book*; 'A Shabby Genteel Story' (in *Fraser's Magazine*)

DRAMA
Hunt: *A Legend of Florence* (publ.)
Landor: *Fra Rupert* (publ.)
Lytton: *Money*
POETRY
Barham: *The Ingoldsby Legends* (first series, second and third series 1847)
Browning, R.: *Sordello*

1841

Peel forms Conservative ministry (–1846); Miners' Association of Great Britain and Ireland formed; Thomas Cook organises a temperance excursion from Leicester to Loughborough; British refugees from Canton seize island of Hong Kong and declare British sovereignty; *Punch, or The London Charivari* started.

PROSE
Ainsworth: *Old St Paul's*
Borrow: *The Zincali, or An Account of the Gypsies of Spain*
Carlyle: *On Heroes, Hero-Worship and the Heroes in History*
Dickens: *Barnaby Rudge*; *The Old Curiosity Shop* (both serialised 1840–1)
Marryat: *Masterman Ready*
Thackeray: *Comic Tales and Sketches*; 'The Great Hoggarty Diamond' (in *Fraser's Magazine*); *The History of Samuel Titmarsh*

DRAMA
Boucicault: *London Assurance*
POETRY
Browning, R.: *Pippa Passes*
Hunt and others: *Chaucer Modernised*

1842

Industrial crisis in England and Scotland; second Chartist Petition rejected by the Commons; 'Rebecca Riots': tollgates attacked by rural poor in Wales (–1844); employment of women and children under 10 in mines forbidden; income tax reintroduced; general anaesthetic first used for an operation, in U.S.A.

PROSE
Burney (*d.*1840): *Diary and Letters* (compl. in 7 vols by 1846)
Dickens: *American Notes for General Circulation*
Lytton: *Zanoni*
Thackeray: 'The Fitzboodle Papers' (in *Fraser's Magazine*)
Wilson: *Recreations of Christopher North*

POETRY
Browning, R.: *Dramatic Lyrics*; *King Victor and King Charles*
Macaulay: *Lays of Ancient Rome*
Tennyson: *Poems* (incl. 'Locksley Hall' and 'Ulysses')
Wordsworth: *Poems Chiefly of Early and Late Years, Including The Borderers*

1843

Establishment of the Free Church of Scotland; factory opens at Deptford for manufacture of super-phosphates (fertilisers); first printed Christmas cards.

PROSE
Ainsworth: *Windsor Castle* (serialised in *Ainsworth's Magazine* 1842–3)
Borrow: *The Bible in Spain*
Carlyle: *Past and Present*
Dickens: *A Christmas Carol in Prose*
Lytton: *The Last of the Barons*
Macaulay: *Critical and Historical Essays*
Mill: *A System of Logic*
Prescott: *The Conquest of Mexico*
Ruskin: *Modern Painters* (vol. i, vol. ii 1846, vols iii–iv 1856, vol. v 1860)

PROSE (*cont.*)
Thackeray: 'Bluebeard's Ghost' (in *Fraser's Magazine*); *An Irish Sketchbook*; 'Men's Wives' (in *Fraser's Magazine*)
DRAMA
Browning, R.: *A Blot in the 'Scutcheon*; *The Return of the Druses* (publ.)
POETRY
Hood: 'The Song of the Shirt' (in *Punch*)

1844

Bank Charter Act fixes principles for issue of banknotes; Rochdale pioneers open first cooperative store; polka arrives in Britain from Bohemia.

PROSE

Dickens: *The Chimes: A Goblin Story*; *Martin Chuzzlewit* (serialised 1843–4)
Disraeli: *Coningsby, or The New Generation*
Haydon: *Lectures on Painting and Design* (compl. 1846)
Hood: *Hood's Magazine and Comic Miscellany* (–1845); *Whimsicalities* (prose and verse)
Kinglake: *Eothen*
Newman (ed.): *Lives of the English Saints*
Thackeray: *The History of the Next French Revolution*

POETRY

Barnes: *Poems of Rural Life, in the Dorset Dialect: With a Dissertation and Glossary* (second collection 1859, third collection 1862)
Browning, E.B.: *Poems*
Browning, R.: *Colombe's Birthday*
Hunt: *Collected Poems* (second edn, with additions, *see* 1832)
Milnes: *Palm Leaves*
Patmore: *Poems*

1845

Famine in Ireland, due to failure of potato crop (–1850); division in the Cabinet about Corn Laws (protecting land owners by taxing imported grain); intense financial speculation on the railways; foundation of College of Chemistry; Newman's conversion to the Church of Rome causes crisis in the Oxford Movement (*see* 1833).

PROSE

Carlyle (ed.): *Letters and Speeches of Cromwell*
Dickens: *The Cricket on the Hearth*
Disraeli: *Sybil, or The Two Nations*
Newman: *An Essay on the Development of Christian Doctrine*
Poe: *Tales of Mystery and Imagination*
Thackeray: 'The Diary of Jeames de la Pluche' (in *Punch*); 'Legend of the Rhine' (in *Cruikshank's Table Book*)

DRAMA

Jerrold: *Time Works Wonders*

POETRY

Browning, R.: *Dramatic Romances and Lyrics*
Poe: *The Raven*
Southey (*d.*1843): *Oliver Newman, and Other Poetical Remains*

1846

Peel repeals Corn Laws; Conservative Party splits over issue, and Peel eventually resigns; Russell becomes Liberal P.M. (–1852); coinage of the term 'folk-lore' (by W.J. Thoms, antiquary).

PROSE

Dickens: *Pictures from Italy*
'George Eliot': *Strauss's Life of Jesus* (transl.)
Lytton: *Lucretia, or Children of the Night*
Marryat: *The Privateer's Man*
Ruskin: *Modern Painters* (vol. ii, *see* 1843)
Thackeray: *Cornhill to Cairo*

POETRY

Brontë, Charlotte, Emily and Anne: *Poems by Currer, Ellis and Acton Bell*
Browning, R.: *Luria: A Soul's Tragedy*; *Bells and Pomegranates* (his last 8 vols collected)
Lear: *Book of Nonsense*

1847

Poor-Law Board set up; Young Ireland insurgent group increases activities; experiments with chloroform lead to development of general anaesthetics; Zeiss opens an optical works for production of microscopes at Jena.

PROSE

Barham (*d.*1845): *The Ingoldsby Legends* (prose and verse, second and third series, *see* 1840)

Brontë, Anne (Acton Bell): *Agnes Grey*

Brontë, Charlotte (Currer Bell): *Jane Eyre*

Brontë, Emily (Ellis Bell): *Wuthering Heights*

Disraeli: *Tancred*

Keble: *Sermons*

Marryat: *The Children of the New Forest*

Medwin: *The Life of Shelley*

Prescott: *The Conquest of Peru*

Surtees: *Hawbuck Grange*

Trollope: *The Macdermots of Ballycloran*

DRAMA

Pitt: *The String of Pearls, or The Fiend of Fleet Street* (*Sweeney Todd*)

POETRY

Landor: *The Hellenics, Enlarged and Completed*

Tennyson: *The Princess*

1848

Revolutions in Paris, Berlin, Vienna, Venice, Rome, Milan, Naples, Prague and Budapest; third Chartist Petition fails; armed rebellion by O'Brien and Young Ireland Party fails; second cholera epidemic in England; Public Health Act sets up Central Board of Health; gold rush begins in California; Millais, Rossetti and Holman Hunt form the Pre-Raphaelite Brotherhood; Marx and Engels: *Communist Manifesto*.

PROSE

Brontë, Anne: *The Tenant of Wildfell Hall*

Dickens: *Dombey and Son* (serialised 1846–8); *The Haunted Man*

Forster: *The Life and Adventures of Oliver Goldsmith*

Gaskell: *Mary Barton*

Keats (*d.*1821): *Life, Letters and Literary Remains* (ed. Milnes)

Landor: *Imaginary Conversation of King Carlo-Alberto and the Duchess of Belgioioso*

Lytton: *Harold, the Last of the Saxon Kings*

Mill: *Principles of Political Economy*

Thackeray: *Our Street*; *Vanity Fair* (serialised 1847–8)

POETRY

Aytoun: *Lays of the Scottish Cavaliers*

Clough: *The Bothie of Toper-na-Fuosich*

Hunt: *A Jar of Honey from Mount Hybla*

1849

Suppression of European uprisings (*see* 1848); Bedford College for women founded in London; Paris Opera uses electric arc-lights; safety pin invented, in U.S.A.; *Notes and Queries* started.

PROSE

Ainsworth: *The Lancashire Witches* (serialised 1848)

Brontë, Charlotte: *Shirley*

(Chateaubriand (*d.*1848): *Mémoires d'outre tombe*, compl. in 12 vols by 1851)

Coleridge (*d.*1834): *Notes and Lectures on Shakespeare and Some of the Old Dramatists*

Hunt: *Readings for Railways*

Macaulay: *The History of England from the Accession of James II* (vols i–ii, vols iii–iv 1855, vol. v 1861)

Ruskin: *The Seven Lamps of Architecture*

Southey (*d.*1843): *Commonplace Book* (compl. in 4 series by 1851)

PROSE (*cont.*)

Thackeray: *Dr Birch and His Young Friends*; *The History of Pendennis* (vol. i, vol. ii 1850, serialised 1848–50)

POETRY

Arnold: *The Strayed Reveller, and Other Poems*

Clough: *Ambarvalia*

1850

Palmerston criticised in Parliament for his aggressive handling of foreign affairs; (*c.*) brass bands become popular in north of England; Public Libraries Act leads to foundation of municipal libraries throughout Britain; population of England and Wales: 18 million; Scotland: 3 million; Ireland: 6.5 million; first underwater cable laid across the Channel; Millais: *Christ in the House of His Parents* (*p.*).

PROSE

Carlyle: *Latter-Day Pamphlets*

Coleridge (*d.*1834): *Essays on His Own Times*

Dickens: *David Copperfield* (serialised 1849–50)

Gaskell: *The Moorland Cottage*

Hawthorne: *The Scarlet Letter*

Hunt: *Autobiography*

Kingsley, Charles: *Alton Locke, Taylor and Poet*

Lytton: *The Caxtons*

Poe (*d.*1849): *Works* (incl. verse)

Thackeray: *The Kickleburys on the Rhine*; *Rebecca and Rowena*

POETRY

Beddoes (*d.*1849): *Death's Jest Book, or The Fool's Tragedy*

Browning, E.B.: *Poems* (incl. 'Sonnets from the Portuguese')

Browning, R.: *Christmas Eve and Easter Day*

POETRY (*cont.*)

Dobell: *The Roman: A Dramatic Poem*

Rossetti, D.G., and others: *The Germ* (incl. 'The Blessed Damozel')

Tennyson: *In Memoriam*

Watts: *Lyrics of the Heart*

Wordsworth (*d.*1850): *The Prelude, or Growth of a Poet's Mind: An Autobiographical Poem* (*see* 1805)

1851

The Great Exhibition of the Industries of All Nations held at the Crystal Palace; in France, Louis-Napoleon overthrows the Republic and procures Presidency for 10 years; Palmerston forced to resign as Foreign Secretary, for acting without consulting colleagues: he had sent his secret approval of the French *coup d'état*; census reveals low church attendance in industrial areas; Singer starts manufacture of practical sewing machine in U.S.A.; gold discovered in Australia; Layard: *Popular Account of Discoveries at Nineveh* (archaeological work).

PROSE
Borrow: *Lavengro*
Carlyle: *The Life of John Sterling*
Dickens: 'A Child's History of England' (serialised in *Household Words* –1853)
Hunt: *Table Talk*
Kingsley, Charles: *Yeast* (in abridged form in *Fraser's Magazine* 1848)
Melville: *Moby Dick*
Ruskin: *Examples of the Architecture of Venice*; *Pre-Raphaelitism*; *The Stones of Venice* (vol. i, vols ii–iii 1853)
Wordsworth (*d.*1850): *Memoirs, Dictated by Himself*
DRAMA
(Labiche: *The Italian Straw Hat*)

POETRY
Beddoes (*d.*1849): *Collected Poems*
Browning, E.B.: *Casa Guidi Windows*
Meredith: *Poems* (incl. 'Love in the Valley')

1852

Conservative administration under Derby formed, following fall of Russell's Liberal administration, but resigns when Disraeli's first budget is defeated; Mayhew: *London Labour and the London Poor* (expanded edn in 4 vols 1861–2); Victoria and Albert Museum opens.

PROSE
Disraeli: *The Life of Lord George Bentinck*
Kingsley, Charles: *Phaethon*
Mitford: *Recollections of a Literary Life*
Newman: *Discourses on the Scope and Nature of University Education*
Stowe: *Uncle Tom's Cabin*
Thackeray: *The Book of Snobs* (serialised in *Punch* 1846–7); *The Fitzboodle Papers* (serialised in *Fraser's Magazine* 1842–3); *The History of Henry Esmond*; *The Luck of Barry Lyndon* (vol. i, vol. ii 1853, serialised in *Fraser's Magazine* 1844)
DRAMA
Boucicault: *The Corsican Brothers*
Taylor and Reade: *Masks and Faces*

POETRY
Arnold: *Empedocles on Etna, and Other Poems*
Tennyson: *Ode on the Death of the Duke of Wellington*

1853

Russians attack Turkish provinces on the Danube, leading to outbreak of the Crimean War in 1854 between Russia, and France and Britain (–1856); Gladstone's first budget furthers free trade; Queen Victoria given chloroform during childbirth, encouraging its acceptance as an anaesthetic; invention of the hypodermic syringe; Verdi: *La Traviata* (opera).

PROSE
Brontë, Charlotte: *Villette*
De Quincey: *Selections Grave and Gay* (compl. in 14 vols by 1860)
Dickens: *Bleak House* (serialised 1852–3)
Gaskell: *Cranford* (serialised in *Household Words* 1851–3); *Ruth*
Haydon (*d.*1846): *Autobiography and Journals*
Kingsley, Charles: *Hypatia*
Lytton: *My Novel*
Reade: *Peg Woffington*
Ruskin: *The Stones of Venice* (vols ii–iii, *see* 1851)
Surtees: *Mr Sponge's Sporting Tour*
Thackeray: *The English Humourists of the Eighteenth Century*
Yonge: *The Heir of Redclyffe*
POETRY
Arnold: *Poems: A New Edition* (incl. 'Sohrab and Rustum' and 'The Scholar Gypsy')

POETRY (*cont.*)
Landor: *Last Fruit off an Old Tree* (prose and verse)
Patmore: *Tamerton Church Tower*
Smith, Alexander: *Life Drama*

1854

British and French begin the siege of Sebastopol (–1855); at Balaclava the Light Brigade suffers heavy losses; severe winter causes great suffering among troops; Northcote–Trevelyan report leads to foundation of Civil Service Commission to supervise recruitment (1855); Liszt: *Les Préludes* (symphonic poem); Holman Hunt: *The Awakened Conscience* (*p.*).

PROSE
Ainsworth: *The Star Chamber*
Dickens: *Hard Times*
Mitford: *Atherton, and Other Tales*
Ruskin: *Lectures on Architecture and Painting*
Surtees: *Handley Cross, or Mr Jorrocks's Hunt*
Thackeray: *The Newcomes* (vol. i, vol. ii 1855, serialised 1853–5)
Thoreau: *Walden, or Life in the Woods*
Yonge: *The Little Duke*
POETRY
Allingham: *Day and Night Songs*
Aytoun: *Firmilian*
Dobell: *Balder*

POETRY (*cont.*)
Patmore: *The Betrothal* (pt i of *The Angel in the House*, pt ii 1856, pt iii 1860, pt iv 1862)
Tennyson: 'The Charge of the Light Brigade' (in *The Examiner*, publ. separately 1855)

1855

The Times reveals mismanagement of Crimean campaign; Palmerston made P.M. (–1858) in place of Aberdeen ministry; Sebastopol falls to the Allies; Florence Nightingale introduces hygienic conditions into military hospitals in the Crimea; modernisation of London sewers begins after outbreaks of cholera; duty on newspapers abolished, leading to expansion of newspaper industry; first publication of the *Daily Telegraph*; Livingstone discovers the Victoria Falls during exploration of the Zambesi river; Brown: *The Last of England (p.)*.

PROSE
Burton: *Personal Narrative of a Pilgrimage to El-Medinah and Mecca* (compl. in 3 vols by 1856)
Gaskell: *Lizzie Leigh, and Other Tales* (serialised 1850–4); *North and South* (serialised in *Household Words* 1854–5)
Kingsley, Charles: *Westward Ho!*
Macaulay: *The History of England* (vols iii–iv, *see* 1849)
Meredith: *The Shaving of Shagpat*

PROSE (*cont.*)
Motley: *The Rise of the Dutch Republic*
Spencer: *Principles of Psychology*
Trollope: *The Warden*
Yonge: *The Lances of Lynwood*
POETRY
Arnold: *Poems, Second Series*
Browning, R.: *Men and Women*
Longfellow: *Hiawatha*
Tennyson: *Maud, and Other Poems*
Whitman: *Leaves of Grass*

1856

Crimean War (*see* 1853) ended by the Treaty of Paris; London General Omnibus Company founded; Bessemer's converter adopted by steel industry; production of first synthetic dye, Perkin's mauve.

PROSE
Froude, J.: *History of England* (compl. in 12 vols by 1870)
Kingsley, Charles: *The Heroes*
Reade: *It Is Never Too Late to Mend*
Ruskin: *Modern Painters* (vols iii–iv, *see* 1843)
Yonge: *The Daisy Chain*

POETRY
Dobell: *England in Time of War*
Patmore: *The Espousals* (pt ii of *The Angel in the House*, *see* 1854)
Rossetti, D.G., Morris and others: *The Oxford and Cambridge Magazine* (poetry and prose)

1857

The Indian Mutiny (–1858): Delhi is taken by the rebels and then recaptured; the Massacre of Cawnpore; Lucknow is besieged and relieved; Matrimonial Causes Act establishes divorce courts in England and Wales; Livingstone: *Missionary Travels and Researches in South Africa*; Pasteur explains role of bacteria in fermentation of lactic acid.

PROSE
Ballantyne: *The Coral Island*
Borrow: *The Romany Rye*
Brontë, Charlotte (*d.*1855): *The Professor*
Carlyle: *Collected Works* (compl. in 16 vols by 1858)
Dickens: *Little Dorrit* (serialised 1855–7)
(Flaubert: *Madame Bovary*)
Gaskell: *The Life of Charlotte Brontë*

PROSE (*cont.*)
Hughes: *Tom Brown's Schooldays*
Meredith: *Farina*
Newman: *Sermons on Various Occasions*
Ruskin: *The Political Economy of Art*
Trollope: *Barchester Towers*
POETRY
(Baudelaire: *Les Fleurs du mal*)
Browning, E.B.: *Aurora Leigh*
Smith, Alexander: *City Poems*

1858

Palmerston defeated over Conspiracy to Murder Bill, introduced following the Orsini plot to assassinate Louis Napoleon of France; abolition of property qualifications for M.P.s; first Atlantic cable laid; Burton and Speke discover Lake Tanganyika; Speke goes on to discover Lake Victoria; Frith: *Derby Day* (*p.*); Offenbach: *Orpheus in the Underworld* (opera).

PROSE

Carlyle: *Frederick the Great* (compl. in 6 vols by 1865)
'George Eliot': *Scenes of Clerical Life*
Farrar: *Eric, or Little by Little*
Hogg, Thomas: *The Life of Shelley*
Lytton: *What Will He Do With It?*
Peacock: 'Memoirs of Shelley' (in *Fraser's Magazine*)
Thackeray: *The Virginians* (vol. i, vol. ii 1859, serialised 1857–9)
Trelawny: *Recollections of the Last Days of Shelley and Byron*
Trollope: *Doctor Thorne*; *The Three Clerks*

POETRY

Clough: *Amours de Voyage*
Kingsley, Charles: *Andromeda, and Other Poems*
Morris: *The Defence of Guenevere, and Other Poems*

1859

Disraeli's Reform Bill defeated; Palmerston P.M. again (–1865); Italian war of liberation from Austrian rule takes place; Austrians defeated at Solferino; De Lesseps starts the Suez Canal (compl. 1869); drilling of first American oil-well (at Titusville, Pennsylvania); Darwin: *On the Origin of Species by Means of Natural Selection, or The Preservation of Favoured Races in the Struggle for Life*; Samuel Smiles: *Self-Help* (advocates thrift and self-improvement); Dickens starts *All the Year Round* (weekly –1895).

PROSE

Arnold: *England and the Italian Question*
Dickens: *A Tale of Two Cities*
'George Eliot': *Adam Bede*; 'The Lifted Veil' (in *Blackwood's Magazine*)
Gaskell: *Round the Sofa* (serialised 1855–8)
Holmes: *The Professor at the Breakfast Table* (prose and verse)
Kingsley, Henry: *The Recollections of Geoffrey Hamlyn*
Meredith: *The Ordeal of Richard Feverel*
Mill: *Dissertations and Discussions* (compl. in 4 vols by 1876); *On Liberty*; *Thoughts on Parliamentary Reform*
Ruskin: *The Two Paths*
Trollope: *The Bertrams*

DRAMA

Boucicault: *The Octoroon*

POETRY

Barnes: *Hwomely Rhymes: A Second Collection of Poems in the Dorset Dialect* (*see* 1844)
Fitzgerald: *The Rubáiyát of Omar Khayyám*
Tennyson: *Idylls of the King*

1860

Lincoln becomes President of U.S.A. (–1865); Gladstone's budget introduces further reductions on tariffs; Garibaldi and Cavour complete unification of Italy; first gas-driven internal combustion engine; Wilson (ed.): *Essays and Reviews* ('Broad Church' religious essays, denounced in 1861 for their liberalism); Burckhardt: *The Civilisation of the Renaissance in Italy*.

PROSE
Collins: *The Woman in White*
Dickens: *The Uncommercial Traveller*
'George Eliot': *The Mill on the Floss*
Gaskell: *Right At Last, and Other Tales* (publ. intermittently 1856–60)
Ruskin: *Modern Painters* (vol. v, *see* 1843)
Trollope: *Castle Richmond*
Yonge: *Pigeon Pie*
DRAMA
Boucicault: *The Colleen Bawn*

POETRY
Browning, E.B.: *Poems before Congress*
Hunt (*d.*1859): *Poetical Works*
Patmore: *Faithful for Ever* (pt iii of *The Angel in the House*, *see* 1854)

1861

Southern States of U.S.A. secede from the Union over the issues of slavery and trade protection; beginning of the American Civil War (–1865); death of Albert, the Prince Consort; lack of supplies of cotton from U.S.A. leads to famine amongst mill workers in Lancashire (–1863); in Russia, emancipation of serfs is proclaimed; first British ironclad ship, the *Warrior*, constructed; completion of telegraph line across U.S.A., leading to the end of the Pony Express; Mrs Beeton: *The Book of Household Management* (serialised 1859–61).

PROSE
Arnold: *On Translating Homer*; *The Popular Education of France, with Notices of That of Holland and Switzerland*
Dickens: *Great Expectations* (serialised in *All the Year Round* 1860–1)
'George Eliot': *Silas Marner*
Kingsley, Henry: *Ravenshoe*
Macaulay (*d.*1859): *The History of England* (vol. v, *see* 1849)
Meredith: *Evan Harrington*
Mill: *Considerations on Representative Government*
Peacock: *Gryll Grange* (serialised in *Fraser's Magazine* 1860)
Reade: *The Cloister and the Hearth: A Tale of the Middle Ages*
Spencer: *Education*
Thackeray: *The Four Georges*; *Lovel the Widower* (both serialised in *The Cornhill Magazine* 1860)
Trollope: *Framley Parsonage*
Wood: *East Lynne*

POETRY
Palgrave (ed.): *The Golden Treasury* (anthology)
Rossetti, D.G.: *Early Italian Poets* (transl.)

1862

Bismarck becomes Prussian premier (–1890); Confederate battle-ship *Alabama* leaves Merseyside shipbuilders, arousing indignation in the Northern States at this breach of neutrality; Gatling patents machine gun.

PROSE
Arnold: *On Translating Homer: Last Words*
Borrow: *Wild Wales*
Collins: *No Name*
(Hugo: *Les Misérables*)
Lytton: *A Strange Story*
Ruskin: 'Unto this Last' (in *The Cornhill Magazine*)
Swinburne: 'Dead Love' (in *Once a Week*)
Thackeray: *The Adventures of Philip* (serialised in *The Cornhill Magazine* 1861–2)
Trollope: *Orley Farm* (serialised 1861–2)
(Turgenev: *Fathers and Sons*)
Wood: *The Channings*
POETRY
Austin: *Human Tragedy*

POETRY (*cont.*)
Barnes: *Poems of Rural Life in the Dorset Dialect: Third Collection* (*see* 1844)
Browning, E.B. (*d.*1861): *Last Poems*
Calverley: *Verses and Translations*
Clough (*d.*1861): *Collected Poems*
Meredith: *Modern Love*; *Poems of the English Roadside*
Patmore: *The Victories of Love* (pt iv of *The Angel in the House*, *see* 1854)
Rossetti, Christina: *Goblin Market, and Other Poems*

1863

Abolition of slavery proclaimed in U.S.A.; Lincoln's Gettysburg Address; construction of the London Underground begins, the first such railway in the world; Broadmoor, institution for the criminally insane, opens; creation of Football Association to formulate rules for Association football; invention of first practical roller-skates leads to skating craze in Europe and U.S.A.; Speke: *Journal of the Discovery of the Source of the Nile*; Manet: *Déjeuner sur l'herbe* (*p.*).

PROSE
'George Eliot': *Romola* (serialised in *The Cornhill Magazine* 1862–3)
Gaskell: *A Dark Night's Work*; *Sylvia's Lovers*
Gilchrist (*d.*1861): *Life of W. Blake, 'Pictor Ignotus', with Selections from His Poems and Other Writing*
Kinglake: *The History of the Crimean War* (compl. in 8 vols by 1887)
Kingsley, Charles: *The Water Babies*
Le Fanu: *The House by the Churchyard*
Mill: *Utilitarianism* (serialised in *Fraser's Magazine* 1861)
Oliphant: *The Rector and The Doctor's Family* (pts i and ii of *The Chronicles of Carlingford*); *Salem Chapel*

PROSE (*cont.*)
Reade: *Hard Cash*
Smith, Alexander: *Dreamthorp*
Thackeray (*d.*1863): *Roundabout Papers* (serialised in *The Cornhill Magazine* 1860–3)
POETRY
Ingelow: *Poems* (first series, second series 1876, third series 1885)
Landor: *Heroic Idylls*

1864

Austria and Germany defeat Denmark, following dispute over control of Schleswig-Holstein; Trade Union Congress founded in England; 'First International' of the Working Men's Association; foundation of the International Red Cross by Dunant, Swiss philanthropist.

PROSE
Gaskell: *Cousin Phillis, and Other Tales* (serialised 1863–4)
Kingsley, Charles: *What Then Does Dr Newman Mean?*
Le Fanu: *Uncle Silas*
Meredith: *Emilia in England* (later called *Sandra Belloni*)
Newman: *Apologia Pro Vita Sua*
Trollope: *Can You Forgive Her?* (serialised 1864–5); *The Small House at Allington*

DRAMA
Boucicault: *Arrah-na-Pogue*
Robertson: *David Garrick*

POETRY
Browning, R.: *Dramatis Personae*
Praed (*d.*1839): *Poetical Works*
Tennyson: *Idylls of the Hearth* (later called *Enoch Arden*)

1865

Surrender of Confederates under General Lee leads to end of the American Civil War (*see* 1861); assassination of Abraham Lincoln; death of Palmerston; Mendel defines laws of heredity that form the basis of modern genetics; Metropolitan Fire Service established; Locomotives on Highways Act, known as the Red Flag Act, restricts vehicles to four miles per hour on the open road; first concrete road in Britain; overarm bowling permitted in cricket; Scott designs station and hotel of St Pancras Station, London, in Gothic revival style.

PROSE
Arnold: *Essays in Criticism* (first series, second series 1888)
'Lewis Carroll': *Alice's Adventures in Wonderland*
Clough (*d.*1861): *Letters and Remains*
Dickens: *Our Mutual Friend* (serialised 1864–5)
Gaskell (*d.*1865): *The Grey Woman, and Other Tales* (publ. intermittently 1861–5)
Kingsley, Henry: *The Hillyars and Burtons*
Meredith: *Rhoda Fleming*
'Ouida': *Strathmore*
Ruskin: *Sesame and Lilies*

DRAMA
Robertson: *Society*

POETRY
Newman: 'The Dream of Gerontius' (in *The Month*, publ. as separate vol. 1866)
Swinburne: *Atalanta in Calydon*

POETRY (*cont.*)
Tennyson: *A Selection from the Works*
Whitman: *Drum-Taps*; *Sequel to Drum-Taps* (compl. 1866)

1866 War between Austria and Prussia: Austria defeated at Sadowa; Russell ministry resigns after defeat of Reform Bill; Derby forms Conservative ministry with Disraeli as leader of the House of Commons (–1868); Fenian conspiracy to make Ireland a republic leads to suspension of Habeas Corpus and arrests; Ku Klux Klan founded in southern states of U.S.A. (dissolved officially 1871); Siemens produces the dynamo; development of the Winchester repeating rifle and the self-propelling torpedo.

PROSE
Blackmore: *Cradock Nowell*
Carlyle: *On the Choice of Books*
Collins: *Armadale*
Dallas: *The Gay Science*
(Dostoevsky: *Crime and Punishment*)
'George Eliot': *Felix Holt*
Gaskell (*d.*1865): *Wives and Daughters*
Kingsley, Charles: *Hereward the Wake*
Macaulay (*d.*1859): *Collected Works*
'Ouida': *Chandos*
Reade: *Griffith Gaunt*
Ruskin: *The Crown of Wild Olive*; *Ethics of the Dust*
Swinburne: *Notes on Poems and Reviews*

PROSE (*cont.*)
Trollope: *The Belton Estate*
Yonge: *The Dove in the Eagle's Nest*
DRAMA
Robertson: *Ours*
POETRY
Lytton: *The Lost Tales of Miletus*
Rossetti, Christina: *The Prince's Progress, and Other Poems*
Swinburne: *Poems and Ballads* (first series, second series 1878, third series 1889)
(Verlaine: *Poèmes saturniens*)
Whittier: *The Works of John Greenleaf Whittier*

1867 The Second Reform Bill, brought by Disraeli, passed by Parliament, adding nearly a million to the electorate and giving a share of political power to the working classes; Fenian rising in Ireland; U.S.A. buys Alaska from Russia; Lister's use of carbolic antiseptic reduces risk of infection in surgery; Nobel patents dynamite; Bagehot: *The English Constitution*; Marx: *Das Kapital* (compl. in 3 vols by 1894); Strauss: *The Blue Danube* (waltz).

PROSE
Arnold: *On the Study of Celtic Literature*
Carlyle: 'Shooting Niagara' (in *Macmillan's Magazine*)
Keble (*d.*1866): *Sermons, Occasional and Parochial*
Meredith: *Vittoria*
'Ouida': *Under Two Flags*
Pater: 'Essay on Winckelmann' (in *Westminster Review*)
Ruskin: *Time and Tide*
Thackeray (*d.*1863): *Denis Duval* (serialised in *The Cornhill Magazine* 1864)
(Tolstoy: *War and Peace*, compl. in 6 vols by 1869)
Trollope: *The Claverings*; *The Last Chronicle of Barset* (serialised 1866–7); *Nina Balatka*

DRAMA
Robertson: *Caste*
POETRY
Arnold: *New Poems*
Gordon: *Sea Spray and Smoke Drift*
Ingelow: *A Story of Doom*
Morris: *The Life and Death of Jason*
Swinburne: *A Song of Italy*

1868

Gladstone becomes Liberal P.M. (–1874); abolition of compulsory church rates in England and Wales; first regular Trade Union Congress, in Manchester; Brahms: *German Requiem*.

PROSE
Alcott: *Little Women*
Collins: *The Moonstone*
Newman: *Collected Works*
Swinburne: *William Blake*
Queen Victoria: *Leaves from a Journal of Our Life in the Highlands*

POETRY
Browning, R.: *The Ring and the Book*
'George Eliot': *The Spanish Gypsy*
Morris: *The Earthly Paradise* (compl. in 3 vols by 1870)
Swinburne: *Siena*

1869

Anglican Church disestablished in Ireland; abolition of imprisonment for debt; Suez Canal opened (*see* 1859); first transcontinental American railway completed; *Cutty Sark* launched.

PROSE
Arnold: *Culture and Anarchy*
Blackmore: *Lorna Doone*
(Flaubert: *Sentimental Education*)
Guiccioli: *Recollections of Lord Byron*
Mill: *On the Subjection of Women*
Robinson (*d*.1867): *Diary*
Ruskin: *The Queen of the Air*
Thackeray (*d*.1863): *Works* (compl. in 24 vols by 1886)

PROSE (*cont*.)
Trollope: *He Knew He Was Right*; *Phineas Finn* (serialised 1867–9)
DRAMA
Robertson: *School*
POETRY
Arnold: *Collected Poems* (*see* 1877)
'George Eliot': *Agatha: A Poem*
Gilbert: *The 'Bab' Ballads*
Tennyson: *The Holy Grail, and Other Poems*

1870

Outbreak of the Franco-Prussian War (–1871); Third Republic proclaimed in Paris after defeat of Napoleon III at Sedan; siege of Paris; Gladstone's first Irish Land Act passed, seeking to regularise relationships between landlords and tenants; Forster's Elementary Education Act sets up school boards; first Married Women's Property Act gives wives right to keep their earnings; Civil Service opened to competitive examination; Tramways Act leads to development of tram service throughout Britain; ferro-concrete building developed; diamond mining starts in South Africa; Brewer: *Dictionary of Phrase and Fable*.

PROSE
Collins: *Man and Wife*
Dickens (*d*.1870): 'The Mystery of Edwin Drood' (serialised, unfinished); *Speeches, Literary and Social*
Disraeli: *Lothair*
Huxley: *Sermons, Addresses and Reviews*
Newman: *An Essay in Aid of a Grammar of Assent*
Ruskin: *Lectures on Art*
(Verne: *Twenty Thousand Leagues under the Sea*)

DRAMA
Gilbert: *The Princess*
Reade: *Free Labour*
POETRY
Gordon (*d*.1870): *Bush Ballads and Galloping Rhymes*
Rossetti, D.G.: *Poems*
Swinburne: *Ode on the Proclamation of a French Republic*

1871 Prussia victorious over France; Paris Commune suppressed; in Britain, Trade Union Act gives unions legal status, but Criminal Law Amendment Act makes picketing illegal; bill passed abolishing religious tests at Oxford and Cambridge Universities, allowing attendance by non-Anglicans; Stanley and Livingstone meet in East Africa; Whymper: *Scrambles amongst the Alps*; Darwin: *The Descent of Man*; Verdi's opera *Aida* performed in Cairo; Buchanan makes pseudonymous attack on Pre-Raphaelite poets in 'The Fleshly School of Poetry' (*Contemporary Review*, October); D.G. Rossetti replies in 'The Stealthy School of Criticism' (*Athenaeum*, December).

PROSE
Ainsworth: *The South-Sea Bubble* (serialised 1868)
Arnold: *Friendship's Garland*
'Lewis Carroll': *Through the Looking Glass*
'George Eliot': *Middlemarch* (compl. in 4 vols by 1872)
Hardy: *Desperate Remedies*
Kingsley, Charles: *At Last*
Lytton: *The Coming Race*
MacDonald: *At the Back of the North Wind*
Meredith: *The Adventures of Harry Richmond*
Reade: *A Terrible Temptation*
Ruskin: *Fors Clavigera: Letters to the Workmen and Labourers of Great Britain* (compl. in 9 vols by 1887)
Whitman: *Democratic Vistas*
DRAMA
Gilbert: *Pygmalion and Galatea*
Lewis: *The Bells*

POETRY
Browning, R.: *Balaustion's Adventure*; *Prince Hohenstiel-Schwangau*
Lear: *Nonsense Songs and Stories*
Swinburne: *Songs before Sunrise*
Whitman: *Passage to India*

1872 Ballot Act secures secret voting; National Agricultural Labourers' Union founded; Eastlake: *A History of the Gothic Revival*; Monet: *Impression, Sunrise* (p., gives rise to the derisive term 'impressionism').

PROSE
Blackmore: *The Maid of Sker*
Butler: *Erewhon*
Hardy: *Under the Greenwood Tree*
MacDonald: *The Princess and the Goblin*
(Nietzsche: *The Birth of Tragedy*)
Reade, William: *The Martyrdom of Man*
Ruskin: *The Eagle's Nest*; *Munera Pulveris*
POETRY
Browning, R.: *Fifine at the Fair*
Calverley: *Fly Leaves*

POETRY (*cont.*)
Lang: *Ballads and Lyrics of Old France*
Lear: *More Nonsense Songs*
Morris: *Love Is Enough: A Morality*
Tennyson: *Gareth and Lynette*

1873

Agricultural and financial depression starts throughout Britain; war waged against the Ashanti, leading in 1874 to enlargement of the Gold Coast Colony; first commercially successful typewriter designed, in U.S.A.; invention of barbed wire, in U.S.A.

PROSE
Arnold: *Literature and Dogma*
Butler: *The Fair Haven*
Collins: *The New Magdalen*
Hardy: *A Pair of Blue Eyes*
(serialised 1872–3)
Lytton (*d.*1873): *Kenelm Chillingly*;
The Parisians
Mill (*d.*1873): *Autobiography*
Pater: *Studies in the Renaissance*
Spencer: *The Study of Sociology*

PROSE (*cont.*)
Trollope: *The Eustace Diamonds*
(serialised 1871–3)
Yonge: *The Pillars of the House*
POETRY
Bridges: *Poems* (first series, second series 1879, third series 1880)
Browning, R.: *Red Cotton Night-Cap Country*
Dobson: *Vignettes in Rhyme*

1874

Disraeli becomes Conservative P.M. (–1880); Building Societies Act encourages home ownership; lawn tennis invented (originally called *Sphairistike*); first Impressionist Exhibition, in Paris (seven more –1886); Bruckner: Symphony No.4 (*Romantic*, first version).

PROSE
Clarke: *For the Term of His Natural Life*
Hardy: *Far from the Madding Crowd*
'Ouida': *Two Little Wooden Shoes*
Ruskin: *Val d'Arno*
Stephen: *Hours in a Library* (all 3 series by 1879)
Trollope: *Phineas Redux* (serialised 1873–4)

PROSE (*cont.*)
Wordsworth, Dorothy (*d.*1855):
Recollections of a Tour Made in Scotland
POETRY
'George Eliot': *The Legend of Jubal*
Thomson: 'The City of Dreadful Night' (in *The National Reformer*)

1875

Social reforms of Disraeli's administration include Public Health Act (creating a Sanitary Authority in every area), Artisans' Dwelling Act (aiming to improve housing) and Sale of Food and Drugs Act (against adulteration); Disraeli buys Britain shares in the Suez Canal; completion of London's main drainage system; Mary Baker Eddy (founder of Christian Science): *Science and Health*; Bizet: *Carmen* (opera).

PROSE
Arnold: *God and the Bible*
Peacock (*d.*1866): *Works*
Ruskin: *Deucalion* (compl. in 8 pts by 1884); *Mornings in Florence* (compl. in 6 pts by 1877); *Proserpina* (compl. in 10 pts by 1886)
Swinburne: *Essays and Studies*
Symonds: *The Renaissance in Italy*
Trollope: *The Way We Live Now* (serialised 1874–5)

POETRY
Browning, R.: *Aristophanes' Apology*; *The Inn Album*
Dobell (*d.*1874): *Collected Poetical Works*
Meynell: *Preludes*
Morris: *The Aeneid of Virgil* (transl.); (with Magnusson): *Three Northern Love Stories from Iceland* (transl.)
Palgrave (ed.): *The Children's Treasury of English Song*
Swinburne: *Songs of Two Nations*
Tennyson: *The Lover's Tale*

1876

Merchant Shipping Act adopts Plimsoll's load-line for ships; in U.S.A., the battle of Little Big Horn, 'Custer's Last Stand' against the Sioux; death of Truganini, known as the last Tasmanian aborigine; Bell invents the modern telephone; Bissel invents the carpet sweeper; Lawson invents the 'Safety' bicycle (driven by chain to rear wheel, unlike the Ordinary or 'penny-farthing'); invention of the ammonium refrigerator; Otto invents four-stroke gas engine; first complete performance of Wagner's opera *Der Ring des Nibelungen* at Bayreuth.

PROSE
Besant and Rice: *The Golden Butterfly*
Bradley, F.H.: *Ethical Studies*
'George Eliot': *Daniel Deronda*
Hardy: *The Hand of Ethelberta* (serialised 1875–6)
James: *Roderick Hudson*
Meredith: *Beauchamp's Career*
Spencer: *The Principles of Sociology* (compl. in 3 vols by 1896)
Thackeray (*d*.1863): *The Orphan of Pimlico*
Trollope: *The Prime Minister* (serialised 1875–6)
'Mark Twain': *The Adventures of Tom Sawyer*
Wordsworth (*d*.1850): *Prose Works* (first collected edn)

DRAMA
Gilbert: *Original Plays* (publ., compl. in 4 series by 1911)
(Ibsen: *Peer Gynt*, with music by Grieg)
Tennyson: *Queen Mary*

POETRY
Bridges: *The Growth of Love*
Browning, R.: *Pacchiarotto, with Other Poems*
'Lewis Carroll': *The Hunting of the Snark*
Ingelow: *Poems: Second Series* (*see* 1863)
Morris: *The Story of Sigurd the Volsung and the Fall of the Niblungs*
Swinburne: *Erechtheus: A Tragedy*

1877

Queen Victoria assumes title of Empress of India; Edison invents the phonograph; frozen meat first exported from Argentina to Europe; first Wimbledon tennis championship; William Morris founds the Society for the Protection of Ancient Buildings from Injudicious Restoration.

PROSE
Arnold: *Last Essays on Church and Religion*
Butler: *Life and Habit*
James: *The American*
Mallock: *The New Republic*
Martineau (*d*.1876): *Autobiography*
Meredith: 'The Idea of Comedy' (in *New Quarterly Magazine*)
Sewell: *Black Beauty*
Swinburne: *Charlotte Brontë*
Trollope: *The American Senator* (serialised 1876–7)

POETRY
Arnold: *Collected Poems* (revised edn, *see* 1869)
Browning, R.: *The Agamemnon of Aeschylus* (transl.)
Dobson: *Proverbs in Porcelain*
Patmore: *The Unknown Eros, and Other Poems*

1878

European powers meet at the Congress of Berlin to discuss the Eastern Question, caused by weakness of Turkey and ambitions of her neighbours, and agree on division of Balkan states; Criminal Investigation Department set up in London (Special Branch, against terrorism, 1883); Cyclists' Touring Club started; Renoir: *Madame Charpentier and Her Children* (*p.*); Whistler wins a farthing damages for Ruskin's criticism of the painting *Nocturne in Black and Gold*; Grove: *Dictionary of Music and Musicians* (compl. in 4 vols by 1889).

PROSE
Besant and Rice: *By Celia's Arbour*; *The Monks of Thelema*
Hardy: *The Return of the Native*
James: *Watch and Ward*
Jefferies: *The Gamekeeper at Home*
Keats (*d.*1821): *Letters to Fanny Brawne* (ed. Forman)
Stanley: *Through the Dark Continent*
Stevenson: *An Inland Voyage*
(Tolstoy: *Anna Karenina*)
Trelawny: *Records of Shelley, Byron and the Author*
Trollope: *Is He Popenjoy?* (serialised 1877–8)

POETRY
Swinburne: *Poems and Ballads* (second series, *see* 1866)

1879

Gladstone, campaigning to be M.P. for Midlothian, denounces the imperialism and domestic record of the Conservative government; British defeat Zulus under Cetewayo and occupy Zululand; massacre of British legation at Kabul by Afghan troops; Parnell becomes leader of Irish Nationalist M.P.s; Edison produces incandescent electric light; electric tram demonstrated in Berlin; Tay Bridge collapses; Degas: *Miss Lala at the Cirque Fernando* (*p.*); Gilbert and Sullivan: *The Pirates of Penzance* (operetta).

PROSE
Arnold: *Mixed Essays*
Butler: *Evolution, Old and New*
'George Eliot': *Theophrastus Such*
Howells: *The Lady of the Aroostook*
James: *Daisy Miller*; *The Europeans*; *The Madonna of the Future*
Meredith: *The Egoist*
Spencer: *The Data of Ethics* (pt i of *The Principles of Ethics*, compl. in 2 pts by 1893)
Stevenson: *Travels with a Donkey in the Cevennes*
Trollope: *Thackeray*
DRAMA
(Ibsen: *A Doll's House*)
Tennyson: *The Falcon*

POETRY
Bridges: *Poems: Second Series* (*see* 1873)
Browning, R.: *Dramatic Idyls* (first series, second series 1880)

1880

Gladstone P.M. for second time (–1885); civil disturbances in Ireland over evictions; Bradlaugh, atheist M.P., not allowed into the House of Commons for refusal to take oath; frozen mutton arrives in Britain from Australia.

PROSE
Butler: *Unconscious Memory*
Dickens (*d.*1870): *Letters* (compl. in 3 vols by 1882)
Disraeli: *Endymion*
(Dostoevsky: *The Brothers Karamazov*)
Gissing: *The Workers in the Dawn*
Hardy: *The Trumpet-Major*
(Maupassant: *Boule de suif*)
Meredith: *The Tragic Comedians*
'Ouida': *Moths*
Ruskin: *Arrows of the Chace*; *Elements of English Prosody*
Shorthouse: *John Inglesant*
Trollope: *The Duke's Children* (serialised 1879–80)

POETRY
Blunt: *Love Sonnets of Proteus*
Bridges: *Poems, Third Series* (*see* 1873)
Browning, R.: *Dramatic Idyls* (second series, *see* 1879)

POETRY (*cont.*)
Lang: *Twenty-Two Ballades in Blue China*
Swinburne: *Songs of the Springtides*; *Studies in Song*
Tennyson: *Ballads, and Other Poems*
Thomson: *The City of Dreadful Night, with Other Poems*

1881

Gladstone passes second Irish Land Act to regularise rents; flogging abolished in the army (abolished in the navy 1879); Natural History Museum opens in Kensington; Pasteur successfully inoculates sheep against anthrax; Panama Canal begun (formally opened 1914).

PROSE
Revised Version of the New Testament (Old Testament 1885)
Besant and Rice: *The Chaplain of the Fleet*
Butler: *Alps and Sanctuaries of Piedmont and the Canton Ticino*
Carlyle (*d.*1881): *Reminiscences*
Hardy: *A Laodicean* (serialised 1880–1)
James: *The Portrait of a Lady*; *Washington Square*
'Mark Rutherford': *The Autobiography of Mark Rutherford*
Stevenson: *Virginibus Puerisque*
Trollope: *Ayala's Angel*; *Dr Wortle's School* (serialised 1880)

DRAMA
Tennyson: *The Cup*

POETRY
Lang: *Thirty-Two Ballades in Blue China*
Rossetti, Christina: *A Pageant, and Other Poems*
Rossetti, D.G.: *Ballads and Sonnets*
Wilde: *Poems*

1882 Irish Secretary and Under-Secretary murdered in Phoenix Park, Dublin, leading to repressive Prevention of Crimes Bill; British defeat Egyptians at Tel-el-Kebir, following Egyptian Nationalist resistance to British and French involvement in Egypt; Britain occupies Egypt and the Sudan; second Married Women's Property Act (*see* 1870); Breuer develops treatment of hysteria by hypnosis, leading to psychoanalysis; electric train in use at Leytonstone in east London; Manet: *The Bar at the Folies-Bergère* (*p.*); Wagner: *Parsifal* (opera).

PROSE
'F. Anstey': *Vice Versa*
Arnold: *Irish Essays and Others*
Besant: *All Sorts and Conditions of Men*
Carlyle (*d.*1881): *The Last Words of Carlyle*; *Reminiscences of My Irish Journey in 1849*
Hardy: *Two on a Tower*
Jefferies: *Bevis, the Story of a Boy*
Morris: *Hopes and Fears for Art*
'Ouida': *In Maremma*
Shaw: *Cashel Byron's Profession*
Stevenson: *Familiar Studies of Men and Books*; *New Arabian Nights*

DRAMA
Dickens (*d.*1870): *Plays and Poems* (publ.)
Henley and Stevenson: *Deacon Brodie*
Jones, H.A.: *The Silver King*

POETRY
Child (ed.): *The English and the Scottish Popular Ballads* (compl. in 5 vols by 1898)
Lang: *Helen of Troy*
Swinburne: *Tristram of Lyonesse, and Other Poems*

1883 Irish terrorist bombings in London; completion of the Brooklyn Bridge in New York; explosion of Krakatoa, causing devastating tidal wave around Java; establishment of the Boys' Brigade, in Glasgow.

PROSE
Carlyle, Jane (*d.*1866): *Letters and Memorials*
Jefferies: *The Story of My Heart*
MacDonald: *The Princess and Curdie*
(Nietzsche: *Thus Spoke Zarathustra*, compl. in 4 pts by 1892)
Schreiner: *The Story of an African Farm*
Shaw: *An Unsocial Socialist*
Stevenson: *Silverado Squatters*; *Treasure Island*
Trollope (*d.*1882): *An Autobiography*

DRAMA
Wilde: *Vera, or The Nihilists* (in New York)

POETRY
Bridges: *Prometheus the Firegiver*
Browning, R.: *Jocoseria*
Carpenter: *Towards Democracy* (all 4 pts by 1902)
'Lewis Carroll': *Rhyme? and Reason?*
Meredith: *Poems and Lyrics of the Joy of Earth*
Swinburne: *A Century of Roundels*

1884

Third Reform Act extends franchise to agricultural labourers; foundation of Socialist League by William Morris; foundation of Fabian Society; foundation of National Society for the Prevention of Cruelty to Children; steam turbine invented by Parsons; artificial silk patented; Burne-Jones: *King Cophetua and the Beggar-Maid* (*p.*); Seurat: *Bathers at Asnières* (*p.*); Brahms: Symphony No. 4; Murray (ed.): *A New English Dictionary on Historical Principles* (work begun 1878, compl. in 125 fascicules by 1928).

PROSE
Austen (*d.*1817): *Letters*
'George Eliot' (*d.*1880): *Essays, and Leaves from a Notebook*
Gissing: *The Unclassed*
James: *Tales of Three Cities*
Lang: *Custom and Myth*
Moore: *A Mummer's Wife*
Ruskin: *The Art of England*
Spencer: *Man Versus the State*
Thomson (*d.*1882): *Satires and Profanities*
'Mark Twain': *The Adventures of Huckleberry Finn*

POETRY
Browning, R.: *Ferishtah's Fancies*
De Vere: *Poetical Works*
Swinburne: *A Midsummer Holiday, and Other Poems*
Symonds: *Wine, Women and Song* (transl. from medieval Latin)
Thomson (*d.*1882): *A Voice from the Nile, and Other Poems*

1885

General Gordon killed by the Mahdi's forces, two days before British troops arrive to relieve the siege of Khartoum; Joseph Arch, an ex-farm labourer, becomes M.P. for Northampton; Burroughs invents his first adding machine (practical model 1892); Daimler develops lightweight petrol engine; Benz develops petrol-driven three-wheel vehicle; Rover Company markets safety bicycle with diamond-shaped frame; Pasteur uses inoculation to cure a child infected with rabies; first vol. of *Dictionary of National Biography* (ed. Stephen, first 21 vols by 1890).

PROSE
Arnold: *Discourses in America*
Burton: *Arabian Nights* (transl., compl. in 16 vols by 1888)
'George Eliot' (*d.*1880): *Life, As Related in Her Letters and Journals*
Haggard: *King Solomon's Mines*
Howells: *The Rise of Silas Lapham*
Hudson: *The Purple Land*
Meredith: *Diana of the Crossways*
Pater: *Marius the Epicurean*
Ruskin: *On the Old Road*; *Praeterita* (compl. in 3 vols by 1888)
'Mark Rutherford': *Mark Rutherford's Deliverance*
Stevenson: *More New Arabian Nights: The Dynamiter*
(Zola: *Germinal*)
DRAMA
Pinero: *The Magistrate*

DRAMA (*cont.*)
Swinburne: *Marino Faliero: A Tragedy* (publ.)
POETRY
Austin: *At the Gate of the Convent, and Other Poems*
Bridges: *Eros and Psyche*
Dobson: *At the Sign of the Lyre*
Ingelow: *Poems: Third Series* (*see* 1863)
Lang: *Rhymes à la Mode*
Morris: *Chants for Socialists*
Stevenson: *A Child's Garden of Verses*
Tennyson: *Tiresias, and Other Poems*

1886

Gladstone prepares Home Rule Bill for Ireland, but is defeated in Parliament and resigns; Irish tenants league together against landlords in the 'Plan of Campaign'; Daimler constructs a four-wheel car; aluminium electrolytically produced; invention of the mantel burner improves gas lighting; appendicitis identified; foundation of the New English Art Club to challenge conventionalism of the Royal Academy.

PROSE
Burnett: *Little Lord Fauntleroy*
Corelli: *A Romance of Two Worlds*
Gissing: *Demos*; *Isabel Clarendon*
Hardy: *The Mayor of Casterbridge*
James: *The Bostonians*; *The Princess Casamassima*
Stevenson: *Dr Jekyll and Mr Hyde*; *Kidnapped*
Symons: *Introduction to Browning*
DRAMA
Pinero: *The Schoolmistress*
POETRY
Kipling: *Departmental Ditties*
Morris: *The Pilgrims of Hope*

POETRY (*cont.*)
Rossetti, D.G. (*d.*1882): *Collected Works*
Tennyson: *Locksley Hall, Sixty Years After*

1887

Queen Victoria's Golden Jubilee; Parnell accused of complicity in the Phoenix Park Murders (*see* 1882); first Colonial Conference held in London; British East Africa Company chartered; incandescent electric light for domestic use developed; Cézanne: *Mont Sainte-Victoire with Large Pine Trees* (*p.*).

PROSE
Blackmore: *Springhaven*
Butler: *Luck or Cunning*
Doyle: *A Study in Scarlet*
Gissing: *Thyrza*
Haggard: *Allan Quartermain*; *She*
Hardy: *The Woodlanders* (serialised 1886–7)
Jefferies (*d.*1887): *Amaryllis at the Fair*
Lang: *Myth, Ritual and Religion*
Pater: *Imaginary Portraits*
'Mark Rutherford': *The Revolution in Tanner's Lane*
Saintsbury: *Elizabethan Literature*
Stevenson: *Memories and Portraits*; *The Merry Men, and Other Tales*
(Zola: *La Terre*)
DRAMA
Pinero: *Dandy Dick*
(Strindberg: *The Father*)
POETRY
Browning, R.: *Parleyings with Certain People*
(Mallarmé: *Poésies*)

POETRY (*cont.*)
Meredith: *Ballads and Poems of Tragic Life*
Morris: *The Odyssey* (transl. of Homer)
Swinburne: *The Question*

1888

Local Government Act establishes county councils; murder of six women in London by 'Jack the Ripper'; development of Dunlop's pneumatic tyre; Satie: *Gymnopédies* (piano music); Van Gogh: *Sunflowers* (*p.*, several versions).

PROSE

Arnold (*d.*1888): *Essays in Criticism* (second series, *see* 1865)
Bellamy: *Looking Backward: 2000–1887*
'Rolf Boldrewood': *Robbery Under Arms*
Butler: *Ex Voto*
Doughty: *Travels in Arabia Deserta*
Garnett: *Twilight of the Gods, and Other Tales*
Gissing: *A Life's Morning*
Hardy: *Wessex Tales* (publ. intermittently 1879–88)
James: *The Aspern Papers*; *Partial Portraits*; *The Reverberator*
Kipling: *Plain Tales from the Hills*; *Soldiers Three*
Moore: *Confessions of a Young Man*
Morris: *A Dream of John Ball, and A King's Lesson*; *Signs of Change*

PROSE (*cont.*)

Stevenson: *The Black Arrow*; *The Wrong Box*
Ward: *Robert Elsmere*
Wilde: *The Happy Prince, and Other Tales*
Yeats: *Fairy and Folk Tales of the Irish Peasantry*

POETRY

Henley: *A Book of Verses*
Meredith: *A Reading of Earth*
Wordsworth (*d.*1850): *The Recluse*

1889

Strikes in the London Docks; Eastman manufactures Kodak camera using roll film; Eiffel Tower constructed; Panhard and Levassor begin French car industry using Daimler engines; National Telephone Company established; Charles Booth: *Life and Labour of the People of London* (final edn compl. in 17 vols by 1903, defines poverty line).

PROSE

Barrie: *A Window in Thrums*
Burney (*d.*1840): *Early Diary, 1768–78, with Letters*
Carpenter: *Civilisation, Its Cause and Cure*
Doyle: *The Sign of Four*
Gissing: *The Nether World*
Jerome: *Three Men in a Boat*
Kipling: *From Sea to Sea*
Meredith: *Sandra Belloni* (*see* 1864)
Morris: *The House of the Wolfings* (incl. verse)
Pater: *Appreciations*
Shaw (with others): *Fabian Essays in Socialism*
Stevenson: *The Master of Ballantrae*

DRAMA

Davidson: *A Romantic Farce*; *Scaramouch in Naxos*; *An Unhistorical Pastoral* (all publ.)

POETRY

Browning, E.B. (*d.*1861): *Poetical Works* (ed. R. Browning, compl. in 6 vols by 1890)
Browning, R. (*d.*1889): *Asolando*
Lear (*d.*1888): *Nonsense Drolleries*
Swinburne: *Poems and Ballads* (third series, *see* 1866)
Tennyson: *Demeter, and Other Poems*
Yeats: *Crossways*; *The Wanderings of Oisin, and Other Poems*

1890

Parnell found innocent of complicity in the Phoenix Park Murders (*see* 1882) but is cited as co-respondent in a divorce case; the scandal causes the Irish Nationalist Party to reject him as leader; Britain, France, Belgium, Germany and Portugal draw up treaties defining their territorial claims in East and West Africa; Rhodes becomes P.M. of Cape Colony (–1896); Wilhelm II, Emperor of Germany, quarrels with and dismisses Bismarck; Deptford Power Station built to supply London's electricity; completion of the Forth Railway Bridge; first entirely steel-framed building, in Chicago; Stanley: *In Darkest Africa*; General William Booth (of Salvation Army): *In Darkest England* (study of poverty).

PROSE
Barrie: *My Lady Nicotine*
Frazer: *The Golden Bough* (third, complete edn in 12 vols by 1915)
Gissing: *The Emancipated*
James, Henry: *The Tragic Muse*
James, William: *Principles of Psychology*
Kipling: *The Light That Failed*
Morris: 'News from Nowhere' (in *The Commonweal*, publ. separately 1891); *The Roots of the Mountains*

DRAMA
Gilbert: *Original Comic Operas* (publ.)
(Ibsen: *Hedda Gabler*)

POETRY
Bridges: *Shorter Poems*
Dickinson (*d.*1886): *Poems*
Gilbert: *Songs of a Savoyard*
Stevenson: *Ballads*
Watson: *Wordsworth's Grave, and Other Poems*

1891

Assisted Education Act makes elementary education free in England; London–Paris telephone line opened; Trans-Siberian railway started (compl. 1904).

PROSE
Barrie: *The Little Minister*
Gissing: *New Grub Street*
Hardy: *A Group of Noble Dames*; *Tess of the d'Urbervilles*
Kipling: *Life's Handicap*
Meredith: *One of Our Conquerors*
Moore: *Impressions and Opinions*
Morris: *The Story of the Glittering Plain*
Schreiner: *Dreams*
Shaw: *The Quintessence of Ibsenism*
Wilde: *A House of Pomegranates*; *Intentions*; *Lord Arthur Savile's Crime, and Other Stories*; *The Picture of Dorian Gray*

DRAMA
(Ibsen: *Ghosts,* first performance in Britain)
James: *The American*
Wilde: *The Duchess of Padua* (in New York)

POETRY
Davidson: *In a Music Hall, and Other Poems*
Morris: *Poems by the Way*

1892

Gladstone returned to office as P.M. (–1894); James Keir Hardie elected Independent Socialist M.P. for West Ham South; Blackwall Tunnel under the Thames started (compl. 1897); severe famine in Russia.

PROSE

Doyle: *The Adventures of Sherlock Holmes*
Du Maurier: *Peter Ibbetson*
Gissing: *Born in Exile*; *Denzil Quarrier*
Grossmith, George and Weedon: *The Diary of a Nobody* (serialised in *Punch* 1888–9)
Henley: *Views and Reviews: Art*
Hudson: *A Naturalist in La Plata*
James: *The Lesson of the Master*
Stevenson: *Across the Plains*; *A Footnote to History*; *The Wrecker*
Zangwill: *Children of the Ghetto*

DRAMA

Shaw: *Widowers' Houses*
Swinburne: *The Sisters: A Tragedy* (publ.)
Tennyson (*d*.1892): *The Foresters* (publ.)
Wilde: *Lady Windermere's Fan*; *Salome* (rehearsed but banned; performed 1896)
Yeats: *The Countess Kathleen* (publ.)

POETRY

Henley: *Lyra Heroica*; *The Song of the Sword, and Other Verse*
Kipling: *Barrack-Room Ballads*
Tennyson (*d*.1892): *The Death of Oenone, Akbar's Dream, and Other Poems*
Watson: *Lachrymae Musarum*

1893

Gladstone's second Irish Home Rule Bill rejected by the Lords; Keir Hardie founds the Independent Labour Party; Lilienthal's first glider flight; Munch: *The Cry* (*p.*); Beardsley's drawings appear in first edn of *The Studio*; Dvořák: Symphony No.9 (*From the New World*); Tchaikovsky: Symphony No.6 (*Pathétique*).

PROSE

Benson: *Dodo*
Bradley, F.H.: *Appearance and Reality*
Corelli: *Barabbas*
Doyle: *The Memoirs of Sherlock Holmes*
Gissing: *The Odd Women*
Hudson: *Idle Days in Patagonia*
James: *The Private Life*
Kipling: *Many Inventions*
Pater: *Plato and Platonism*
Patmore: *Religio Poetae*
Stevenson: *Catriona*
Yeats: *The Celtic Twilight*

DRAMA

Pinero: *The Second Mrs Tanqueray*
Tennyson (*d*.1892): *Becket*

DRAMA (*cont.*)

Wilde: *A Woman of No Importance*

POETRY

Davidson: *Fleet Street Eclogues*
Meynell: *Poems*
Thompson: *Poems* (incl. 'The Hound of Heaven')

1894

Parish Councils Act completes long process of regularising local government; in France, the Dreyfus treason case excites controversy and anti-semitism; Manchester Ship Canal opens; Debussy: *Prélude à l'après-midi d'un faune* (orchestral music); Mahler: Symphony No.2 (*Resurrection*); *The Yellow Book* (illustrated magazine of 'decadent' artists and writers, –1897).

PROSE
Blackmore: *Perlycross*
Du Maurier: *Trilby*
Gissing: *In the Year of the Jubilee*
Hardy: *Life's Little Ironies*
'Anthony Hope': *The Prisoner of Zenda*
Kipling: *The Jungle Book*
Meredith: *Lord Ormont and His Aminta*
Moore: *Esther Waters*
Morris: *The Wood beyond the World*
Pater (*d.*1894): *The Child in the House*
Stevenson (*d.*1894): *Collected Works* (compl. in 28 vols by 1898); *The Ebb-Tide*

PROSE (*cont.*)
Swinburne: *Studies in Prose and Poetry*
DRAMA
Davidson: *Collected Plays* (publ.)
Jones, H.A.: *The Masqueraders*
Shaw: *Arms and the Man*
Yeats: *The Land of Heart's Desire*
POETRY
Davidson: *Ballads and Songs*
Watson: *Odes, and Other Poems*

1895

Factory and Workshops Act consolidates reforms of conditions and safety at work; Jameson Raid (–1896) on Transvaal in abortive attempt to overthrow Kruger; 50,000 Armenians massacred in Constantinople by Turks; Röntgen experiments with X-rays; Lumière brothers patent cinematograph; completion of the Kiel Canal; Oscar Wilde imprisoned for homosexual offences (–1897).

PROSE
Coleridge (*d.*1834): *Anima Poetae*; *Letters*
Conrad: *Almayer's Folly*
Corelli: *The Sorrows of Satan*
Crane: *The Red Badge of Courage*
Gissing: *Eve's Ransom*; *The Paying Guest*; *Sleeping Fires*
Hardy: *Jude the Obscure* (serialised 1894–5 in early form)
James: *Terminations*
Kipling: *The Second Jungle Book*
Meredith: *The Amazing Marriage*
Moore: *Celibates*
Morris: *Child Christopher and Goldilind the Fair*
Pater (*d.*1894): *Greek Studies*; *Miscellaneous Studies*
Patmore: *The Rod, the Root and the Flower*
Stevenson (*d.*1894): *The Body-Snatcher*; *Vailima Letters*
Wells: *The Time Machine*

DRAMA
Pinero: *The Notorious Mrs Ebbsmith*
Wilde: *An Ideal Husband*; *The Importance of Being Earnest*
POETRY
Johnson: *Poems*
Thompson, Francis: *Sister Songs*
Thomson, James (*d.*1882): *Poetical Works*
Yeats: *Poems*

1896

Conciliation Act sets up boards to settle industrial disputes if both sides agree; Marconi demonstrates wireless telegraphy on Salisbury Plain; Becquerel reports discovery of radio-activity; repeal of Locomotive Act increases maximum speed of powered vehicles to 14 miles per hour; discovery of gold in Bonanza Creek, Klondike, U.S.A.; Nobel prizes established; first modern Olympic Games held in Athens; Richard Strauss: *Also sprach Zarathustra* (symphonic poem); Morris prints the Kelmscott Press edn of the works of Chaucer.

PROSE
Barrie: *Margaret Ogilvie*; *Sentimental Tommy*
Beerbohm: *Works of Max Beerbohm*
Carpenter: *Love's Coming of Age*
Conrad: *An Outcast of the Islands*
Corelli: *The Mighty Atom*
Jacobs: *Many Cargoes*
James: *Embarrassments*; *The Other House*
Lawson: *While the Billy Boils*
Meynell: *The Colour of Life, and Other Essays*
Morris (*d.*1896): *The Well at the World's End*
Pater (*d.*1894): *Gaston de Latour*
Stevenson (*d.*1894): *Fables*; *The Strange Case of Dr Jekyll and Mr Hyde, with Other Fables*; *Weir of Hermiston*
Wells: *The Island of Dr Moreau*; *The Wheels of Chance*

DRAMA
Jones, H.A.: *Michael and His Lost Angel*
POETRY
Belloc: *A Bad Child's Book of Beasts*
Browning, R. (*d.*1889): *Collected Works*
Housman: *A Shropshire Lad*
Kipling: *The Seven Seas*
Paterson: *The Man from Snowy River*
Rossetti, Christina (*d.*1894): *Poems, Unpublished or Uncollected*
Stevenson (*d.*1894): *Songs of Travel*
Swinburne: *The Tale of Balen*

1897

Queen Victoria's Diamond Jubilee; Workmen's Compensation Act ensures workers compensation for injuries at work; malaria identified; research on cathode rays leads to identification of the electron; Diesel demonstrates his engine; Havelock Ellis: *Studies in the Psychology of Sex* (final edn in 8 vols 1905–28).

PROSE
Butler: *The Authoress of the Odyssey*
Conrad: *The Nigger of the Narcissus*
Du Maurier (*d.*1896): *The Martian*
Gissing: *The Whirlpool*
Hardy: *The Well-Beloved* (serialised 1892)
James: *The Spoils of Poynton*; *What Maisie Knew*
Kipling: *Captains Courageous*
Maugham: *Liza of Lambeth*
Meredith: *An Essay on Comedy*
Stoker: *Dracula*
Wells: *The Invisible Man*; *The Plattner Story*
Yeats: *The Secret Rose*

DRAMA
Jones, H.A.: *The Liars*
Shaw: *Candida*; *The Devil's Disciple*; *The Man of Destiny*
POETRY
Davidson: *New Ballads*
Meynell: *The Flower of the Mind*
Newbolt: *Admirals All, and Other Verses*
Thompson: *New Poems*
Watts-Dunton: *The Coming of Love, and Other Poems*

1898

Chinese government grants Britain 99-year lease of mainland Hong Kong; in the Sudan, France and Britain clash in the Fashoda Incident; British conquer the Sudan to protect interests in Egypt; Zola publishes open letter, entitled '*J'accuse*', in defence of Dreyfus (*see* 1894); electrification of the underground railway in London begins (*see* 1863); Rodin: *The Kiss* (sc.).

PROSE
Conrad: *Tales of Unrest*
Falkner: *Moonfleet*
Gissing: *Human Odds and Ends*; *The Town Traveller*
'Anthony Hope': *Rupert of Hentzau*
James: *In the Cage*; *The Two Magics: The Turn of the Screw, and Covering End*
Kipling: *The Day's Work*
Saintsbury: *A Short History of English Literature*
Shaw: *The Perfect Wagnerite* (revised edn 1907)
Wells: *The War of the Worlds*

DRAMA
Pinero: *Trelawny of the 'Wells'*
Shaw: *Plays Pleasant and Unpleasant* (publ., contains *Arms and the Man* (first performed 1894); *Candida* (1897); *The Man of Destiny* (1897); *Mrs Warren's Profession* (1902); *The Philanderer* (1905); *Widowers' Houses* (1892); *You Never Can Tell* (1899))

POETRY
Bridges: *Poetical Works* (compl. in 6 vols by 1905)
Hardy: *Wessex Poems, and Other Verses*
Newbolt: *The Island Race*
Phillips: *Poems*
Wilde: *The Ballad of Reading Gaol*

1899

British and Boers at war in South Africa (–1902); Court of Arbitration for international affairs set up at the Hague; in France, further controversy over Dreyfus (*see* 1894), who is found guilty again but pardoned; wireless telegraphy begins between England and France; Elgar: *Enigma Variations* (orchestral music); Schoenberg: *Verklärte Nacht* (music for string sextet); Sibelius: *Finlandia* (symphonic poem).

PROSE
Beerbohm: *More*
Browning, E.B. (*d.*1861) and R. (*d.*1889): *Letters*
Gissing: *The Crown of Life*
James: *The Awkward Age*
Kipling: *Stalky and Co.*
Meynell: *The Spirit of Place, and Other Essays*
Somerville and Ross: *Some Experiences of an Irish R.M.*
Watts-Dunton: *Aylwin*
Wells: *When the Sleeper Wakes*

POETRY
Davidson: *The Last Ballad, and Other Poems*
Henley: *Hawthorn and Lavender*
Watson: *Collected Poems*
Yeats: *The Wind among the Reeds*

1900 Labour Party initiated at the Labour Representation Committee; in South Africa, the relief of Mafeking (defended by Baden-Powell for 215 days); Britain annexes the Orange Free State and the Transvaal; Northern Nigeria becomes a British Protectorate; in China, the Boxer rebellion against foreigners suppressed by an international European army; first Zeppelin constructed; escalator exhibited at Paris Exposition; population of England and Wales: 33 million; Scotland: 4.5 million; Ireland: 4.5 million; Freud: *The Interpretation of Dreams*; Elgar: *The Dream of Gerontius* (oratorio); Puccini: *Tosca* (opera).

PROSE
Butler: *Odyssey* (transl. of Homer)
Conrad: *Lord Jim*
Corelli: *The Master Christian*
Dreiser: *Sister Carrie*
Saintsbury: *A History of Criticism*
  (compl. in 3 vols by 1904)
Wells: *Love and Mr Lewisham*
DRAMA
Jones, H.A.: *Mrs Dane's Defence*
Shaw: *Captain Brassbound's Conversion*

POETRY
Henley: *For England's Sake*
Lear (d.1888): *The Jumblies*

1901 Death of Queen Victoria; accession of Edward VII (–1910); Taff Vale judgement establishes principle that trade unions can be sued for damages (–1906); union anger helps consolidation of movement towards Labour Party; Theodore Roosevelt becomes President of U.S.A. (–1909) after assassination of McKinley; Commonwealth of Australia inaugurated; Marconi transmits morse signals across the Atlantic; first electric tram in London; British navy orders its first submarine from U.S.A.; Rowntree: *Poverty* (social survey).

PROSE
Belloc: *Robespierre*
Butler: *Erewhon Revisited*
Franklin: *My Brilliant Career*
Gissing: *By the Ionian Sea*
Jacobs: *Light Freights*
Kipling: *Kim*
Lawson: *Joe Wilson and His Mates*
(Mann: *Buddenbrooks*)
Moore: *Sister Teresa*
Wells: *The First Men in the Moon*
DRAMA
(Chekhov: *Three Sisters*)
Davidson: *Self's the Man* (publ.)
Phillips: *Herod*
Pinero: *Iris*
Shaw: *Three Plays for Puritans*
  (publ., contains *Captain Brassbound's Conversion* (first performed 1900); *Caesar and Cleopatra* (1907); *The Devil's Disciple* (1897))

POETRY
Hardy: *Poems of the Past and Present*
Meredith: *A Reading of Life*
Meynell: *Later Poems*
Newbolt: *The Sailing of the Long Ships*
Yeats: *Poems*

1902

Peace of Vereeniging ends the Boer War (*see* 1899); alliance between Britain and Japan; Education Act replaces school boards by local education authority and brings church schools into state system; Caruso makes his first gramophone record; Hobson: *Imperialism: A Study*.

PROSE
Baynton: *Bush Studies*
Bell: *Wee MacGreegor*
Belloc: *The Path to Rome*
Bennett: *Anna of the Five Towns*;
The Grand Babylon Hotel
Chesterton: *Robert Browning*
Conrad: *Youth: A Narrative, and
Two Other Stories* ('Heart of
Darkness' and 'The End of the
Tether')
Doyle: *The Hound of the Baskervilles*
Jacobs: *The Lady of the Barge*
James, Henry: *The Wings of the
Dove*
James, William: *The Varieties of
Religious Experience*
Kipling: *Just So Stories*
Nesbit: *Five Children and It*
Potter: *Peter Rabbit*
DRAMA
Barrie: *The Admirable Crichton*;
Quality Street

DRAMA (*cont.*)
Granville-Barker: *The Marrying of
Ann Leete*
Phillips: *Paulo and Francesca*
Yeats: *Cathleen Ni Houlihan*
POETRY
Masefield: *Salt-Water Ballads*

1903

Joseph Chamberlain resigns his Cabinet post to campaign against free trade and for customs reforms favouring British colonies; Women's Social and Political Union founded to demand votes for women; Irish Land Act facilitates land purchase by tenants; beginning of *Entente Cordiale* between France and Britain; Letchworth founded as first garden-city; in U.S.A., the Wright brothers fly a heavier than air biplane 852 feet, and Ford founds his motor company; speed limit on British roads increased to 20 miles per hour; Gillette manufactures safety razor; Bertrand Russell: *Principles of Mathematics*; Delius: *Sea Drift* (choral work).

PROSE
Butler (*d*.1902): *The Way of All
Flesh*
Childers: *The Riddle of the Sands*
'Tom Collins': *Such Is Life*
Conrad: *Typhoon*; (with F.M.
Hueffer): *Romance*
Gissing (*d*.1903): *The Private Papers
of Henry Ryecroft*
James: *The Ambassadors*
London: *The Call of the Wild*
Wells: *Mankind in the Making*
DRAMA
Synge: *In the Shadow of the Glen*

POETRY
Kipling: *The Five Nations*
Noyes: *The Flower of Old Japan*
Traherne (*d*.1674): *Poetical Works*
Watson: *For England: Poems Written
During Estrangement*

1904

Entente Cordiale (see 1903) strengthened by agreements between Britain and France on colonial interests; outbreak of Russo-Japanese War over rivalry in the Far East (–1905); Royce produces his first car (combines with Rolls 1906); C.R. Mackintosh designs The Willow Tea Rooms, Glasgow; (*c.*) Cézanne: *The Bathers* (*p.*, several with this title); Puccini: *Madame Butterfly* (opera); Abbey Theatre, Dublin, opens.

PROSE
Bradley, A.C.: *Shakespearean Tragedy*
Chesterton: *The Napoleon of Notting Hill*
Conrad: *Nostromo*
Hudson: *Green Mansions*
James, Henry: *The Golden Bowl*
James, M.R.: *Ghost Stories of an Antiquary*
Rolfe: *Hadrian the Seventh*
Wells: *The Food of the Gods*
DRAMA
Barrie: *Peter Pan*
(Chekhov (*d.*1904): *The Cherry Orchard*)
Hardy: *The Dynasts, Pt I* (publ.)
Shaw: *John Bull's Other Island*
Synge: *Riders to the Sea*
Yeats: *The Shadowy Waters*

POETRY
Bridges: *Demeter: A Mask*
Newbolt: *Songs of the Sea*
Swinburne: *A Channel Passage, and Other Poems*

1905

Royal Commission on the Poor Law (–1909); Sinn Fein party organised in Ireland; revolution in Russia following defeat by Japan and general strike; St Petersburg Soviet formed under Trotsky; Herbert Austin opens car factory; motorbuses first used in London; in Pittsburg, U.S.A., first purpose-built cinema; Matisse, and other artists exhibiting in Paris, called pejoratively '*les fauves*' ('the wild beasts'); start of Fauvism.

PROSE
Doyle: *The Return of Sherlock Holmes*
Forster: *Where Angels Fear to Tread*
Gissing (*d.*1903): *Will Warburton*
Kipling: *They*
London: *White Fang*
Masefield: *A Mainsail Haul*
Orczy: *The Scarlet Pimpernel*
Swinburne: *Love's Cross-Currents*
Wells: *Kipps*; *A Modern Utopia*
Wharton: *The House of Mirth*
Wilde (*d.*1900): *De Profundis* (compl. text 1949)
DRAMA
Granville-Barker: *The Voysey Inheritance*

DRAMA (*cont.*)
Shaw: *Major Barbara*; *Man and Superman*
Synge: *The Well of the Saints*
POETRY
Dowson (*d.*1900): *Poems*

1906

Liberals achieve big victory in General Election, and gain support of Irish Nationalists and Labour Party in the Commons; Trades Disputes Act improves legal position of trade unions; in France, Dreyfus honourably readmitted to the army (*see* 1894); launching of first modern battleship, H.M.S. *Dreadnaught*; Simplon tunnel in the Alps opened; severe earthquake in San Francisco; Lutyens designs buildings for the newly founded Hampstead Garden Suburb; Matisse: *Joie de vivre* (*p.*); Picasso: *Portrait of Gertrude Stein* (*p.*); Fowler: *The King's English*.

PROSE
Barrie: *Peter Pan in Kensington Gardens*
Belloc: *Esto Perpetua*
Conrad: *Mirror of the Sea*
De Morgan: *Joseph Vance*
Galsworthy: *The Man of Property* (*see* 1922)
Kipling: *Puck of Pook's Hill*
Moore: *Memoirs of My Dead Life*
Nesbit: *The Railway Children*
Saintsbury: *A History of English Prosody* (all 3 vols by 1910)
Sinclair: *The Jungle*
Wallace: *The Four Just Men*
DRAMA
Galsworthy: *The Silver Box*
Hardy: *The Dynasts, Pt II* (publ.)
Pinero: *His House in Order*
Shaw: *The Doctor's Dilemma*

POETRY
De la Mare: *Poems*
Doughty: *The Dawn in Britain*

1907

Triple Entente between France, Russia and Britain; Gandhi begins campaign of civil disobedience in South Africa; Picasso: *Les Demoiselles d'Avignon* (*p.*); beginnings of Cubism.

PROSE
Conrad: *The Secret Agent*
De Morgan: *Alice-for-Short*
Forster: *The Longest Journey*
Galsworthy: *The Country House*
Gosse: *Father and Son*
Kipling: *The Brushwood Boy*
Queen Victoria (*d.*1901): *Letters, 1837–1861*
DRAMA
Granville-Barker: *Waste*
Maugham: *Lady Frederick*
Synge: *The Playboy of the Western World*
POETRY
Belloc: *Cautionary Tales for Children*
Colum: *Wild Earth*
Davidson: *The Triumph of Mammon*
Flecker: *The Bridge of Fire*

POETRY (*cont.*)
Hodgson: *The Last Blackbird, and Other Lines*
Joyce: *Chamber Music*
Service: *Songs of a Sourdough*

1908

Asquith becomes Liberal P.M. (–1916); *Daily Telegraph* interview with Kaiser Wilhelm of Germany, in which he claims that the German people are hostile to Britain; Women's Freedom League founded; Votes for Women rally in Hyde Park; Territorial Force introduced; first production of the Model T Ford; first Boy Scout Troop set up by Baden-Powell.

PROSE
Belloc: *Mr Clutterbuck's Election*
Bennett: *The Old Wives' Tale*
Chesterton: *The Man Who Was Thursday*
Davies: *The Autobiography of a Super-Tramp*
Doughty: *Wanderings in Arabia* (abridgement of *Travels in Arabia Deserta, see* 1888)
Forster: *A Room with a View*
Grahame: *The Wind in the Willows*
London: *The Iron Heel*
Montgomery: *Anne of Green Gables*
'Henry Handel Richardson': *Maurice Guest*
Wells: *The War in the Air*

DRAMA
Barrie: *What Every Woman Knows*
Gregory: *The Workhouse Ward*
Hardy: *The Dynasts, Pt III* (publ.)
Pinero: *The Thunderbolt*
Shaw: *Getting Married*

POETRY
Abercrombie: *Interludes and Poems*
Davidson: *Mammon and His Message*; *The Testament of John Davidson*
Doughty: *Adam Cast Forth*
Yeats: *Collected Works*

1909

Lloyd George introduces his 'People's Budget', taxing large incomes; its rejection by the Lords leads to constitutional crisis; Old Age Pension in force, giving pensions to over-70s; suffragettes on hunger strike in prison force-fed; Blériot makes first cross-Channel flight; opening of Selfridges department store in London; Beveridge: *Unemployment: A Problem of Industry.*

PROSE
Bradley, A.C.: *Oxford Lectures on Poetry*
Buchan: *Prester John*
Kipling: *Actions and Reactions*
Stein: *Three Lives*
Wells: *Ann Veronica*; *Tono Bungay*

DRAMA
Galsworthy: *Strife*
Masefield: *The Tragedy of Nan, and Other Plays* (publ.)

POETRY
Binyon: *England, and Other Poems*
Hardy: *Time's Laughingstocks, and Other Verses*
Meredith (*d.*1909): *Last Poems*

POETRY (*cont.*)
Noyes: *The Enchanted Island, and Other Poems*
Pound: *Exultations*; *Personae*
Synge (*d.*1909): *Poems and Translations*

1910

Death of Edward VII; accession of George V (–1936); Liberals introduce Parliament Bill to reduce the power of the Lords, and fight General Election on the issue; Dominion of South Africa formed out of united colonies; Zeppelin forms company to carry passengers in his airships; Ehrlich discovers cure for syphilis; Crippen, the murderer, arrested, after a radio message to the ship on which he was travelling.

PROSE
Bennett: *Clayhanger* (*see* 1925)
Forster: *Howards End*
James: *The Finer Grain*
Morris (*d.*1896): *Collected Works*
Wells: *The History of Mr Polly*
DRAMA
Galsworthy: *Justice*
Granville-Barker: *The Madras House*
Shaw: *Misalliance*

POETRY
Belloc: *Verses*
Flecker: *Thirty-Six Poems*
Masefield: *Ballads and Poems* (incl.
  'Cargoes')
Noyes: *Collected Poems* (compl. in 4
  vols by 1927)
Yeats: *Poems: Second Series*
Young: *Songs of Night*

1911

Parliament Act reduces power of the Lords and shortens life of Parliaments; M.P.s given annual salary; dockers and railwaymen in strikes, part of general industrial unrest; National Insurance Act provides insurance in cases of unemployment and sickness; German dispatch of gunboat to Agadir causes international incident; liberal reforms in Russia end with assassination of Stolypin; in China, Sun Yat-Sen overthrows Manchu emperors; Amundsen reaches the South Pole; air-mail service begun in Britain between Hendon and Windsor; aircraft used for first time in war, by the Italians in Libya; self-starter for cars invented; Duchamp: *Nude Descending a Staircase* (*p.*); Gilman, Gore and Sickert form the Camden Town Group of artists.

PROSE
Beerbohm: *Zuleika Dobson*
Bennett: *The Card*; *Hilda Lessways*
  (*see* 1925)
Burnett: *The Secret Garden*
Chesterton: *The Innocence of Father
  Brown*
Conrad: *Under Western Eyes*
Douglas: *Siren Land*
Forster: *The Celestial Omnibus*
'O. Henry' (*d.*1910): *Collected Works*
James, M.R.: *More Ghost Stories of
  an Antiquary*
Lawrence: *The White Peacock*
Leacock: *Nonsense Novels*
'Katherine Mansfield': *In a German
  Pension*
Moore: *Hail and Farewell* (vol. i, vol.
  ii 1912, vol. iii 1914)
Wallace: *Sanders of the River*
Walpole: *Mr Perrin and Mr Traill*
Wells: *The Country of the Blind*; *The
  New Machiavelli*
Wharton: *Ethan Frome*

DRAMA
Ervine: *Mixed Marriage*
POETRY
Brooke: *Poems*
Davies: *Songs of Joy, and Others*
Drinkwater: *Poems of Men and
  Hours*
Masefield: *The Everlasting Mercy*
Pound: *Canzoni*

1912

War in the Balkans between the Bulgarian League and the Turks (–1913); Ulster Unionists sign 'solemn covenant' to defeat Home Rule; miners' strike leads to agreement on minimum wages; British telephone system nationalised (except Hull); Scott's expedition reaches the South Pole but all perish soon afterwards; S.S. *Titanic* sinks after collision with an iceberg; first parachute descent from an aircraft; Jung: *The Psychology of the Unconscious*; Kandinsky: *Painting with the Black Arch* (*p.*, early example of abstract art).

PROSE
Belloc: *The Servile State*
Butler (*d.*1902): *Notebooks*
Conrad: *'Twixt Land and Sea*
Doyle: *The Lost World*
Lawrence: *The Trespasser*
(Mann: *Death in Venice*)
Moore: *Hail and Farewell* (vol. ii, *see* 1911)
Saintsbury: *The History of English Prose Rhythm*
'Saki': *The Unbearable Bassington*
Stephens: *The Crock of Gold*
Wells: *Marriage*
DRAMA
Houghton: *Hindle Wakes*

POETRY
Abercrombie: *Emblems of Love*
De la Mare: *The Listeners, and Other Poems*
Marsh (ed.): *Georgian Poetry 1911–12*
Pound: *Ripostes*

1913

Trade Union Act allows unionists voluntary payment of political contributions; suffragette killed by George V's horse at Derby; first woman magistrate in Britain; completion of the Panama Canal; Geiger invents radiation counter; Epstein: *The Rockdrill* (vorticist sc.); Stravinsky: *The Rite of Spring* (ballet); Chaplin makes his film debut.

PROSE
(Alain-Fournier: *Le Grand Meaulnes*)
Bentley: *Trent's Last Case*
Conrad: *Chance*
James: *A Small Boy and Others*
Lawrence: *Sons and Lovers*
Mackenzie: *Sinister Street* (vol. i, vol. ii 1914)
(Proust: *A la recherche du temps perdu*, compl. in 8 pts and 13 vols by 1928)
Walpole: *Fortitude*
DRAMA
Ervine: *Jane Clegg*
Galsworthy: *The Fugitive*
Shaw: *Androcles and the Lion*
POETRY
De la Mare: *Peacock Pie*
Flecker: *The Golden Journey to Samarkand*
Frost: *A Boy's Will*
Lawrence: *Love Poems*

POETRY (*cont.*)
Masefield: *Dauber*
Meynell: *Collected Poems*
Squire: *The Three Hills, and Other Poems*
Watson: *The Muse in Exile*
Williams, W.C.: *The Tempers*

1914

The murder at Sarajevo of Archduke Franz-Ferdinand of Austria results in Austria declaring war on Serbia; the European nations divide into two hostile groups, Germany, allied with Austria and, later, Turkey, and the Triple Entente of Britain, Russia and France; trench warfare develops from the Channel to Switzerland, with other areas of conflict all over Europe, at sea and in the colonies of the various powers (–1918); Home Rule Act for Ireland, establishing an Irish Parliament with limited powers, suspended after outbreak of war; first Zeppelin raid; British build first single-seater fighter planes.

PROSE
Bradley, F.H.: *Truth and Reality*
Chesterton: *The Wisdom of Father Brown*
James: *Notes on Novelists*
Joyce: *Dubliners*
Lawrence: *The Prussian Officer*
Moore: *Hail and Farewell* (vol. iii, *see* 1911)
'Saki': *Beasts and Superbeasts*
Stein: *Tender Buttons*
'Robert Tressell' (*d.*1911): *The Ragged Trousered Philanthropists*
Walpole: *The Duchess of Wrexe*
Yeats: *Responsibilities*

DRAMA
Jones, H.A.: *The Lie*
Shaw: *Pygmalion*
POETRY
Blunt: *Poetical Works*
Brennan: *Poems*
Dickinson (*d.*1886): *The Single Hound*
Frost: *North of Boston*
Hardy: *Satires of Circumstance*

1915

Huge casualties in trench warfare on the Western Front; battles of Ypres, Neuve Chapelle and Loos; Italy joins the Allies and declares war on Austria; Allied attempt to defeat Turkey by landing at Gallipoli fails; Austrian forces drive Russians out of Austria and Poland; anger in U.S.A. at sinking of the *Lusitania* by Germany; Nurse Cavell executed by Germans; Germans use poison gas and flame-thrower; first Women's Institute in Britain; Einstein elaborates general theory of relativity; tango craze in Europe and America; Griffith: *The Birth of a Nation* (*f.*); all copies of Lawrence's *The Rainbow* withdrawn and destroyed as obscene.

PROSE
Buchan: *The Thirty-Nine Steps*
Conrad: *Victory*; *Within the Tides: Tales*
Douglas: *Old Calabria*
Doyle: *The Valley of Fear*
Ford: *The Good Soldier*
Lawrence: *The Rainbow*
Maugham: *Of Human Bondage*
Richardson: *Pointed Roofs* (first of 12 vols, variously titled, publ. in 1938 as *Pilgrimage*)
Woolf: *The Journey Out*
Yeats: *Reveries over Childhood and Youth*
DRAMA
Brighouse: *Hobson's Choice*
Ervine: *John Ferguson*

POETRY
Aldington: *Images*
Brooke (*d.*1915): *1914, and Other Poems*
Chesterton: *Poems*
Dennis: *The Songs of a Sentimental Bloke*
Flecker (*d.*1915): *The Old Ships*
Marsh (ed.): *Georgian Poetry 1913–15*
Masters: *The Spoon River Anthology*
Monro: *Trees*
Pound: *Cathay*
Read: *Songs of Chaos*
Sitwell, E.: *The Mother, and Other Poems*

1916

Battles of Verdun and Somme on the Western Front; at the Somme the Allies advance nine miles; British losses alone are over 400,000; sea battle of Jutland indecisive; T.E. Lawrence supports Arab revolt against the Turks; Easter rebellion by Irish Nationalists in Dublin suppressed; compulsory military service introduced in Britain; Lloyd George forms coalition government (–1922); first tank, *Little Willie*, in use in battle; in U.S.A., birth control clinic opens in Brooklyn; Monet: *Water-Lilies* (*p.*, first in sequence –1922); Holst: *The Planets* (orchestral suite); Griffith: *Intolerance* (epic *f.*).

PROSE
Bennett: *These Twain* (*see* 1925)
Bridges (ed.): *The Spirit of Man* (anthology of prose and verse)
Buchan: *Greenmantle*
Joyce: *A Portrait of the Artist as a Young Man*
Lawrence: *Twilight in Italy*
Moore: *The Brook Kerith*
Quiller-Couch: *The Art of Writing*
Walpole: *The Dark Forest*
Wells: *Mr Britling Sees It Through*
DRAMA
Barrie: *A Kiss for Cinderella*
Chu Chin Chow (musical comedy, runs for 2,238 shows)

POETRY
Brooke (*d.*1915): *Collected Poems*
Davies: *Collected Poems* (second series 1923)
Drinkwater: *Olton Pools*
Flecker (*d.*1915): *Collected Poems*
Gibson: *Battle*
Graves: *Over the Brazier*
Lawrence: *Amores*
Masefield: *Sonnets and Poems*
Mew: *The Farmer's Bride*
Pound: *Lustra*
Sandburg: *Chicago Poems*
the Sitwells (ed.): *Wheels: An Anthology of Verse* (annually –1921)

1917

Germany attempts to starve Britain of supplies by submarine warfare; attacks on shipping bring U.S.A. into the war; battles of Passchendaele and Cambrai; Allenby captures Jerusalem from the Turks; the Russian Revolution; Bolsheviks sign an armistice with Germany; Balfour issues declaration of intent to establish Jewish homeland in Palestine; British Tank Corps formed; first bombing raid by aeroplanes (rather than airships) on London; Duchamp exhibits a urinal as sculpture entitled *Fountain*.

PROSE
Conrad: *The Shadow Line: A Confession*
Douglas: *South Wind*
Doyle: *His Last Bow: Some Reminiscences of Sherlock Holmes*
James (*d.*1916): *The Middle Years*
Kipling: *A Diversity of Creatures*
'Henry Handel Richardson': *Australia Felix*
Wells: *God the Invisible King*
DRAMA
Barrie: *Dear Brutus*
POETRY
Binyon: *For the Fallen, and Other Poems*
Bridges: *Ibant Obscuri*
Drinkwater: *Poems 1908–14*
Eliot: *Prufrock, and Other Observations*

POETRY (*cont.*)
Gibson: *Livelihood*
Graves: *Fairies and Fusiliers*
Gurney: *Severn and Somme*
Hodgson: *Poems*
Kipling: *The Years Between*
Lawrence: *Look! We Have Come Through!*
Marsh (ed.): *Georgian Poetry 1916–17*
Meynell: *A Father of Women*
Monro: *Strange Meetings*
Sassoon: *The Old Huntsman, and Other Poems*
Squire: *The Lily of Malud*
Thomas, Edward (*d.*1917): *Poems*
Williams, W.C.: *Al Que Quiere!*
Yeats: *The Wild Swans at Coole*

1918

German attempts to force a victory in the face of Allied naval supremacy and strength on the Western Front fail; the Kaiser abdicates; Armistice of 11 November; in Britain, Parliamentary Reform Act gives vote to men over 21 and women over 30; worldwide influenza epidemic (–1919) kills an estimated 20 million people; school-leaving age raised to 14; Marie Stopes: *Married Love and Wise Parenthood*; Nash: *We Are Making a New World (p.)*; Bartók: *Duke Bluebeard's Castle* (opera); Stravinsky: *Ragtime*.

PROSE
Bridges: *The Necessity of Poetry*
Galsworthy: *Five Tales*
Lewis, Wyndham: *Tarr*
Lindsay: *The Magic Pudding*
Quiller-Couch: *Studies in Literature* (all 3 series by 1929)
Strachey: *Eminent Victorians*
DRAMA
Joyce: *Exiles* (publ., first performed 1925)
Pinero: *The Freaks*
POETRY
(Apollinaire (*d.*1918): *Calligrammes*)
De la Mare: *Motley, and Other Poems*

POETRY (*cont.*)
Gibson: *Whin*
Hopkins (*d.*1889): *Poems* (ed. Bridges)
Lawrence: *New Poems*
Sassoon: *Counter-Attack, and Other Poems*
Sitwell, E.: *Clowns' Houses*
Squire: *Poems: First Series* (second series 1922)
Thomas, Edward (*d.*1917): *Last Poems*

1919

Peace treaties (at Versailles, St Germain and Neuilly) signed, dividing Europe; Austro-Hungarian Empire split up; President Wilson establishes the League of Nations; Spartacist revolutionary uprising in Berlin crushed; Hitler founds National Socialist German Workers' Party; Mussolini founds Fascist Party in Italy; German fleet scuttled at Scapa Flow; civil war in Russia between Bolsheviks and 'White' Russians; British government bans Sinn Fein; Amritsar Massacre in the Punjab: troops fire on crowd protesting in favour of Indian self-government; first aeroplane flights across the Atlantic (also by airship) and to Australia; Gropius founds Bauhaus school of architecture and design (closed by Nazis in 1933); Elgar: Cello Concerto.

PROSE
Ashford: *The Young Visiters*
'W.N.P. Barbellion' (*d.*1919): *The Journal of a Disappointed Man*
Buchan: *Mr Standfast*
Conrad: *The Arrow of Gold*
Firbank: *Valmouth*
Galsworthy: *Saint's Progress*
Maugham: *The Moon and Sixpence*
Woolf: *Night and Day*
DRAMA
Bennett: *Sacred and Profane Love*
Maugham: *Caesar's Wife*; *Home and Beauty*
Shaw: *Heartbreak House* (publ.)
Yeats: *Two Plays for Dancers* (publ.)

POETRY
Aldington: *Images of Desire*
Gurney: *War's Embers, and Other Verses*
Hardy: *Collected Poems*; *Moments of Vision, and Miscellaneous Verse*
Masefield: *Reynard the Fox*
Pound: *Quia Pauper Amavi*
Read: *Naked Warriors*
Sassoon: *The War Poems*
Squire: *The Birds, and Other Poems*

1920

Government of Ireland Act passed, partitioning Ireland; Sinn Fein rejects terms and clashes violently with British government forces; martial law declared; Anglican Church disestablished in Wales; first meeting of the Council of the League of Nations; American women given the vote; prohibition of alcohol in U.S.A. starts (–1933); De Havilland Aircraft Company formed; Marconi opens public broadcasting station; women allowed to take degrees at Oxford University; Welwyn Garden City established.

PROSE
Chesterton: *The Uses of Diversity*
Christie: *The Mysterious Affair at Styles*
(Colette: *Chéri*)
Conrad: *The Rescue*
Eliot: *The Sacred Wood*
Fitzgerald: *This Side of Paradise*
Fry, Roger: *Vision and Design*
Galsworthy: *Awakening*; *In Chancery* (*see* 1922)
James (*d.*1916): *Letters*
Lawrence: *The Lost Girl*; *Women in Love*
'Katherine Mansfield': *Bliss, and Other Stories*
Wells: *The Outline of History*
Wharton: *The Age of Innocence*
DRAMA
Barrie: *Mary Rose*
Galsworthy: *The Skin Game*

DRAMA (*cont.*)
O'Neill: *Beyond the Horizon*; *The Emperor Jones*
POETRY
Blunden: *The Waggoner, and Other Poems*
Eliot: *Poems*
Gibson: *Neighbours*
Graves: *Country Sentiment*
Owen (*d.*1918): *Poems*
Pound: *Hugh Selwyn Mauberley*; *Umbra*
Sandburg: *Smoke and Steel*
Sitwell, E.: *The Wooden Pegasus*
Thomas, Edward (*d.*1917): *Collected Poems*
Yeats: *Michael Robartes and the Dancer*

1921

Rebellion in Ireland ends in establishment of Ulster and the Irish Free State, with Dominion status; Indian Central Legislature set up with limited powers, but Gandhi and the National Congress not satisfied; 1 million unemployed in Britain; lockouts in the coal industry in England; in Russia, Lenin begins 'new economic policy' during period of severe famine; first birth control clinic in London; first Austin Seven produced.

PROSE
De la Mare: *Memoirs of a Midget*
Galsworthy: *To Let* (*see* 1922)
Huxley: *Crome Yellow*
Lawrence: *Psychoanalysis and the Unconscious*; *Sea and Sardinia*
Lubbock: *The Craft of Fiction*
Richards (with Ogden and Wood): *The Foundation of Aesthetics*
Russell, Bertrand: *The Analysis of Mind*
Strachey: *Queen Victoria*
DRAMA
Barrie: *Shall We Join the Ladies?*
(Čapek: *The Insect Play*)

DRAMA (*cont.*)
Drinkwater: *Mary Stuart*; *Oliver Cromwell* (publ.)
Maugham: *The Circle*
(Pirandello: *Six Characters in Search of an Author*)
Shaw: *Back to Methuselah* (publ.)
Yeats: *Four Plays for Dancers* (publ.)
POETRY
De la Mare: *The Veil, and Other Poems*
Graves: *The Pier-Glass*
Lawrence: *Tortoises*
Sackville-West: *Orchard and Vineyard*

1922

Conservatives break with Lloyd George; Bonar Law becomes P.M. (–1923); Sinn Fein rejects Dominion status in Ireland, leading to further civil war (–1923); Mussolini becomes premier of Italy (–1943); in Russia, Stalin becomes Secretary of the Communist Party; British Broadcasting Company starts radio broadcasts; Tutankhamun's tomb discovered at Luxor; Vaughan Williams: Symphony No.3 (*Pastoral*).

PROSE
Austen (*d.*1817): *Love and Friendship*
Cummings: *The Enormous Room*
Fitzgerald: *The Beautiful and the Damned*
Galsworthy: *The Forsyte Saga* (complete in 1 vol., contains *The Man of Property* (1906); *In Chancery* (1920); *Awakening* (1920); *To Let* (1921))
Garnett: *Lady into Fox*
Gerhardie: *Futility*
Harris: *My Life and Loves* (compl. in 4 vols by 1927)
Joyce: *Ulysses*
Lawrence: *Aaron's Rod*; *England, My England*; *Fantasia of the Unconscious*
Lewis, Sinclair: *Babbitt*
'Katherine Mansfield': *The Garden Party*
Walpole: *The Cathedral*
'Rebecca West': *The Judge*

PROSE (*cont.*)
Woolf: *Jacob's Room*
DRAMA
Coward: *The Young Idea*
Flecker (*d.*1915): *Hassan* (publ.)
Galsworthy: *Loyalties*
Pinero: *The Enchanted Cottage*
POETRY
Blunden: *The Shepherd, and Other Poems*
Davies: *Child Lovers, and Other Poems*
Drinkwater: *Preludes*
Eliot: *The Waste Land*
Hardy: *Late Lyrics and Earlier*
Housman: *Last Poems*
Monro: *Real Property*
Sitwell, E.: *Façade*
Sitwell, S.: *A Hundred and One Harlequins*
Squire: *Poems: Second Series* (see 1918)
Yeats: *Later Poems*

1923

France occupies the Ruhr to compel Germany to pay war debts; Hitler's Nazi *putsch* in Munich fails; serious inflation in Germany; Ottoman Empire ends with proclamation of republic under Mustapha Kemal; in Russia, civil war ends with the Union of Soviet Socialist Republics; Julian Huxley: *Essays of a Biologist*; Spencer starts painting *Resurrection, Cookham* (compl. 1926); Walton: *Façade* (musical setting for Edith Sitwell's poems).

PROSE
Bennett: *Riceyman Steps*
Chambers: *The Elizabethan Stage*
Chesterton: *St Francis of Assisi*
(Colette: *The Ripening Seed*)
Conrad: *The Rover*
Huxley: *Antic Hay*
Lawrence: *Kangaroo*; *Studies in Classic American Literature*
'Katherine Mansfield' (*d.*1923): *The Dove's Nest, and Other Stories*
Stephens: *Deirdre*
DRAMA
O'Casey: *The Shadow of a Gunman*

DRAMA (*cont.*)
Shaw: *Saint Joan*
POETRY
Aldington: *Exile, and Other Poems*
Belloc: *Sonnets and Verse*
Blunden: *To Nature*
Davies: *Collected Poems* (second series, see 1916)
Drinkwater: *Collected Poems*
Frost: *New Hampshire*
Lawrence: *Birds, Beasts and Flowers*
Masefield: *Collected Poems*
(Rilke: *Duino Elegies*)
Stevens: *Harmonium*

1924

Labour Party takes office for the first time, under Ramsay Mac-Donald; publication of forged 'Zinoviev Letter' suggests Labour are dealing with communists in U.S.S.R.; Conservatives take power again (–1929); death of Lenin; Gershwin: *Rhapsody in Blue* (music for piano and orchestra).

PROSE
Eliot: *Homage to John Dryden*
Ford: *Some Do Not*
Forster: *A Passage to India*
Lawrence (with Skinner): *The Boy in the Bush*
(Mann: *The Magic Mountain*)
Melville (*d.*1891): *Billy Budd*
Walpole: *The Old Ladies*
Webb: *Precious Bane*
Wodehouse: *The Inimitable Jeeves*

DRAMA
Coward: *The Vortex*
O'Casey: *Juno and the Paycock*
O'Neill: *Desire under the Elms*

POETRY
Davies: *Secrets*
Sitwell, E.: *The Sleeping Beauty*
Squire: *Grub Street Nights*

1925

At the Treaty of Locarno Germany agrees on frontiers with Belgium and France, and accedes to arbitration conventions; France evacuates the Ruhr (*see* 1923); Britain returns to the gold standard; teaching of theory of evolution banned in Tennessee; first Surrealist Exhibition in Paris; Charleston dance craze; Louis Armstrong playing with Hot Five and Hot Seven; Berg: *Wozzeck* (opera); Chaplin in *The Gold Rush* (*f.*); Eisenstein: *The Battleship Potemkin* (*f.*); Hitler: *Mein Kampf* ('My Struggle').

PROSE
Austen (*d.*1817): *Sanditon*
Bennett: *The Clayhanger Family* (contains *Clayhanger* (1910); *Hilda Lessways* (1911); *These Twain* (1916))
Compton-Burnett: *Pastors and Masters*
Conrad (*d.*1924): *Suspense*
Dreiser: *An American Tragedy*
Fitzgerald: *The Great Gatsby*
Ford: *No More Parades*
Huxley: *Those Barren Leaves*
(Kafka (*d.*1924): *The Trial*)
Lawrence: *St Mawr and the Princess*
Loos: *Gentlemen Prefer Blondes*
Maugham: *The Painted Veil*
Stein: *The Making of Americans*
Wallace: *The Gaunt Stranger* (later called *The Ringer*)
Walpole: *Portrait of a Man with Red Hair*
Whitehead: *Science and the Modern World*
Woolf: *The Common Reader*; *Mrs Dalloway*
Yeats: *A Vision* (publ. privately)

DRAMA
Coward: *Fallen Angels*; *Hay Fever*
Travers: *A Cuckoo in the Nest*

POETRY
Blunden: *English Poems*
Bottomley: *Poems of Thirty Years*
Bridges: *New Verse Written in 1921*
Davies: *A Poet's Alphabet*
Drinkwater: *New Poems*
Eliot: *Poems 1909–25*
Graves: *Welchman's Hose*
Hardy: *Human Shows, Far Fantasies*
Lowell, Amy (*d.*1925): *What's O'Clock*
'Hugh MacDiarmid': *Sangschaw*
Muir: *First Poems*
Pound: *A Draft of XVI Cantos*
Sitwell, E.: *Troy Park*

1926

The General Strike: workers in key industries strike in support of miners' fight against threatened wage cuts; T.U.C. calls off strike after nine days; adoption of children legalised in England; General Electricity Board established, coordinating supplies into national grid; first liquid fuel rocket, in U.S.A.; Jelly Roll Morton records 'Red Hot Peppers' jazz sessions.

PROSE
Christie: *The Murder of Roger Ackroyd*
Firbank: *Concerning the Eccentricities of Cardinal Pirelli*
Fitzgerald: *All the Sad Young Men*
Ford: *A Man Could Stand Up*
Galsworthy: *The Silver Spoon*
Hemingway: *The Sun Also Rises*
Lawrence, D.H.: *The Plumed Serpent*
Lawrence, T.E.: *The Seven Pillars of Wisdom*
Milne: *Winnie-the-Pooh*
Prichard: *Working Bullocks*
Wells: *The World of William Clissold*

DRAMA
Coward: *Easy Virtue*
Galsworthy: *Escape*
Maugham: *The Constant Wife*
O'Casey: *The Plough and the Stars*
Travers: *Rookery Nook*

POETRY
Hughes, Langston: *The Weary Blues*
Jeffers: *Roan Stallion, Tamar, and Other Poems*
'Hugh MacDiarmid': *A Drunk Man Looks at the Thistle*; *Penny Wheep*
Muir: *Chorus of the Newly Dead*
Pound: *Personae: Collected Poems*
Sassoon: *Satirical Poems*
Sitwell, E.: *Elegy on Dead Fashion*

1927

Trades Union Act makes 'sympathetic' strikes illegal; Trotsky expelled by Stalin from Russian Communist Party; Lindbergh makes first solo flight across the Atlantic; widespread use of the telephone leads to the modernisation of London's phone system; British army abandons lance as weapon; Duke Ellington's band start playing at the Cotton Club, New York (–1932); first 'talkie': *The Jazz Singer*.

PROSE
Bowen: *The Hotel*
Cather: *Death Comes for the Archbishop*
Forster: *Aspects of the Novel*
Granville-Barker: *Prefaces to Shakespeare* (all 5 series by 1948)
Hemingway: *Men Without Women*
Lawrence: *Mornings in Mexico*
Lewis, Sinclair: *Elmer Gantry*
Lowes: *The Road to Xanadu*
Mottram: *The Spanish Farm Trilogy*
Myers: *The Near and the Far*
Sinclair: *Oil!*
Wilder: *The Bridge of San Luis Rey*
Williamson: *Tarka the Otter*
Woolf: *To the Lighthouse*

DRAMA
Maugham: *The Letter*
Travers: *Thark*

POETRY
Chesterton: *Collected Poems*
Davies: *A Poet's Calendar*
De la Mare: *Stuff and Nonsense*
Joyce: *Pomes Penyeach*
Marquis: *archy and mehitabel*
Sandburg: *The American Songbag*
Sitwell, E.: *Rustic Elegies*
Sitwell, S.: *The Cyder Feast*
Yeats: *October Blast*

1928

U.S.A. and U.S.S.R., along with 63 other nations, renounce war in the Kellogg Pact; women over 21 given the vote in Britain; effective government established in China by the Kuomintang under Chiang Kai-Shek; Kingsford-Smith flies across the mid-Pacific; Fleming discovers bacteria-killing properties of penicillin (*see* 1940); foam rubber developed; B.B.C. transmits still television pictures; Louis Armstrong: *West End Blues* (jazz).

PROSE
Blunden: *Undertones of War*
Eliot: *For Lancelot Andrewes*
Ford: *Last Post*
Forster: *The Eternal Moment*
Huxley: *Point Counter Point*
Joyce: *Anna Livia Plurabelle*
Lawrence: *Lady Chatterley's Lover*;
The Woman Who Rode Away
Lewis, Wyndham: *The Childermass*
(vol. i of *The Human Age*, vols ii–iii 1955)
Maugham: *Ashenden*
Milne: *The House at Pooh Corner*
Powys, T.F.: *Mr Weston's Good Wine*
Sassoon: *Memoirs of a Fox-Hunting Man*
Sayers: *Lord Peter Views the Body*
Shaw: *The Intelligent Woman's Guide to Socialism*
Waugh: *Decline and Fall*
Woolf: *Orlando*
DRAMA
(Brecht: *The Threepenny Opera*)

DRAMA (*cont.*)
Maugham: *The Sacred Flame*
Sherriff: *Journey's End*
POETRY
Abercrombie: *Twelve Idylls, and Other Poems*
Blunden: *Japanese Garland*; *Retreat*;
Winter Nights
Day-Lewis: *Country Comets*
Gibson: *The Golden Room*
Lawrence: *Collected Poems*
Monro: *The Earth for Sale*
Sandburg: *Good Morning, America*
Sassoon: *The Heart's Journey*
Sitwell, E.: *Five Poems*
Yeats: *The Tower*

1929

Collapse of New York stock exchange heralds world depression; second Labour government under Ramsay MacDonald (–1931); Maginot initiates construction of fortifications along eastern frontier of France; election of fascist parliament in Italy.

PROSE
Aldington: *Death of a Hero*
Bowen: *The Last September*
(Cocteau: *Les Enfants terribles*)
Compton-Burnett: *Brothers and Sisters*
Eliot: *Dante*
Faulkner: *The Sound and the Fury*
Graves: *Goodbye to All That*
'Henry Green': *Living*
Greene: *The Man Within*
Hemingway: *A Farewell to Arms*
Hughes, Richard: *A High Wind in Jamaica*
Powys, J.C.: *Wolf Solent*
Prichard: *Coonardoo*
Priestley: *The Good Companions*

PROSE (*cont.*)
(Remarque: *All Quiet on the Western Front*)
Woolf: *A Room of One's Own*
DRAMA
O'Casey: *The Silver Tassie*
Shaw: *The Apple Cart*
POETRY
Blunden: *Near and Far*
Bridges: *The Testament of Beauty*
Davies: *Ambition, and Other Poems*
Lawrence: *Pansies*
MacNeice: *Blind Fireworks*
Russell, 'AE': *Dark Weeping*
Sitwell, E.: *Gold Coast Customs*
Yeats: *The Winding Stair*

1930

Occupation of the Rhineland by Allied troops ended; 107 Nazis elected to the Reichstag; Stalin starts repression of Kulaks in U.S.S.R.; in India, Gandhi defies British government monopoly of salt production; he is imprisoned for civil disobedience; destruction of airship R101 leads to abandonment of airship construction; Whittle experiments with gas turbines for jet propulsion; Stravinsky: *Symphony of Psalms* (choral work).

PROSE
Bennett: *Imperial Palace*
Charteris: *Enter the Saint*
Empson: *Seven Types of Ambiguity*
Faulkner: *As I Lay Dying*
Hammett: *The Maltese Falcon*
Lawrence: *The Virgin and the Gipsy*
Lewis, Wyndham: *The Apes of God*
Maugham: *Cakes and Ale*
Priestley: *Angel Pavement*
Ransome: *Swallows and Amazons*
Sackville-West: *The Edwardians*
Sassoon: *Memoirs of an Infantry Officer*
Walpole: *Rogue Herries* (all 4 vols of *The Herries Chronicle* by 1933)
Waugh: *Vile Bodies*
Williams, Charles: *War in Heaven*
DRAMA
'James Bridie': *The Anatomist*
Coward: *Private Lives*
Maugham: *The Breadwinner*
Sherriff: *Badger's Green*
POETRY
Abercrombie: *Collected Poems*
Auden: *Poems*
Belloc: *New Cautionary Tales*

POETRY (*cont.*)
Blunden: *Poems 1914–30*
Bottomley: *Festival Preludes*
Crane: *The Bridge*
Eliot: *Ash Wednesday*
Gibson: *Hazards*
'Hugh MacDiarmid': *To Circumjack Cencrastus*
Russell, 'AE': *Enchantment*
Sassoon: *In Sicily*
Sitwell, E.: *Collected Poems*

1931

Financial crisis in Britain; nearly 3 million unemployed; burden of war debts to U.S.A. and unemployment benefits bring the Government near to bankruptcy; gold standard abandoned and pound devalued; MacDonald forms the 'National Government' (–1935); Mosley leaves the Labour Party to found the New Party; Gandhi visits London to insist on all-India government; invention of the electric razor.

PROSE
Aldington: *The Colonel's Daughter*
Compton-Burnett: *Men and Wives*
Faulkner: *Sanctuary*
Lawrence: *The Man Who Died*
Powell: *Afternoon Men*
Wilson, Edmund: *Axel's Castle*
Woolf: *The Waves*
DRAMA
Coward: *Cavalcade*
O'Neill: *Mourning Becomes Electra*

POETRY
Binyon: *Collected Poems*
Bridges (*d.*1930): *Shorter Poems*
Davies: *In Winter*
Day-Lewis: *From Feathers to Iron*
Russell, 'AE': *Vale, and Other Poems*

1932

Chamberlain's Import Duties Act introduces trade protection in Britain; Roosevelt elected President of U.S.A. (–1945); (c.) Stalin starts purges of 'Old Bolsheviks', 'intelligentsia' and army officers; first motorway built, from Bonn to Cologne.

PROSE
Bennett (d.1931): *Journals* (all 3 vols by 1933)
Bowen: *To the North*
Dos Passos: *1919*
Eliot: *Selected Essays 1917–32*
Faulkner: *Light in August*
Gibbons: *Cold Comfort Farm*
Greene: *Stamboul Train*
Hemingway: *Death in the Afternoon*
Huxley: *Brave New World*
Lawrence (d.1930): *Letters* (ed. Huxley)
Leavis: *New Bearings in English Poetry*
Lehmann: *Invitation to the Waltz*
Powell: *Venusberg*
Runyon: *Guys and Dolls*
Shaw: *The Adventures of the Black Girl in Her Search for God*

PROSE (cont.)
Thurber: *The Seal in the Bedroom, and Other Predicaments*
Waugh: *Black Mischief*
DRAMA
Maugham: *For Services Rendered*
Priestley: *Dangerous Corner*
Shaw: *Too True to Be Good*
POETRY
Auden: *The Orators*
Blunden: *Halfway House*
Davies: *Poems 1930–1*
De la Mare: *Old Rhymes and New*
Eliot: *Sweeney Agonistes*
Hardy (d.1928): *Collected Poems*
'Hugh MacDiarmid': *First Hymn to Lenin*; *Scots Unbound*
Muir: *Six Poems*
Yeats: *Words for Music Perhaps, and Other Poems*

1933

Hitler appointed Chancellor in Germany (–1945); communists blamed for Reichstag fire in Berlin; Enabling Law gives Hitler dictatorial powers; concentration camps started; Germany withdraws from the League of Nations and the Geneva Disarmament Conference; in U.S.A., Roosevelt seeks to counter financial depression and unemployment with the New Deal (–1939); prohibition of alcohol repealed in U.S.A. (*see* 1920); Oxford Union Society supports motion refusing to fight for 'King and Country'; invention of polythene; *King Kong* (*f.*).

PROSE
Aldington: *All Men Are Enemies*
Brittain: *Testament of Youth*
Compton-Burnett: *More Women Than Men*
Eliot: *The Use of Poetry and the Use of Criticism*
Greenwood: *Love on the Dole*
Hemingway: *Winner Take Nothing*
Hilton: *Lost Horizon*
Lowry: *Ultramarine*
(Malraux: *La Condition humaine*)
'George Orwell': *Down and Out in Paris and London*
Powell: *From a View to a Death*
Powys, J.C.: *A Glastonbury Romance*
Stein: *The Autobiography of Alice B. Toklas*
Thurber: *My Life and Hard Times*
West: *Miss Lonelyhearts*

DRAMA
(Lorca: *Blood Wedding*)
O'Neill: *Ah, Wilderness!*
Priestley: *Laburnum Grove*
POETRY
Barker: *Thirty Preliminary Poems*
Crane (d.1932): *Collected Poems*
Day-Lewis: *The Magnetic Mountain*
De la Mare: *The Fleeting, and Other Poems*
Lawrence (d.1930): *Last Poems*; *The Ship of Death*
Monro (d.1932): *Collected Poems*
Read: *The End of a War*
Sackville-West: *Collected Poems*
Sassoon: *The Road to Ruin*
Spender: *Poems*
Yeats: *Collected Poems*

1934

Hitler purges followers in 'Night of the Long Knives'; Austrian chancellor Dolfuss murdered in attempted Nazi coup; Mao Tse-Tung starts 'Long March' across China (–1935), under attack from Chiang Kai-Shek; British government subsidises construction of the *Queen Mary*; in U.S.A., Clyde Barrow and Bonnie Parker ambushed after four years of bank-robbing.

PROSE
Beckett: *More Pricks Than Kicks*
Bowen: *The Cat Jumps*
Eliot: *After Strange Gods*
Fitzgerald: *Tender Is the Night*
Graves: *I Claudius; Claudius the God*
Greene: *It's a Battlefield*
Hilton: *Good-Bye, Mr Chips*
James (*d*.1916): *The Art of the Novel*
Miller, Henry: *Tropic of Cancer*
O'Hara, John: *Appointment in Samarra*
'George Orwell': *Burmese Days*
Pound: *The A.B.C. of Reading*
Rhys: *Voyage in the Dark*
Rolfe (*d*.1913): *The Desire and Pursuit of the Whole*
Saroyan: *The Daring Young Man on the Flying Trapeze*
Sayers: *The Nine Taylors*
Symons: *The Quest for Corvo*
Toynbee: *A Study of History* (compl. in 12 vols by 1961)

PROSE (*cont.*)
Waugh: *A Handful of Dust*
Wells: *An Experiment in Autobiography*

DRAMA
Auden: *The Dance of Death*
O'Casey: *Within the Gates*
O'Neill: *Days Without End*
Priestley: *Eden End*

POETRY
Blunden: *Choice or Chance*
Eliot: *The Rock* (pageant play)
Muir: *Variations on a Time Theme*
Russell, 'AE': *The House of the Titans*
Spender: *Vienna*
Thomas, Dylan: *Eighteen Poems*
Williams, W.C.: *Collected Poems*
Yeats: *The King of the Great Clock Tower*

1935

Baldwin succeeds MacDonald as P.M. for the third time (–1937); conscription introduced in Germany, and anti-Jewish Nuremberg Decrees adopted; Italy invades Abyssinia; in Britain, Hore-Belisha introduces pedestrian crossings on roads and 30 mile per hour speed limit in built-up areas; Gershwin: *Porgy and Bess* (musical); introduction of paper-covered Penguin books, priced sixpence; Left Book Club started (–1948).

PROSE
Bowen: *The House in Paris*
(Canetti: *Auto da Fé*)
Compton-Burnett: *A House and Its Head*
Connolly: *The Rock Pool*
Forester: *The African Queen*
Greene: *England Made Me*
Hemingway: *The Green Hills of Africa*
Isherwood: *Mr Norris Changes Trains*
Myers: *The Root and the Flower*
O'Hara, John: *Butterfield 8*
'George Orwell': *A Clergyman's Daughter*
Stead: *Seven Poor Men of Sydney*
Steinbeck: *Tortilla Flat*

PROSE (*cont.*)
Thurber: *The Middle-Aged Man on the Flying Trapeze*

DRAMA
Eliot: *Murder in the Cathedral*
Novello: *Glamorous Night*
Odets: *Waiting for Lefty*
Williams, Emlyn: *Night Must Fall*

POETRY
Barker: *Poems*
Davies: *Love Poems*
Day-Lewis: *A Time to Dance, and Other Poems*
MacNeice: *Poems*
Sassoon: *Vigils*
Stevens: *Ideas of Order*
Williams, W.C.: *An Early Martyr*

1936

Death of George V; accession of Edward VIII; because of his wish to marry Mrs Simpson, Edward abdicates the throne to his brother, who becomes George VI (–1952); 200 shipyard workers march from Jarrow to London, one of several hunger marches; Mosley's Blackshirts prevented from marching through London's East End at the 'Battle of Cable Street'; revolt by Franco's Falange leads to start of the Spanish Civil War (–1939); Germany reoccupies the Rhineland; eleventh modern Olympic Games at Berlin under Hitler's patronage; Butlin's first holiday camp opens, at Skegness; Keynes: *A General Theory of Employment, Interest and Money*; *New Writing* begun (–1939).

PROSE
Barnes: *Nightwood*
Eliot: *Essays Ancient and Modern*
Faulkner: *Absalom, Absalom!*
Forster: *Abinger Harvest*
Holtby (*d.*1935): *South Riding*
Huxley: *Eyeless in Gaza*
Lewis, C.S.: *The Allegory of Love*
'George Orwell': *Keep the Aspidistra Flying*
Powys, J.C.: *Maiden Castle*
Sassoon: *Sherston's Progress*
Smith, 'Stevie': *Novel on Yellow Paper*

DRAMA
Auden and Isherwood: *The Dog beneath the Skin*

DRAMA (*cont.*)
Barrie: *The Boy David*
Novello: *Careless Rapture*
Rattigan: *French Without Tears*
Shaw: *The Millionairess*

POETRY
Auden: *Look, Stranger!*
Roberts (ed.): *The Faber Book of Modern Verse*
Sandburg: *The People, Yes!*
Stevens: *Owl's Clover*
Thomas, Dylan: *Twenty-Five Poems*
Williams, W.C.: *Adam and Eve and the City*
Yeats (ed.): *The Oxford Book of Modern Verse*

1937

Chamberlain becomes P.M. (–1940); Guernica, Spain, bombed by Germans; air raid precautions introduced in Britain; divorce legalised for grounds other than adultery; completion of designs for the Spitfire fighter plane; Picasso: *Guernica* (*p.*); Orff: *Carmina Burana* (cantata); Disney's first full-length cartoon: *Snow White and the Seven Dwarfs*.

PROSE
Auden and MacNeice: *Letters from Iceland* (prose and verse)
Blixen: *Out of Africa*
Compton-Burnett: *Daughters and Sons*
Cronin: *The Citadel*
Hemingway: *To Have and Have Not*
Hopkins (*d.*1889): *Notebooks and Papers*
Kipling (*d.*1936): *Something of Myself*
Lewis, Wyndham: *Blasting and Bombardiering*; *The Revenge for Love*
'George Orwell': *The Road to Wigan Pier*
Steinbeck: *Of Mice and Men*
Thurber: *Let Your Mind Alone*
Tolkien: *The Hobbit*
Williams, Charles: *Descent into Hell*

DRAMA
Auden and Isherwood: *The Ascent of F6*
Coward: *Design for Living*
MacNeice: *Out of the Picture*
Priestley: *I Have Been Here Before*; *Time and the Conways*
Yeats: *Nine One-Act Plays* (publ.)

POETRY
Barker: *Calamiterror*
Blunden: *An Elegy, and Other Poems*
De la Mare: *This Year, Next Year*
Jones, David: *In Parenthesis*
Muir: *Journeys and Places*
Rosenberg (*d.*1918): *Collected Works* (incl. prose)
Stevens: *The Man with the Blue Guitar*
Tate: *Selected Poems*

1938

Germany annexes Austria; Chamberlain (P.M.) pursues policy of appeasement with Hitler, condemned by Churchill and others; Munich Agreement establishes peace pact with Germany and allows Germany to seize Czech Sudetenland; first anti-Jewish measures in Italy; gas masks distributed in Britain; Women's Voluntary Service founded; Biro invents first practical ball-point pen.

PROSE
Beckett: *Murphy*
Bowen: *The Death of the Heart*
Connolly: *Enemies of Promise*
Du Maurier: *Rebecca*
'Rumer Godden': *Black Narcissus*
Greene: *Brighton Rock*
Hemingway: *The Fifth Column and the First Forty-Nine Stories* (incl. drama)
Herbert: *Capricornia*
Hughes, Richard: *In Hazard*
Kilvert (*d.*1879): *Diaries*
Lewis, C.S.: *Out of the Silent Planet*
Maugham: *The Summing Up*
'George Orwell': *Homage to Catalonia*
Richardson: *Pilgrimage* (*see* 1915)
(Sartre: *Nausea*)
Waugh: *Scoop*
White, T.H.: *The Sword in the Stone*

PROSE (*cont.*)
Woolf: *The Years*
DRAMA
Auden and Isherwood: *On the Frontier*
Fry: *The Boy with a Cart*
Priestley: *Music at Night*; *When We Are Married*
Smith, Dodie: *Dear Octopus*
Spender: *Trial of a Judge*
Wilder: *Our Town*
POETRY
Cummings: *Collected Poems*
Day-Lewis: *Overtures to Death, and Other Poems*
De la Mare: *Memory, and Other Poems*
Gibson: *Coming and Going*
MacNeice: *The Earth Compels*
Yeats: *New Poems*

1939

Germany invades Czechoslovakia; U.S.S.R. and Germany sign non-aggression pact; conscription introduced in Britain; Germany invades Poland; Britain declares war in support of Poland; outbreak of the Second World War (–1945); British troops sent to France; Nationalists under Franco win the Spanish Civil War after fall of Barcelona and Madrid; first jet aircraft flown, in Germany; discovery of nuclear fission; Sikorsky builds first helicopter, in U.S.A.; *Gone with the Wind* (*f.*); Ford: *Stagecoach* (*f.*); *The Wizard of Oz* (*f.*).

PROSE
Cary: *Mister Johnson*
Compton-Burnett: *A Family and a Fortune*
Eliot: *The Idea of a Christian Society*
Faulkner: *The Wild Palms*
Forester: *Captain Hornblower, R.N.*
Greene: *The Confidential Agent*
Huxley: *After Many a Summer*
Isherwood: *Goodbye to Berlin*
Joyce: *Finnegans Wake*
O'Brien, Flann: *At Swim-Two-Birds*
'George Orwell': *Coming Up for Air*
Powell: *What's Become of Waring*
Steinbeck: *The Grapes of Wrath*
Thompson, Flora: *Lark Rise to Candleford*

DRAMA
'James Bridie': *What Say They?*
Eliot: *The Family Reunion*
Novello: *The Dancing Years*
Shaw: *In Good King Charles's Golden Days*
POETRY
Eliot: *Old Possum's Book of Practical Cats*
Frost: *Collected Poems*
Housman (*d.*1936): *Collected Poems*
MacNeice: *Autumn Journal*
Spender: *The Still Centre*
Thomas, Dylan: *The Map of Love* (incl. prose)
Yeats (*d.*1939): *Last Poems and Two Plays*

1940

Fall of Denmark, Norway, Holland, Belgium and France to Germany; evacuation of British forces from Dunkirk; in the battle of Britain the Germans fail to destroy the R.A.F.; the London 'Blitz'; Churchill becomes P.M. of Coalition ministry (–1945); Pétain becomes P.M. of government of occupied France, at Vichy (–1945); British offensive against the Italians in the Western Desert; Japan signs Tripartite Pact with Germany and Italy; formation of the Home Guard in Britain and introduction of food rationing; development of penicillin as an antibiotic (*see* 1928); discovery of prehistoric wall-paintings at Lascaux; *Penguin New Writing* (–1950).

PROSE
Chandler: *Farewell, My Lovely*
Greene: *The Power and the Glory*
Hemingway: *For Whom the Bell Tolls*
Koestler: *Darkness at Noon*
McCullers: *The Heart Is a Lonely Hunter*
Muir: *The Story and the Fable*
'George Orwell': *Inside the Whale, and Other Essays*
Snow: *Strangers and Brothers*
Thomas, Dylan: *Portrait of the Artist as a Young Dog*
DRAMA
Priestley: *The Long Mirror*
POETRY
Abercrombie (*d*.1938): *Lyrics and Unfinished Poems*
Auden: *Another Time*
Barker: *Lament and Triumph*

POETRY (*cont.*)
Betjeman: *Old Lights for New Chancels*
Blunden: *Poems 1930–40*
Cummings: *Fifty Poems*
Davies (*d*.1940): *Poems of W.H. Davies, 1940*
Day-Lewis: *Poems in Wartime*
Eliot: *East Coker* (*see* 1943)
Kipling (*d*.1936): *Rudyard Kipling's Verse*
Read: *Thirty-Five Poems*
Sassoon: *Rhymed Ruminations*
Sitwell, E.: *Poems New and Old*

1941

Germany breaks pact and invades U.S.S.R.; siege of Leningrad starts (–1944); Rommel's Afrika Korps lands in Libya to strengthen Italian forces on the Western Desert front; Japan bombs the American fleet at Pearl Harbor; U.S.A. under Roosevelt joins the Allies against the Axis powers; Blitz on Coventry; income tax at 10 shillings in the pound; Shostakovich: Symphony No. 7 (*Leningrad*); Tippett: *A Child of Our Time* (oratorio); Orson Welles: *Citizen Kane* (*f*.).

PROSE
Cary: *Herself Surprised*
Churchill: *Into Battle*
Compton-Burnett: *Parents and Children*
Fitzgerald (*d*.1940): *The Last Tycoon*
Gallico: *The Snow Goose*
Gunn: *The Silver Darlings*
'George Orwell': *The Lion and the Unicorn: Socialism and the English Genius*
Ransom: *The New Criticism*
Warner: *The Aerodrome*
Woolf (*d*.1941): *Between the Acts*

DRAMA
(Brecht writes *Mother Courage*, performed 1949)
Coward: *Blithe Spirit*
POETRY
Auden: *New Year Letter*
Davies (*d*.1940): *Common Joys*
De la Mare: *Bells and Grass*
Eliot: *Burnt Norton*; *The Dry Salvages* (*see* 1943)
Gibson: *The Alert*
MacNeice: *Plant and Phantom*
Watkins: *The Ballad of the Mari Lwyd*

1942

Fall of Singapore to the Japanese; further Japanese advances in the South Pacific held by the battle of Midway; Russians defeat German army near Stalingrad; after many setbacks the Eighth Army under Montgomery defeats Rommel's forces at El Alamein in Egypt; Allied bombing of Germany increases; Beveridge Report defines schemes of social insurance to cover the whole community.

PROSE
(Camus: *The Stranger*)
Cary: *To Be a Pilgrim*
Faulkner: *Go Down Moses*
Lewis, C.S.: *The Screwtape Letters*
Thurber: *My World — and Welcome to It*
Waugh: *Put Out More Flags*; *Work Suspended*
Woolf (*d.*1941): *The Death of the Moth*

DRAMA
Coward: *This Happy Breed*
Rattigan: *Flare Path*

POETRY
De la Mare: *Collected Poems*; *Time Passes, and Other Poems*
Eliot: *Little Gidding* (*see* 1943)
('Paul Éluard': *Poetry and Truth*)
Lewis, Alun: *Raider's Dawn*
Masefield: *A Generation Risen*; *Land Workers*
Sitwell, E.: *Street Songs*
Spender: *Ruins and Visions*
Stevens: *Parts of a World*

1943

Allies invade Sicily after defeat of Axis resistance in North Africa; German army surrenders at Stalingrad; fall of Mussolini; Italy concludes armistice with Allied forces, but German resistance in Italy continues; further increase of 'round-the-clock' bombing raids on Germany; Americans start to push back the Japanese in the Pacific by 'island-hopping'; part-time work made compulsory for British women; Ministry of Town and County Planning set up to avoid haphazard building after the war; Rodgers and Hammerstein: *Oklahoma* (musical); Sartre: *Being and Nothingness: An Essay in Phenomenological Ontology*.

PROSE
Graves: *Wife to Mr Milton*
Greene: *The Ministry of Fear*
Koestler: *Arrival and Departure*
Plomer: *Double Lives*
Woolf (*d.*1941): *A Haunted House*

DRAMA
(Brecht: *The Good Woman of Setzwan*; *Life of Galileo*)
'James Bridie': *Mr Bolfry*
O'Casey: *Red Roses for Me*
Priestley: *Desert Highway*; *They Came to a City*
Rattigan: *While the Sun Shines*
(Sartre: *The Flies*)

POETRY
Day-Lewis: *Word Over All*
Eliot: *Four Quartets* (in U.S., 1944 in Britain, comprises *East Coker* (1940); *Burnt Norton* (1941); *The Dry Salvages* (1941); *Little Gidding* (1942))

POETRY (*cont.*)
Gascoyne: *Poems 1937–42*
Gibson: *The Searchlights*
Muir: *The Narrow Place*
Raine, Kathleen: *Stone and Flower*
Thomas, Dylan: *New Poems*

1944

Anzio landings; Rome surrenders to the Allies; Russians liberate the Baltic states and advance into Poland; D Day landings in Normandy; English and American troops drive the Germans out of France, but attempts to take Arnhem and other Rhine bridges fail; Americans liberate the Pacific islands as far as the Philippines; attempt to assassinate Hitler fails; Germans launch V1 flying bombs and V2 rockets against England; proposal for British National Health Service made in Parliament; Butler's Education Act revises secondary education.

PROSE
Bates: *Fair Stood the Wind for France*
(Borges: *Fictions*)
Cary: *The Horse's Mouth*
Comfort: *The Powerhouse*
Compton-Burnett: *Elders and Betters*
Hartley: *The Shrimp and the Anemone*
Joyce (*d.*1941): *Stephen Hero*
Lehmann: *The Ballad and the Source*
Maclaren-Ross: *The Stuff to Give the Troops*
Maugham: *The Razor's Edge*

DRAMA
(Anouilh: *Antigone*)
'James Bridie': *The Forrigan Reel*; *It Depends What You Mean*
Rattigan: *Love in Idleness*
(Sartre: *In Camera*)
Williams, 'Tennessee': *The Glass Menagerie*

POETRY
Auden: *For the Time Being*
Barker: *Eros in Dogma*
Betjeman: *New Bats in Old Belfries*
Blunden: *Shells by a Stream*
De la Mare: *Collected Rhymes and Verses*
Gibson: *The Outpost*
MacNeice: *Springboard*
Read: *A World within a War*
Sitwell, E.: *Green Song*
Williams, W.C.: *The Wedge*

1945

Allies advance into Germany from east and west; Hitler commits suicide; unconditional surrender of Germany; atomic bombs dropped on Hiroshima and Nagasaki; surrender of Japan; *c.*55 million people killed during the war; United Nations Organisation established; Nuremberg trials of war-criminals begin (–1946); in Britain, Labour wins General Election and Attlee becomes P.M. (–1951); Britten: *Peter Grimes* (opera).

PROSE
Bowen: *The Demon Lover*
Connolly: *The Unquiet Grave*
Fitzgerald (*d.*1940): *The Crack-Up*
'Henry Green': *Loving*
Isherwood: *Prater Violet*
Mitford: *The Pursuit of Love*
'George Orwell': *Animal Farm*
Thurber: *The Thurber Carnival*
Waugh: *Brideshead Revisited*
Wells: *Mind at the End of Its Tether*

DRAMA
'James Bridie': *Lancelot*
(Lorca (*d.*1936): *The House of Bernarda Alba*)

DRAMA (*cont.*)
Novello: *Perchance to Dream*
Priestley: *An Inspector Calls*

POETRY
De la Mare: *The Burning Glass, and Other Poems*
Larkin: *The North Ship*
Lewis, Alun (*d.*1944): *Ha! Ha! Among the Trumpets*
Pitter: *The Bridge*
Ransom: *Selected Poems*
Sitwell, E.: *The Song of the Cold*
Watkins: *The Lamp and the Veil*

1946

National Insurance Act establishes comprehensive insurance system based on Beveridge scheme; National Health Act provides free health care to all; Bank of England and coal industry nationalised; United Nations Assembly meets; Russian power of veto on the Security Council reveals political divide; Churchill coins the term 'Iron Curtain'; Hindu–Moslem riots in India; U.S. atomic bomb tests at Bikini and other islands; B.B.C. television broadcasts resumed; Spock: *The Commonsense Book of Baby and Child Care*.

PROSE
Cary: *The Moonlight*
(Colette: *Gigi*)
'Lewis Grassic Gibbon' (*d.*1935): *A Scots Quair* (contains *Sunset Song* (1932); *Cloud Howe* (1933); *Grey Granite* (1934))
'Henry Green': *Back*
Larkin: *Jill*
McCullers: *The Member of the Wedding*
'George Orwell': *Critical Essays*
Peake: *Titus Groan*

DRAMA
Fry: *A Phoenix Too Frequent*
O'Neill: *The Iceman Cometh*
Rattigan: *The Winslow Boy*

POETRY
De la Mare: *The Traveller*
Muir: *The Voyage*
Raine, Kathleen: *Living in Time*
Read: *Collected Poems*
Thomas, Dylan: *Deaths and Entrances*
Williams, W.C.: *Paterson: Book One* (compl. in 5 bks by 1958)
Wright: *The Moving Image*

1947

Economic crisis in Britain; food rations diminished; nationalisation of electrical industry and road and rail transport; U.S.A. offers Marshall Aid financial help to Europe to avert starvation and bankruptcy; partition of India, creating Dominions of India and Pakistan; first British nuclear reactor built, at Harwell; first supersonic flight; Dior's first show launches 'New Look' fashion; discovery of the Dead Sea Scrolls.

PROSE
(Camus: *The Plague*)
Compton-Burnett: *Manservant and Maidservant*
Graves: *The White Goddess*
Hartley: *Eustace and Hilda*
Lowry: *Under the Volcano*
Mackenzie: *Whisky Galore*
Maclaren-Ross: *Of Love and Hunger*
Potter: *The Theory and Practice of Gamesmanship, or The Art of Winning Games without Actually Cheating*
Snow: *The Light and the Dark*
Woolf (*d.*1941): *The Moment*

DRAMA
'James Bridie': *Dr Angelus*; *John Knox*
Coward: *Peace in Our Time*
Miller: *All My Sons*

DRAMA (*cont.*)
Priestley: *The Linden Tree*
Williams, 'Tennessee': *A Streetcar Named Desire*

POETRY
Sassoon: *Collected Poems*
Sitwell, E.: *The Shadow of Cain*
Spender: *Poems of Dedication*
Stevens: *Transport to Summer*

1948

Russians blockade West Berlin (–1949); communist coup in Cze-choslovakia; Zionist Jews declare new state of Israel in Palestine, following end of British mandate; in India, Gandhi assassinated; Malayan communists begin terrorist campaign (–1955); in Britain, Representation of the People Act abolishes plural voting; World Health Organisation established; Kinsey: *Sexual Behaviour in the Human Male*.

PROSE
Churchill: *The Second World War*
Eliot: *Notes Towards the Definition of Culture*
Faulkner: *Intruder in the Dusk*
Greene: *The Heart of the Matter*
James (*d.*1916): *The Art of Fiction*
Leavis: *The Great Tradition*
Mailer: *The Naked and the Dead*
(Mann: *Dr Faustus*)
Paton: *Cry, the Beloved Country*
Waugh: *The Loved One*
DRAMA
Fry: *The First-Born*; *The Lady's Not for Burning*
Rattigan: *The Browning Version*

POETRY
Auden: *The Age of Anxiety*
Betjeman: *Selected Poems*
Day-Lewis: *Collected Poems 1929–36*; *Poems 1943–7*
Graves: *Collected Poems 1914–47*
MacNeice: *Holes in the Sky*
Watkins: *The Lady with the Unicorn*

1949

North Atlantic Treaty signed by Western states; pound devalued; Eire secedes from the Empire; civil war in China results in collapse of Kuomintang regime and establishment of Communist govern-ment; Orson Welles in *The Third Man* (*f.*); Beauvoir: *The Second Sex*.

PROSE
Bates: *The Jacaranda Tree*
Bowen: *The Heat of the Day*
Cary: *A Fearful Joy*
Compton-Burnett: *Two Worlds and Their Ways*
Faulkner: *Knight's Gambit*
Mitford: *Love in a Cold Climate*
'George Orwell': *Nineteen-Eighty-Four*
Snow: *Time of Hope*
Wilson, Angus: *The Wrong Set*
DRAMA
(Brecht: *Mother Courage*)
'James Bridie': *Daphne Laureola*
Eliot: *The Cocktail Party*
Miller: *Death of a Salesman*
Novello: *King's Rhapsody*
O'Casey: *Cock a Doodle Dandy*
POETRY
Blunden: *After the Bombing, and Other Short Poems*
Empson: *Collected Poems*
Frost: *Complete Poems*

POETRY (*cont.*)
MacNeice: *Collected Poems 1925–48*
Muir: *The Labyrinth*
Pound: *Pisan Cantos*
Raine, Kathleen: *The Pythoness, and Other Poems*
Sitwell, E.: *The Canticle of the Rose*
Tate: *Poems 1922–47*
Wright: *Woman to Man*

1950

Nationalisation of iron and steel industry announced; in U.S.A., Senator McCarthy claims State Department to be full of communists; communist North Korean army invades South Korea; U.S.A. sends military assistance; population of England and Wales: 44 million; Scotland: 5.25 million; Northern Ireland: 1.36 million; samba the popular dance; *Eagle* comic launched.

PROSE
Boswell (*d*.1795): *London Journal 1762–3*
Bowen: *Collected Impressions*
'William Cooper': *Scenes from Provincial Life*
Hemingway: *Across the River and into the Trees*
Lessing: *The Grass Is Singing*
Lewis, C.S.: *The Lion, the Witch and the Wardrobe*
'George Orwell' (*d*.1950): *Shooting an Elephant, and Other Essays*
Peake: *Gormenghast*
Waugh: *Helena*
Wilson, Angus: *Such Darling Dodos*

DRAMA
'James Bridie': *Mr Gillie*; *The Queen's Comedy*
Fry: *Ring round the Moon* (adaptation of Anouilh); *Venus Observed*
Rattigan: *Who Is Sylvia?*
Shaw (*d*.1950): *Far-Fetched Fables*
Sherriff: *Home at Seven*

POETRY
Auden: *Collected Shorter Poems 1930–44*
Barker: *The Dead Seagull*; *The True Confession of George Barker*
De la Mare: *Inward Companion*
Gascoyne: *A Vagrant, and Other Poems*
Sitwell, E.: *Poor Men's Music*
Young: *Collected Poems*

1951

Bevan, Minister of Labour, resigns over health charges and defence spending; Conservatives win General Election; Churchill becomes P.M. (–1955); Burgess and Maclean defect to U.S.S.R.; armistice talks in Korea (*see* 1950); Kingdom of Libya created; Festival of Britain opens on the South Bank; 42,000 homes in Britain have T.V. sets; X certificates introduced for films unsuitable for persons under 16; Le Corbusier plans city of Chandigarh in the Punjab according to his modernist vision (compl. 1956); *The Lavender Hill Mob* (British film comedy); *The Archers* radio serial begins.

PROSE
Bradbury, Ray: *The Illustrated Man*
Forster: *Two Cheers for Democracy*
Greene: *The End of the Affair*
Monsarrat: *The Cruel Sea*
Powell: *A Question of Upbringing*
Salinger: *The Catcher in the Rye*
Snow: *The Masters*
'John Wyndham': *The Day of the Triffids*

DRAMA
Fry: *A Sleep of Prisoners*
Ustinov: *The Love of Four Colonels*
Whiting: *A Penny for a Song*; *Saint's Day*

POETRY
Auden: *Nones*

1952 Death of George VI; accession of Elizabeth II; European Coal and Steel Community starts to work towards political community in Europe; Nkrumah assumes control of the Gold Coast; Mau Mau activities in Kenya; contraceptive pill first made; U.S.A. explodes hydrogen bomb; first British atomic bomb exploded; last London tram makes farewell journey; Cage: *4'33"* (musical work consisting of the noise of the place where it is played); Gene Kelly in *Singin' in the Rain* (f.); *The Goon Show* (radio comedy –1960).

PROSE
Ellison: *Invisible Man*
Hemingway: *The Old Man and the Sea*
Leavis: *The Common Pursuit*
Lessing: *Martha Quest*
Powell: *A Buyer's Market*
Waugh: *Men at Arms*
Wilson, Angus: *Hemlock and After*

DRAMA
'James Bridie' (*d.*1951): *The Baikie Charivari*
Christie: *The Mousetrap*
Priestley: *Dragon's Mouth*
Rattigan: *The Deep Blue Sea*

POETRY
Jones, David: *The Anathemata*
Thomas, Dylan: *Collected Poems 1934–52*

1953 Coronation of Elizabeth II; death of Stalin; anti-Soviet uprising in East Berlin swiftly suppressed; Churchill proposes meeting of major world powers; armistice in Korea (*see* 1950); French troops occupy Dien Bien Phu (*see* 1954); Egypt becomes a republic; Hillary and Tensing climb Everest; Watson and Crick reveal the structure of D.N.A. molecule; myxomatosis epidemic kills millions of rabbits.

PROSE
(Barthes: *Writing Degree Zero*)
Beckett: *Watt*
Bellow: *The Adventures of Augie March*
Brophy: *Hackenfeller's Ape*
Cary: *Except the Lord*
Fleming: *Casino Royale*
Hartley: *The Go-Between*
Lehmann: *The Echoing Grove*
Wain: *Hurry on Down*

DRAMA
(Anouilh: *The Lark*)
(Beckett: *En attendant Godot*, *see* 1955)
Eliot: *The Confidential Clerk*
Greene: *The Living Room*
Miller: *The Crucible*
Rattigan: *The Sleeping Prince*
Williams, Emlyn: *Someone Waiting*
Williams, 'Tennessee': *Camino Real*

POETRY
Day-Lewis: *An Italian Visit*
Graves: *Poems 1953*
Mew (*d.*1928): *Collected Poems*

1954

Russians oppose reunification of Germany at foreign ministers' conference; British reach agreement with Egypt over the Suez Canal zone; Vietnamese Communists' capture of Dien Bien Phu followed by cease-fire in Indo-China; food rationing ends in Britain; Russians explode hydrogen bomb; Bannister runs a mile in under four minutes; Independent Television Authority established; Hepworth: *Two Figures: Menhirs* (*sc.*); Bratby: *Dustbins* (*p.*); Varèse: *Déserts* (music for ensemble and tape-recorder); Marlon Brando in *On the Waterfront* (*f.*).

PROSE
Amis: *Lucky Jim*
Bradbury, Ray: *Fahrenheit 451*
Golding: *Lord of the Flies*
Huxley: *The Doors of Perception*
Lessing: *A Proper Marriage*
Lewis, Wyndham: *Self Condemned*
Masters: *Bhowani Junction*
Muir: *Autobiography*
(Sagan: *Bonjour Tristesse*)
Snow: *The New Men*
Tolkien: *The Fellowship of the Ring*;
 The Two Towers (pts i-ii of *The Lord of the Rings*, pt iii *The Return of the King* 1955)

DRAMA
Behan: *The Quare Fellow*

DRAMA (*cont.*)
Fry: *The Dark Is Light Enough*
Rattigan: *Separate Tables*
Thomas, Dylan (*d.*1953): *Under Milk Wood* (radio)
Whiting: *Marching Song*

POETRY
Barker: *A Vision of Beasts and Gods*
Betjeman: *A Few Late Chrysanthemums*
Cummings: *Poems 1923–54*
Day-Lewis: *Collected Poems*
Gurney (*d.*1937): *Poems*
MacNeice: *Autumn Sequel*; *The Other Wing*

1955

Churchill espouses nuclear arms as deterrent, before retiring as P.M.; Eden becomes P.M. (–1957); 'credit squeeze' introduced to counter inflation; West Indian immigration to Britain increases; Eastern bloc nations sign Warsaw Pact; in U.S.S.R., Krushchev starts to dominate in struggle for power; state of emergency in Cyprus, with EOKA demanding union with Greece; West Germany joins NATO; black boycott of bus company in Montgomery, Alabama, following dispute over racial segregation; road modernisation schemes begun in Britain; commercial television and V.H.F. broadcasting begin; bill for suppression of 'horror comics'.

PROSE
Amis: *That Uncertain Feeling*
Becket: *Molloy* (French version 1951)
Cary: *Not Honour More*
Donleavy: *The Ginger Man*
Golding: *The Inheritors*
Greene: *Loser Takes All*; *The Quiet American*
Lewis, C.S.: *Surprised by Joy*
Nabokov: *Lolita*
Powell: *The Acceptance World*
Tolkien: *The Return of the King* (*see* 1954)
Waugh: *Officers and Gentlemen*
White: *The Tree of Man*

DRAMA
Beckett: *Waiting for Godot* (in French as *En attendant Godot* 1953)
Lawler: *The Summer of the Seventeenth Doll*
Miller: *A View from the Bridge*
Williams, 'Tennessee': *Cat on a Hot Tin Roof*

POETRY
Bishop: *North and South: A Cold Spring*
Larkin: *The Less Deceived*
Spender: *Collected Poems 1928–53*
Thomas, R.S.: *Song at the Year's Turning*

1956

Archbishop Makarios deported from Cyprus in attempt to stop violence; President Nasser of Egypt nationalises the Suez Canal; Israel attacks Egypt; Britain and France send troops; ceasefire call by U.N. is accepted; Bulganin and Krushchev visit Britain; 'de-Stalinisation' of East European countries; revolt in Hungary in favour of greater democratic freedoms ended by Russian invasion; first Aldermaston march organised by the Campaign for Nuclear Disarmament; rebuilding of Coventry Cathedral by Spence started (consecrated 1962); beginnings of rock 'n' roll music; Elvis Presley: *Heartbreak Hotel* (song).

PROSE
Baldwin: *Giovanni's Room*
Beckett: *Malone Dies* (in French as *Malone meurt* 1951)
Churchill: *A History of the English-Speaking Peoples* (compl. in 4 vols by 1958)
Golding: *Pincher Martin*
Macaulay: *The Towers of Trebizond*
Wilson, Angus: *Anglo-Saxon Attitudes*
Wilson, Colin: *The Outsider*

DRAMA
O'Neill (*d*.1953): *Long Day's Journey into Night*
Osborne: *Look Back in Anger*
Whiting: *The Gates of Summer*
POETRY
Conquest (ed.): *New Lines*
Ginsberg: *Howl, and Other Poems*

1957

Macmillan takes over from Eden as P.M. (–1963); government White Paper proposes cutting down on conventional forces and relying on nuclear deterrent; Wolfenden report on homosexuality and prostitution; Ghana and Malaya granted independence, part of general decolonisation of British territory during the next decade; in U.S.A., protests over racial segregation in schools cause violent reaction; in U.S.S.R., Krushchev made First Secretary (–1964); 'Asian flu' epidemic; first British hydrogen bomb exploded; Russians launch *Sputniks I* and *II*; extensive exploration of the Antarctic; Bacon: *Screaming Nurse* (*p*.); Bernstein: *West Side Story* (musical).

PROSE
Braine: *Room at the Top*
Durrell: *Bitter Lemons*; *Justine* (pt i of *The Alexandria Quartet*, which includes *Balthazar* (1958); *Mountolive* (1958); *Clea* (1960))
Hartley: *The Hireling*
Kerouac: *On the Road*
Lessing: *The Habit of Loving*
Murdoch: *The Sandcastle*
Naipaul: *The Mystic Masseur*
(Pasternak: *Dr Zhivago*)
Powell: *At Lady Molly's*
(Robbe-Grillet: *Jealousy*)
Waugh: *The Ordeal of Gilbert Pinfold*
White: *Voss*
DRAMA
Arden: *The Waters of Babylon*
Beckett: *All That Fall*

DRAMA (*cont.*)
Bolt: *Flowering Cherry*
(Genet: *The Balcony*)
Greene: *The Potting Shed*
Osborne: *The Entertainer*
Pinter: *The Room*
Simpson: *A Resounding Tinkle*
POETRY
Barker: *Collected Poems 1950–55*
Day-Lewis: *Pegasus, and Other Poems*
Fuller: *Brutus's Orchard*
Gunn: *The Sense of Movement*
Hughes, Ted: *The Hawk in the Rain*
MacNeice: *Visitations*
Smith, 'Stevie': *Not Waving but Drowning: Poems*

1958

Rebellion by French settlers in Algeria; De Gaulle becomes President of France (–1969); race rioting in Notting Hill, London; Alton East Estate at Roehampton built, one of the first of many high-rise housing estates and example of modernist 'New Brutalist' architecture; first parking meter, in Mayfair, London; stereophonic records introduced; Moore: *Reclining Figure* (*sc.*).

PROSE
Achebe: *Things Fall Apart*
Amis: *I Like It Here*
Bates: *The Darling Buds of May*
Beckett: *The Unnameable* (in French as *L'Innomable* 1953)
Behan: *Borstal Boy*
Durrell: *Balthazar; Mountolive* (*see* 1957)
Greene: *Our Man in Havana*
(Lampedusa (*d.*1957): *The Leopard*)
Lessing: *A Ripple from the Storm*
Murdoch: *The Bell*
Naipaul: *The Suffrage of Elvira*
'Mary Renault': *The King Must Die*
Sillitoe: *Saturday Night and Sunday Morning*
Snow: *The Conscience of the Rich*
Spark: *Robinson*

PROSE (*cont.*)
Wilson, Angus: *The Middle Age of Mrs Eliot*
DRAMA
Arden: *Live Like Pigs*
Beckett: *Endgame; Krapp's Last Tape*
Behan: *The Hostage*
Delaney: *A Taste of Honey*
Eliot: *The Elder Statesman*
(Frisch: *The Fire-Raisers*)
Jellicoe: *The Sport of My Mad Mother*
O'Casey: *The Drums of Father Ned*
Pinter: *The Birthday Party*
Shaffer: *Five Finger Exercise*
Wesker: *Chicken Soup with Barley*
POETRY
Betjeman: *Collected Poems*
Thomas, R.S.: *Poetry for Supper*

1959

Macmillan returned as P.M. (–1963); Street Offences Act aimed at removing prostitution from the streets; Makarios becomes President of Cyprus (–1977); following expulsion of President Batista from Cuba, Castro becomes premier; first British motorway opened (London to Birmingham); hovercraft developed; first Mini sold; hula-hoop craze; Marilyn Monroe in *Some Like It Hot* (*f.*).

PROSE
Bellow: *Henderson the Rain King*
Bradbury, Malcolm: *Eating People Is Wrong*
Burroughs: *The Naked Lunch*
Cary (*d.*1957): *The Captive and the Free*
Compton-Burnett: *A Heritage and Its History*
Golding: *Free Fall*
(Grass: *The Tin Drum*)
Huxley: *Brave New World Revisited*
Lee: *Cider with Rosie*
MacInnes: *Absolute Beginners*
Naipaul: *Miguel Street*
Peake: *Titus Alone*
Sillitoe: *The Loneliness of the Long Distance Runner*
Snow: *The Two Cultures and the Scientific Revolution*
Spark: *Memento Mori*

PROSE (*cont.*)
Waterhouse: *Billy Liar*
DRAMA
Albee: *The Zoo Story*
(Anouilh: *Beckett*)
Arden: *Serjeant Musgrave's Dance*
Greene: *The Complaisant Lover*
Osborne: *The World of Paul Slickey*
Pinter: *A Slight Ache*
Simpson: *One Way Pendulum*
Wesker: *The Kitchen; Roots*
Williams, 'Tennessee': *Sweet Bird of Youth*
POETRY
Berryman: *Homage to Mistress Bradstreet, and Other Poems*
Graves: *Collected Poems 1959*
Hill, Geoffrey: *For the Unfallen: Poems 1952–8*
Lowell: *Life Studies*
MacNeice: *Eighty-Five Poems*

1960

Macmillan makes 'Wind of Change' speech in Cape Town, acknowledging inevitability of African independence; Sharpeville Massacre in South Africa; Nigeria gains independence; secession of Katanga leads to civil war in the Congo (–1963); Kennedy becomes President of U.S.A. (–1963); international summit conference breaks up after shooting down of American U-2 spy plane by U.S.S.R.; Britain agrees to harbour Polaris-equipped submarines in Holy Loch; farthing discontinued; last British tram runs in Sheffield (*see* 1952); fashion for stiletto-heeled shoes; Fellini: *La Dolce Vita* (Italian *f.*); Penguin Books acquitted of publishing an obscene work, the unexpurgated version of *Lady Chatterley's Lover*.

PROSE

Amis: *Take a Girl Like You*
Banks: *The L-Shaped Room*
Barstow: *A Kind of Loving*
Barth: *The Sot-Weed Factor*
Day-Lewis: *The Buried Day*
Durrell: *Clea* (*see* 1957)
Lawrence (*d*.1930): *Lady Chatterley's Lover*
Lee, Harper: *To Kill a Mockingbird*
O'Brien, Edna: *The Country Girls*
Powell: *Casanova's Chinese Restaurant*
Snow: *The Affair*
Spark: *The Ballad of Peckham Rye*
Storey: *Flight into Camden*; *This Sporting Life*

DRAMA

Arden: *The Business of Good Government: A Christmas Play*; *The Happy Haven*
Bolt: *A Man for All Seasons*
Coward: *Waiting in the Wings*
Delaney: *The Lion in Love*
(Ionesco: *Rhinoceros*)
Pinter: *The Caretaker*; *The Dumb Waiter*
Rattigan: *Ross*
Wesker: *I'm Talking about Jerusalem*

POETRY

Auden: *Homage to Clio*
Betjeman: *Summoned by Bells*
Durrell: *Collected Poems*
Hughes, Ted: *Lupercal*
Plath: *The Colossus, and Other Poems*; *A Winter Ship*
Scannell: *The Masks of Love*

1961

Berlin Wall built; opponents to Algerian independence attempt to assassinate De Gaulle; South Africa withdraws from the Commonwealth; 'Bay of Pigs' abortive invasion of Cuba backed by U.S.A.; beginning of big expansion of British and Commonwealth universities; first manned satellites orbit the earth.

PROSE

New English Bible (New Testament, Old Testament 1970)
Compton-Burnett: *The Mighty and Their Fall*
Greene: *A Burnt-Out Case*
Heller: *Catch-22*
Hughes, Richard: *The Fox in the Attic*
Macaulay (*d*.1958): *Letters to a Friend*
Murdoch: *A Severed Head*
Naipaul: *A House for Mr Biswas*
Narayan: *The Man-Eater of Malgudi*
Spark: *The Prime of Miss Jean Brodie*
Waugh: *Unconditional Surrender*
White: *Riders in the Chariot*
Wilson, Angus: *The Old Men at the Zoo*

DRAMA

Albee: *The American Dream*
Beckett: *Happy Days*
Fry: *Curtmantle*
Fugard: *The Blood Knot*
Jellicoe: *The Knack*
Osborne: *Luther*
Pinter: *The Collection*
Whiting: *The Devils*
Williams, 'Tennessee': *The Night of the Iguana*

POETRY

Graves: *More Poems 1961*
Gunn: *My Sad Captains, and Other Poems*
Masefield: *The Bluebells, and Other Verse*

1962

Algeria gains independence from France; U.S.A. and U.S.S.R. in confrontation over Russian missile base in Cuba; U.S.S.R. finally dismantles Cuban base; in Britain, Commonwealth Immigrants Act passed to control numbers of immigrants; end of post-war National Service; Pope John XXIII organises the Second Vatican Council (first since 1870), to discuss ecumenism and Church unity (–1964); launch of telecommunications satellite Telstar, enabling live T.V. signals between U.S.A. and Europe; sedative drug Thalidomide withdrawn after discovery that it deforms unborn babies; Britten: *War Requiem* (music for choir and orchestra, incl. settings of poems by Wilfred Owen, performed at dedication of the new Coventry Cathedral); *Private Eye* begins publication.

PROSE
Ballard: *The Drowned World*
Brophy: *Flesh*
Burgess: *A Clockwork Orange*
Faulkner (*d*.1962): *The Reivers*
Kesey: *One Flew Over the Cuckoo's Nest*
Lessing: *The Golden Notebook*
Mortimer: *The Pumpkin Eater*
Murdoch: *An Unofficial Rose*
Nabokov: *Pale Fire*
Powell: *The Kindly Ones*
'Mary Renault': *The Bull from the Sea*
(Solzhenitsyn: *One Day in the Life of Ivan Denisovich*)

DRAMA
Albee: *Who's Afraid of Virginia Woolf?*
(Dürrenmatt: *The Physicists*)
Rudkin: *Afore Night Come*
Wesker: *Chips with Everything*

POETRY
Alvarez (ed.): *The New Poetry* (anthology)
Barker: *The View from a Blind I*
Day-Lewis: *The Gate, and Other Poems*
Fuller: *Collected Poems 1936–61*
Gunn and Ted Hughes: *Selected Poems*

1963

President Kennedy of U.S.A. assassinated; Martin Luther King makes 'I have a dream' speech on civil rights in Washington; South Vietnam government overthrown in coup; in Britain, Profumo, Secretary of State for War, involved in sex scandal; Macmillan resigns; Home P.M. (–1964); Philby revealed as spy and defects to U.S.S.R.; 'Great Train Robbery'; Robinson (Bishop of Woolwich): *Honest to God* (controversial theology); Rachel Carson (ecologist): *Silent Spring*; *The Freewheelin' Bob Dylan* (LP record).

PROSE
Amis: *One Fat Englishman*
Burgess: *Inside Mr Enderby*
Drabble: *A Summer Bird-Cage*
'John le Carré': *The Spy Who Came in from the Cold*
McCarthy: *The Group*
Murdoch: *The Unicorn*
Naipaul: *Mr Stone and the Knight's Companion*
O'Connor: *My Oedipus Complex, and Other Stories*
Plath ('Victoria Lucas'): *The Bell Jar*
Pynchon: *V*
Storey: *Radcliffe*
DRAMA
Arden: *Ironhand*
Beckett: *Play*

DRAMA (*cont.*)
Chilton and Theatre Workshop: *Oh, What a Lovely War!*
Pinter: *The Lover*
Rattigan: *Man and Boy*
Wood: *Cockade*
POETRY
Clarke: *Flight to Africa, and Other Poems*
Ginsberg: *Reality Sandwiches*
Grigson: *Collected Poems 1924–62*
Hobsbaum and Lucie-Smith (eds): *A Group Anthology*
MacNeice (*d*.1963): *The Burning Perch*
Redgrove: *At the White Monument, and Other Poems*

1964

Labour wins General Election and Wilson becomes P.M. (–1970); Commons vote to end death penalty; U.S.A. becomes increasingly embroiled in struggle between South Vietnamese government and Vietcong communists; President Johnson signs Civil Rights Act; Krushchev ousted from power in U.S.S.R by Brezhnev and Kosygin; U.N. prevents fighting between Greek and Turkish communities in Cyprus; China explodes hydrogen bomb; *The Sun* newspaper starts; B.B.C. 2 begins broadcasting; Radio Caroline broadcasts from a ship in the Channel.

PROSE
Achebe: *Arrow of God*
Beckett: *How It Is* (French version *Comment c'est* 1961)
Bellow: *Herzog*
Dahl: *Charlie and the Chocolate Factory*
Golding: *The Spire*
Hemingway (*d.*1961): *A Moveable Feast*
Koestler: *The Act of Creation*
Murdoch: *The Italian Girl*
Powell: *The Valley of Bones*
Snow: *Corridors of Power*
Wilson, Angus: *Late Call*

DRAMA
Arden: *Armstrong's Last Goodnight*
Greene: *Carving a Statue*
Orton: *Entertaining Mr Sloane*

DRAMA (*cont.*)
Osborne: *Inadmissible Evidence*
Shaffer: *The Royal Hunt of the Sun*

POETRY
Berryman: *77 Dreamsongs*
Douglas (*d.*1944): *Selected Poems* (ed. Ted Hughes)
Ginsberg: *Kaddish, and Other Poems*
Graves: *Man Does, Woman Is*
Larkin: *The Whitsun Weddings*
Lowell: *For the Union Dead*
Sexton: *Selected Poems*

1965

Vietnam War escalates; U.S.A. sends more troops and bombs North Vietnam; race riots in U.S.A.; Rhodesia, under Smith, makes Unilateral Declaration of Independence; in Britain, Wilson announces economic sanctions against Smith regime; Race Relations Act sets up Race Relations Board; death of Winston Churchill; natural gas discovered in the North Sea; *The Sound of Music* (*f.* musical); Chomsky: *Aspects of a Theory of Syntax*.

PROSE
'John le Carré': *The Looking-Glass War*
Lessing: *Landlocked*
Mailer: *An American Dream*
Murdoch: *The Red and the Green*
Spark: *The Mandelbaum Gate*
Trevor: *The Boarding-House*
Wolfe: *The Kandy-Kolored Tangerine-Flake Streamline Baby*

DRAMA
Albee: *Tiny Alice*
Arden: *Left-Handed Liberty*
Bond: *Saved*
Marcus: *The Killing of Sister George*
Mercer: *Ride a Cock-Horse*

DRAMA (*cont.*)
Pinter: *The Homecoming*; *Tea Party*
Shaffer: *Black Comedy*
Simpson: *The Cresta Run*
Wesker: *The Four Seasons*

POETRY
Graves: *Collected Poems 1965*
Heath-Stubbs: *Selected Poems*
Plath (*d.*1963): *Ariel*
Scannell: *Walking Wounded*
Silkin: *Nature with Man*

1966

Failure of talks between Wilson and Smith about RI
U.D.I.; Wilson imposes pay and wages freeze; Chairmai
Red Guards start 'Cultural Revolution' in China (–1972); /
mining village disaster; England wins football World Cup;
ing London': Carnaby Street and mini-skirts in fashion.

PROSE

Achebe: *A Man of the People*
Barth: *Giles Goat-Boy*
Capote: *In Cold Blood*
Fowles: *The Magus*
Frayn: *The Russian Interpreter*
Greene: *The Comedians*
Malamud: *The Fixer*
Murdoch: *The Time of the Angels*
Powell: *The Soldier's Art*
Pynchon: *The Crying of Lot 49*
Rhys: *Wide Sargasso Sea*
Scott: *The Jewel in the Crown* (pt i of
the *Raj Quartet*, which includes *The
Day of the Scorpion* (1968); *The
Towers of Silence* (1971); *A
Division of the Spoils* (1975))
Sontag: *Against Interpretation*
White: *The Solid Mandala*

DRAMA

Beckett: *Come and Go: Dramat....c*
Coward: *A Song at Twilight*
Mercer: *Belcher's Luck*
Orton: *Loot*
Osborne: *A Bond Honoured*; *A
Patriot for Me*
Wood: *Fill the Stage with Happy
Hours*

POETRY

Auden: *Collected Shorter Poems
1927–57*
Heaney: *Death of a Naturalist*
MacNeice (*d.*1963): *Collected Poems*
Roethke (*d.*1963): *Collected Poems*
Sexton: *Live or Die*
Smith, 'Stevie': *The Frog Prince, and
Other Poems*

1967

Six Day War between Israel and Arab states; army coup in Greece;
secession of Biafra leads to civil war in Nigeria (–1970); 'Che'
Guevara killed during guerilla warfare in Bolivia; many anti-Vietnam War demonstrations in U.S.A. and Europe; British troops
leave Aden after intensification of rioting; in Britain, devaluation
of pound sterling; homosexual acts between consenting adults
legalised in England and Wales; abortion legalised; first heart
transplant operation, in South Africa; new Radio One devoted
exclusively to pop music; first British colour T.V. broadcast; Hock-
ney: *A Bigger Splash* (*p.*); Beatles: *Sergeant Pepper's Lonely
Hearts' Club Band* (LP record); *Bonnie and Clyde* (*f.*).

PROSE

(Derrida: *Of Grammatology*; *Writing
and Difference*)
Golding: *The Pyramid*
Isherwood: *A Meeting by the River*
Kavan: *Ice*
McCarthy: *Vietnam*
Mailer: *Why Are We in Vietnam?*
(Márquez: *One Hundred Years of
Solitude*)
Naipaul: *The Mimic Men*
Narayan: *The Vendor of Sweets*
Ngugi: *A Grain of Wheat*
O'Brien, Flann: *The Third Policeman*
Richardson (*d.*1957): *March Moonlight*
(last vol. of *Pilgrimage, see* 1915)
Sontag: *Death Kit*
Wilson, Angus: *No Laughing Matter*

DRAMA

Ayckbourn: *Relatively Speaking*
Nichols: *A Day in the Death of Joe
Egg*
Stoppard: *Rosencrantz and
Guildenstern Are Dead*
'Peter Terson': *Zigger Zagger*
Wood: *Dingo*

POETRY

Ashbery: *Selected Poems*
Gunn: *Touch*
Henri, McGough, Patten: *The Mersey
Sound: Penguin Modern Poets 10*
Hughes, Ted: *Wodwo* (incl. prose)
Jennings: *Collected Poems*
Lowell: *Near the Ocean*
Soyinka: *Idanre, and Other Poems*

1968

Nixon becomes President of U.S.A. (–1974); assassination of American civil rights leader Martin Luther King in Memphis; Dubček's liberal reforms in Czechoslovakia ended by Russian invasion; French students riot in Paris; anti-Vietnam War demonstrations in London broken up violently by police; Commonwealth Immigration Act restricts entry of Kenyan Asians; Enoch Powell makes controversial speech about British immigration policies; censorship of the theatre by the Lord Chamberlain abolished.

PROSE
Amis: *I Want It Now*
Barth: *Lost in the Funhouse*
Lowry (*d.*1957): *Dark As the Grave Wherein My Friend Is Laid*
Mailer: *The Armies of the Night*
Moore, Brian: *I Am Mary Dunne*
Murdoch: *The Nice and the Good*
Powell: *The Military Philosophers*
Pritchett: *A Cab at the Door*
Scott: *The Day of the Scorpion* (*see* 1966)
Snow: *The Sleep of Reason*
(Solzhenitsyn: *Cancer Ward*; *The First Circle* (both transl.))
Updike: *Couples*
Vidal: *Myra Breckinridge*

DRAMA
Arden: *The Hero Rises Up*
Bennett: *Forty Years On*
Bond: *Early Morning*; *Narrow Road to the Deep North*
Osborne: *The Hotel in Amsterdam*; *Time Present*
Pinter: *Landscape*
Stoppard: *The Real Inspector Hound*
'Peter Terson': *The Apprentices*
POETRY
Auden: *Collected Longer Poems*
Bunting: *Collected Poems*
Fuller: *New Poems*
Graves: *Poems 1965–8*
Hill, Geoffrey: *King Log*

1969

Legal age of majority (including right to vote) reduced from 21 to 18; Divorce Reform Act makes breakdown of marriage cause for divorce; civil disturbances in Northern Ireland; troops sent to restore order; in France, De Gaulle resigns after losing constitutional referendum; Pompidou becomes President (–1974); *Apollo 11* lands on the moon, transmitting T.V. pictures of man's first moonwalk; maiden flight of *Concorde*; foundation of the Open University; in U.S.A., actress Sharon Tate is among those murdered by followers of cult-leader Charles Manson; *Easy Rider* (*f.*).

PROSE
Amis: *The Green Man*
Atwood: *The Edible Woman*
Blythe: *Akenfield: Portrait of an English Village*
Brautigan: *Trout Fishing in America*
Fowles: *The French Lieutenant's Woman*
Greene: *Travels with My Aunt*
Lee: *As I Walked Out One Midsummer Morning*
Lessing: *The Four-Gated City*
Murdoch: *Bruno's Dream*
Nabokov: *Ada*
Roth: *Portnoy's Complaint*
Upward: *The Rotten Elements*
Vonnegut: *Slaughterhouse-Five*
DRAMA
Jellicoe: *The Giveaway*

DRAMA (*cont.*)
Livings: *Honour and Offer*
Orton (*d.*1967): *What the Butler Saw*
Pinter: *Silence*
Storey: *In Celebration*; *The Contractor*
Wood: *H: Being Monologues at Front of Burning Cities*
POETRY
Auden: *City without Walls, and Other Poems*
Berryman: *His Toy, His Dream, His Rest*
Bishop: *The Complete Poems*
Dunn: *Terry Street*
Enright: *Selected Poems*
Lowell: *Notebook 1967–8*
Soyinka: *Poems from Prison*

1970

Conservatives win General Election; Heath becomes P.M. (–1974); many strikes in protest at the Industrial Relations Bill; emergency power cuts; controversy over the provision of arms for South Africa; riots in Ulster and internment of I.R.A. supporters; after death of 2 million in civil war, Biafran rebels surrender to Federal Nigerian government (*see* 1967); U.S. planes bomb Cambodia; students killed at anti-Vietnam War demonstrations at Kent State University, Ohio; Millett: *Sexual Politics*.

PROSE
(Barthes: *S/Z*)
Bellow: *Mr Sammler's Planet*
Davies: *Fifth Business* (pt i of *The Deptford Trilogy*, which includes *The Manticore* (1972); *World of Wonders* (1975))
Farrell: *Troubles*
Hill, Susan: *I'm the King of the Castle*
Kavan (*d*.1968): *Julia and the Bazooka*
Murdoch: *A Fairly Honourable Defeat*
O'Brien, Edna: *A Pagan Place*
Spark: *The Driver's Seat*
Updike: *Bech: A Book*
DRAMA
Beckett: *Breath*
Bolt: *Vivat, Vivat Regina*
Fry: *A Yard of Sun*

DRAMA (*cont.*)
Hampton: *The Philanthropist*
Hare: *Slag*
Mercer: *After Haggerty*
Mortimer: *A Voyage round My Father*
Rattigan: *Bequest to the Nation*
Storey: *Home*
Wesker: *The Friends*
POETRY
Ashbery: *The Double Dream of Spring*
Berryman: *Love and Fame*
Graham: *Malcolm Mooney's Land*
Harrison: *The Loiners*
Hughes, Ted: *Crow* (*see* 1972)
Lowell: *Notebook* (revised edn, *see* 1969)
Porter: *The Last of England*
Singer (*d*.1964): *Collected Poems*

1971

Introduction of decimal currency; 'Angry Brigade' bombs home of Secretary of State for Employment; Rolls-Royce aircraft engine makers go into liquidation and are nationalised; East Pakistan breaks from West Pakistan and declares itself republic of Bangladesh; Greer: *The Female Eunuch*; Illich: *Deschooling Society*; Skinner: *Beyond Freedom and Dignity* (behavourist psychology).

PROSE
Amis: *Girl 20*
Forster (*d*.1970): *Maurice*
Lessing: *Briefing for a Descent into Hell*
Murdoch: *An Accidental Man*
Naipaul: *In a Free State*
Powell: *Books Do Furnish a Room*
Pritchett: *Midnight Oil*
Scott: *The Towers of Silence* (*see* 1966)
DRAMA
Bennett: *Getting On*
Bond: *Lear*
Gray: *Butley*
Osborne: *West of Suez*
Pinter: *Old Times*
Storey: *The Changing Room*

POETRY
Gunn: *Moly*
Hill, Geoffrey: *Mercian Hymns*
MacBeth: *Collected Poems 1958–70*
O'Hara (*d*.1966): *Collected Poems*
Plath (*d*.1963): *Crossing the Water*; *Winter Trees*

1972

Unemployment in Britain rises to a million; miners' strike leads to electricity blackouts; 13 civilians killed by British troops on 'Bloody Sunday' in Northern Ireland; introduction of direct rule from London instead of Stormont Parliament; Icelandic gunboat sinks two British trawlers in start of 'Cod War' over fishing rights in the North Sea (–1973, 1976); Common Market increases in membership from six to ten, including Britain; President Amin of Uganda expels Asians from his country, many of whom come to Britain; heavy U.S. bombings of North Vietnam followed by suspension and withdrawal of combat troops; President Nixon visits China; bomb outrages in West Germany after arrests of Baader and Meinhof, leaders of the extremist group Red Army Faction.

PROSE
Atwood: *Surfacing*
(Calvino: *Invisible Cities*)
Davies: *The Manticore* (*see* 1970)
Keneally: *The Chant of Jimmie Blacksmith*
Storey: *Pasmore*
DRAMA
Ayckbourn: *Absurd Person Singular*
Osborne: *A Sense of Detachment*
Stoppard: *Jumpers*
Wesker: *The Old Ones*
Wood: *Veterans, or Hairs in the Gates of the Hellespont*
POETRY
Dunn: *The Happier Life*

POETRY (*cont.*)
Fuller, John: *Cannibals and Missionaries*
Heaney: *Wintering Out*
Hope: *Collected Poems 1930–70*
Hughes, Ted: *Crow* (revised edn, *see* 1970)
Smith, 'Stevie' (*d.*1971): *Scorpion, and Other Poems*
Soyinka: *A Shuttle in the Crypt*

1973

Bomb attacks by the Provisional I.R.A. in England; civil disturbance continues in Northern Ireland; food prices and mortgage rates rise to new high levels; miners' overtime ban causes short supplies of coal, resulting in state of emergency; 'Three Day Week' introduced to save energy; 'Yom Kippur' war in the Middle East leads to cuts in supply of oil; cease-fire in the Vietnam War; President Nixon implicated in the Watergate affair; Schumacher: *Small Is Beautiful: A Study of Economics As If People Mattered.*

PROSE
Amis, Martin: *The Rachel Papers*
Greene: *The Honorary Consul*
Lessing: *The Summer before the Dark*
Murdoch: *The Black Prince*
Powell: *Temporary Kings*
Pynchon: *Gravity's Rainbow*
Storey: *A Temporary Life*
Trevor: *Elizabeth Alone*
White: *The Eye of the Storm*
Wilson, Angus: *As If by Magic*
DRAMA
Ayckbourn: *The Norman Conquests*
Bond: *Bingo: Scenes of Money and Death (and Passion)*; *The Sea*

DRAMA (*cont.*)
Hampton: *Savages*
Osborne: *A Place Calling Itself Rome*
Shaffer: *Equus*
Storey: *Cromwell*
POETRY
Heath-Stubbs: *Artorius*
Lowell: *The Dolphin*; *For Lizzie and Harriet*; *History*
Thomas, R.S.: *Selected Poems 1946–68*
Walcott: *Another Life*

1974

Government and miners continue confrontation; Heath loses General Election; minority Labour government under Wilson; second General Election increases Labour's majority (–1979); inflation reaches 16%; I.R.A. bomb in Birmingham pub kills 16; Turkish invasion of Cyprus leads to civil war and evacuations; Nixon resigns as President of U.S.A.; Ford becomes President (–1976).

PROSE

Bainbridge: *The Bottle Factory Outing*
Gordimer: *The Conservationist*
Hill, Susan: *In the Springtime of the Year*
'John le Carré': *Tinker, Tailor, Soldier, Spy*
Lessing: *The Memoirs of a Survivor*
Lurie: *The War between the Tates*
Murdoch: *The Sacred and Profane Love Machine*
Pirsig: *Zen and the Art of Motorcycle Maintenance*
Spark: *The Abbess of Crewe: A Modern Morality Tale*
White: *The Cockatoos*

DRAMA

Rudkin: *Ashes*
Stoppard: *Travesties*

POETRY

Dunn: *Love or Nothing*
Larkin: *High Windows*
Thwaite: *New Confessions*

1975

Civil war begins in Lebanon; South Vietnam surrenders to North Vietnam; civil war begins in Angola; death of General Franco of Spain; Australian P.M. Whitlam sacked by Governor-General in constitutional crisis; in Britain, inflation at 25%; T.U.C. agrees to maximum weekly pay increase in attempt to defeat inflation; unemployment continues to increase; 216 civilians and 30 members of the security forces killed in Northern Ireland disturbances; Equal Opportunities Commission established to counter sex discrimination; Margaret Thatcher defeats Heath for leadership of the Conservative Party.

PROSE

Amis, Martin: *Dead Babies*
(Barthes: *Roland Barthes*)
Bellow: *Humboldt's Gift*
Bradbury, Malcolm: *The History Man*
Davies: *World of Wonders* (see 1970)
Drabble: *The Realms of Gold*
Jhabvala: *Heat and Dust*
McEwan: *First Love, Last Rites*
Murdoch: *A Word Child*
Naipaul: *Guerrillas*
Powell: *Hearing Secret Harmonies*
Scott: *A Division of the Spoils* (see 1966)
Theroux: *The Great Railway Bazaar: By Train through Asia*
Trevor: *Angels at the Ritz, and Other Stories*

DRAMA

Frayn: *Donkey's Years*
Gray: *Otherwise Engaged*
Griffiths: *Comedians*
Osborne: *The End of Me Old Cigar*
Pinter: *No Man's Land*

POETRY

Causley: *Collected Poems 1951–75*
Heaney: *North*
Hope: *A Late Picking: Poems 1965–74*
Porter: *Living in a Calm Country*
Scannell: *The Loving Game*
Smith, 'Stevie' (d.1971): *Collected Poems*

Callaghan becomes P.M. (–1979) after Wilson's resignation; efforts to reduce inflation result in annual rate falling to 15%; Britain's ambassador to Dublin assassinated; Jeremy Thorpe resigns as leader of the Liberal Party after allegations about homosexuality; nationalist guerrillas intensify activity against Ian Smith's rule in Rhodesia; Israeli commandos rescue hostages at Entebbe Airport in Uganda; in U.S.A., Carter elected President (–1980); Foucault: *The History of Sexuality*; opening of the National Theatre in London.

PROSE
(Kundera: *The Farewell Party*)
Murdoch: *Henry and Cato*
Rhys: *Sleep It Off Lady*
Waugh (*d.*1966): *The Diaries of Evelyn Waugh*
White: *A Fringe of Leaves*
DRAMA
Ayckbourn: *Just between Ourselves*
Brenton: *Weapons of Happiness*
Rosenthal: *Bar Mitzvah Boy*
POETRY
Ashbery: *Self-Portrait in a Convex Mirror*
Dylan: *The Songs of Bob Dylan 1966–75*
Gunn: *Jack Straw's Castle*
Levi: *Collected Poems 1955–75*

POETRY (*cont.*)
Murray: *Selected Poems: The Vernacular Republic*
Walcott: *Sea Grapes*

1977 By-election losses make Labour lose a working majority in Parliament; pact arranged with the Liberals; aircraft and shipbuilding industries nationalised; unions agree to voluntary wage restraint after refusing to renew pay pact with Government; strike at Grunwick film-processing works, London, over union recognition (–1978); Queen Elizabeth's Silver Jubilee; General Zia topples President Bhutto in Pakistan; feminist publishing house Virago publishes its first independent title; 'punk' in fashion; *Never Mind the Bollocks, Here's the Sex Pistols* (LP record).

PROSE
Desai: *Fire on the Mountain*
Fowles: *Daniel Martin*
Lively: *The Road to Lichfield*
Narayan: *The Painter of Signs*
Ngugi: *Petals of Blood*
Pym: *Quartet in Autumn*
Scott: *Staying On*
DRAMA
Bennett: *The Old Country*
Stoppard: *Professional Foul*
POETRY
Ashbery: *Houseboat Days*
Bishop: *Geography III*
Garioch: *Collected Poems*
Graham: *Implements in Their Places*

POETRY (*cont.*)
Hughes, Ted: *Gaudete*
Lowell: *Day by Day*
MacCaig: *Tree of Strings*
Walcott: *Selected Poems*

1978

President Carter organises Israeli–Egyptian summit at Camp David; Shah of Iran imposes martial law to quell riots against his rule; Soviet-backed coup by army in Afghanistan; Italian politician Moro kidnapped and murdered by the Red Brigade; in Britain, unions reject 5% as guide line for pay increases; Louise Brown, world's first test-tube baby, born; election of John Paul II, first non-Italian Pope for 450 years.

PROSE
Amis, Kingsley: *Jake's Thing*
Amis, Martin: *Success*
Byatt: *The Virgin in the Garden*
Greene: *The Human Factor*
(Kundera: *The Book of Laughter and Forgetting*)
McEwan: *In between the Sheets*; *The Cement Garden*
Murdoch: *The Sea, the Sea*
Weldon: *Praxis*
DRAMA
Hare: *Plenty*
Potter: *Brimstone and Treacle*
POETRY
Harrison: *The School of Eloquence, and Other Poems*

POETRY (*cont.*)
Hill, Geoffrey: *Tenebrae*
Porter: *The Cost of Seriousness*
Raine, Craig: *The Onion, Memory*
Tomlinson: *Selected Poems 1951–74*

1979

President Sadat of Egypt and P.M. Begin of Israel sign peace treaty; Shah of Iran flees; followers of Ayatollah Khomeini take U.S. embassy staff in Teheran hostage; U.S.S.R. invades Afghanistan; President Somoza ousted by the Sandinistas in Nicaragua; Lancaster House agreement between factions in Rhodesia leads to elections and independence; in Britain, strikes by lorry drivers and public services cause national disruption in the 'winter of discontent'; Conservatives win General Election; Thatcher becomes Britain's first woman P.M.; I.R.A. assassinate M.P. Airey Neave and Lord Mountbatten; fewer than one third of voters participate in first elections to the European Parliament.

PROSE
Barth: *Letters*
(Calvino: *If on a Winter's Night a Traveller*)
Golding: *Darkness Visible*
Lessing: *Shikasta*
Lively: *Treasures of Time*
Naipaul: *A Bend in the River*
DRAMA
Shaffer: *Amadeus*
POETRY
Dunn: *Barbarians*
Graham: *Collected Poems 1942–75*
Heaney: *Field Work*
Hughes, Ted: *Moortown*
Levertov: *Collected Earlier Poems 1940–60*

POETRY (*cont.*)
Murray: *The Boys Who Stole the Funeral*
Raine, Craig: *A Martian Sends a Postcard Home*

1980

Reagan becomes President of U.S.A. (–1988); Mugabe elected premier of new state of Zimbabwe (formerly Rhodesia); in Poland, Solidarity, an anti-government coalition of trade unions, is formed; in Britain, privatisation plans announced for mail services, electricity, telephones and docks; dissident Labour M.P.s William Rodgers, Shirley Williams and David Owen publish an 'open letter', the first moves towards creation of the Social Democratic Party (1981); unemployment at more than 2 million; inflation at more than 21%; S.A.S. rescue hostages in Iranian embassy in London; decision taken to base U.S. cruise missiles at Greenham Common near Newbury; Brenton's play *The Romans in Britain* arouses accusations of obscenity.

PROSE
Bainbridge: *Winter Garden*
Burgess: *Earthly Powers*
Drabble: *The Middle Ground*
Golding: *Rites of Passage*
Greene: *Dr Fischer of Geneva, or The Bomb Party*
Hazzard: *The Transit of Venus*
'John le Carré': *Smiley's People*
Lessing: *The Marriages between Zones Three, Four and Five*
Weldon: *Puffball*

POETRY
Baxter: *Collected Poems*
Muldoon: *Why Brownlee Left*
Walcott: *The Star-Apple Kingdom*

Index of authors

All writers mentioned in the chronology are listed alphabetically, along with the following information: their dates of birth and death (if known and where appropriate); a note as to the kind of writing
for which they are chiefly remembered; and the year or years where their works, or works about
them, or addressed to them, appear in the text (the date or dates at the end of each entry). These
dates may also sometimes refer to years in which writers are mentioned, for various reasons, in the
historical sections of the text. Unless otherwise indicated, the writer is English.

200 · Index

DRAYTON, Michael (1563–1631), poet: 1591, 1593–7, 1599, 1603–7, 1612, 1622, 1627, 1630
DREISER, Theodore (1871–1945), American, novelist: 1900, 1925
DRINKWATER, John (1882–1937), poet, critic and dramatist: 1911, 1916–17, 1921–3, 1925
DRUMMOND, William, of Hawthornden (1585–1649), Scottish, poet: 1616–17, 1623
DRYDEN, John (1631–1700), poet, critic and dramatist: 1649, 1659–65, 1667–72, 1675, 1677–82, 1684–98, 1700, 1717, 1924
DU BARTAS, Guillaume de Salluste (1544–90), French, soldier and poet: 1578, 1592, 1605
DU BELLAY, Joachim (1522–60), French, poet: 1549
DU FRESNOY, Charles-Alphonse (1611–68), French, painter, art critic and poet: 1695
DU MAURIER, Daphne (1907–89), novelist: 1938
DU MAURIER, George (1834–96), artist, illustrator and novelist: 1892, 1894, 1897
DUCK, Stephen (1705–56), poet: 1730
DUNBAR, William (c.1460–c.1520), Scottish, poet: 1508
DUNN, Douglas (b.1942), Scottish, poet: 1969, 1972, 1974, 1979
D'URFEY, Thomas (1653–1723), dramatist and songwriter: 1676, 1698, 1719
DURRELL, Lawrence (b.1912), poet, novelist and travel-writer: 1957–8, 1960
DÜRRENMATT, Friedrich (b.1921), Swiss, dramatist: 1962
DYER, John (1699–1757), Welsh, poet: 1727, 1740, 1757
DYLAN, Bob (b.1941), American, song-writer: 1963, 1976

EARLE, John (c.1601–65), writer of miscellaneous prose, including essays and characters: 1628
EASTLAKE, Charles Locke (1836–1906), art critic: 1872
EDEN, Richard (c.1521–76), travel-writer: 1577
EDGEWORTH, Maria (1767–1849), Anglo-Irish, novelist: 1795–6, 1798, 1800–1, 1804, 1806, 1809, 1812, 1814, 1817
EDWARDS, Richard (c.1523–66), dramatist: 1565, 1576
EDWARDS, Thomas (dates unknown): 1595
EGAN, Pierce (1772–1849), sporting and miscellaneous writer: 1818, 1821, 1828
EINHARD (c.770–840), Frankish, historian and biographer: 832
ELIOT, George, pseud. of Marian or Mary Ann Evans (1819–80), novelist: 1846, 1858–61, 1863, 1866, 1868–9, 1871, 1874, 1876, 1879, 1884–5
ELIOT, Thomas Stearns (1888–1965), American and British, poet, dramatist and critic: 1917, 1920, 1922, 1924–5, 1928–30, 1932–6, 1939–43, 1948–9, 1953, 1958
ELLIOTT, Ebenezer (1781–1849), the 'Corn Law Rhymer', poet: 1831
ELLIS, Henry Havelock (1859–1939), writer on sex: 1897
ELLISON, Ralph (b.1914), American, novelist: 1952
ÉLUARD, Paul, pseud. of Eugène Grindal (1895–1952), French, poet: 1942
ELYOT, Sir Thomas (c.1490–1546), diplomat, moral philosopher and miscellaneous writer: 1531, 1533–4, 1538–40, 1545

EMPSON, William (1906–84), poet and critic: 1930, 1949
ENRIGHT, Dennis Joseph (b.1920), poet and novelist: 1969
EPICTETUS (fl.c.90), Greek, Stoic philosopher: 1567
ERASMUS, Desiderius (1466–1536), Dutch, religious and miscellaneous writer, and humanist philosopher: 1500, 1503, 1510–12, 1516, 1527, 1533, 1542, 1548, 1680
ERVINE, St John Greer (1883–1971), Anglo-Irish, dramatist: 1911, 1913, 1915
ETHEREGE, Sir George (c.1635–92), dramatist: 1664, 1668, 1676
EURIPIDES (c.480–406BC), Greek, tragedian: 1502
EVANS, Evan (1731–89), Welsh, anthologist: 1764
EVANS, Marian, see Eliot, George
EVELYN, John (1620–1706), diarist, miscellaneous writer and courtier: 1641, 1659, 1661, 1664, 1818

FAIRFAX, Edward (c.1580–1635), scholar and translator: 1600
FAIRFIELD, Cecily Isabel, see West, Rebecca
FALKNER, John Meade (1858–1932), novelist and businessman: 1898
FARQUHAR, George (c.1677–1707), Irish, dramatist: 1698–9, 1706–7
FARRAR, Frederick William (1831–1903), clergyman and novelist: 1858
FARRELL, James Gordon (1935–79), novelist: 1970
FAULKNER, William Harrison (1897–1962), American, novelist: 1929–32, 1936, 1939, 1942, 1948–9, 1962
FÉNELON, François (1651–1715), French, churchman and miscellaneous writer: 1699
FENTON, Sir Geoffrey (1539–1608), translator: 1567, 1572, 1575, 1579
FERGUSSON, Robert (1750–74), Scottish, poet: 1773, 1779
FERRIER, Susan (1782–1854), Scottish, novelist: 1818, 1824, 1831
FIELD, Barron (1786–1846), Australian, poet and anthologist: 1819
FIELD, Nathan (1587–c.1620), actor and dramatist: 1609, 1611–12, 1618–19
FIELDING, Henry (1707–54), novelist: 1728, 1730, 1732–3, 1736, 1741–3, 1749–51, 1755
FIRBANK, Ronald (1886–1926), novelist: 1919, 1926
FISH, Simon (d.1531): 1529
FISHER, John, Bishop of Rochester (1469–1535), churchman: 1535
FITZGERALD, Edward (1809–83), scholar and poet: 1859
FITZGERALD, Scott (1896–1940), American, novelist: 1920, 1922, 1925–6, 1934, 1941, 1945
FITZHERBERT, John (dates unknown), miscellaneous writer: 1523
FITZ-NIGEL, Richard (12th century), bishop and treasurer of England: 1195
FLAUBERT, Gustave (1821–80), French, novelist: 1857, 1869
FLECKER, James Elroy (1884–1915), poet: 1907, 1910, 1913, 1915–16, 1922
FLECKNOE, Richard (c.1600–78), possibly Irish, miscellaneous writer: 1653, 1658, 1661
FLEMING, Ian (1908–64), spy novelist: 1953

Index of anonymous works

The author of this Handbook

MARTIN GRAY was educated at the universities of Perugia, Oxford and London. Since 1972 he has been lecturer in the Department of English Studies at the University of Stirling, where he teaches a wide variety of different kinds of literature, including autobiographical writing and Australian novels and poetry. He is currently co-director of a postgraduate course on modern poetry, and is attached to the Centre of Commonwealth Studies and the Centre for Publishing Studies. His publications include *A Dictionary of Literary Terms* (Longman–York Press) and *The Penguin Book of the Bicycle* (with R. Watson). Since 1988 he has been editor of an inter-disciplinary academic journal, *Australian Studies*.